Requiem
for a Female Serial Killer

Also by Phyllis Chesler from New English Review Press

Islamic Gender Apartheid: Exposing A Veiled War Against Women (2017)

A Family Conspiracy: Honor Killing (2018)

Requiem
for a
Female Serial Killer

Phyllis Chesler

Published by New English Review Press
a subsidiary of World Encounter Institute
PO Box 158397
Nashville, Tennessee 37215
&
27 Old Gloucester Street
London, England, WC1N 3AX

Cover Art & Design by Kendra Mallock

ISBN: 978-1-943003-43-3

First Edition

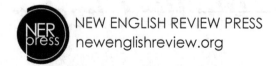

NEW ENGLISH REVIEW PRESS
newenglishreview.org

If men would keep their money in their pockets and their penises in their pants, there would be no prostitution.

— Aileen Carol Wuornos

Aileen (age 20) with her husband. Lewis Gratz Fell.

CONTENTS

INTRODUCTION

Haunted by a Serial Killer

Florida, USA, 1990

Two women are being sought as possible suspects in the shooting deaths of eight to twelve middle-aged men who were lured to their deaths on the Florida highways. Suspect #1 is a white female, five foot eight to five foot ten, with blonde hair. Suspect #2 is also a white female, five foot four to five foot six, with a heavy build and short brown hair. These women are armed and dangerous and may be our nation's first female serial killers. Investigators feel compelled to warn the public, particularly middle-aged white men traveling alone.

THIS NEWS BROADCAST sounded unreal, almost mythical—as diabolically whimsical as Orson Welles' 1938 broadcast on the Martian invasion. What was Everywoman's most forbidden fantasy and Everyman's worst nightmare doing on the airwaves? Was this some kind of joke?

It was not. For the first time in American history, a woman stood accused of being a serial killer—of having killed seven or eight adult male motorists, one by one, in just over a year, after accompanying them to wooded areas off Highway I-75 in Florida, a state well known for its sun, surf, and serial killers. What made this unique was that all the men were strangers, not husbands, not intimates.

Were these two women members of that radical feminist collective in Gainesville, the university town where countless female students had been serially raped, mutilated, killed and ritually posed? Or were they apolitical swamp creatures, criminal outlaws, perhaps prostitutes, finally driven mad by their lives on the Killing Fields?

I would soon find out. I got Ailee/Aileen (Lee) Carol Wuornos to call me a few months after she was arrested. Once on the line, I knew I'd only have a few seconds to gain her attention.

"Lee, I represent a feminist government in exile. We know that you've been captured and we'd like to help."

"Far fuckin' out! You're the Women's Lib, right?"

"Yes."

"Tell the women out there that I'm innocent. Tell them that men hate our guts. I was raped and I defended myself. It was self-defense. I could not stop hustling just because some asshole was going around Florida raping and killing women. I still had to hustle. Can you tell me why men think sex is so important? Why do they have to behave like animals, pant, pant. I can just live masturbating. Why can't men?"

And that's how it all began.

* * *

This book is about a female serial killer and about the way in which her badass deeds pried the world's imagination wide open. Here was a "nobody" who became a "somebody," a throwaway child who became the whore who shot down Johns. Someone anonymous who became famous, a kickass folk hero like Jesse James or Bonnie and Clyde.

Wuornos hit the ground running before either Thelma or Louise came to town. She fired some shots heard round the world, shots which we hoped would warn male serial killers that they might just end up dead if they continued to rape and murder women. Her bullets shattered the silence about violence against prostituted women, about what happens to them when they refuse to take it anymore.

No small feat.

Wuornos, the hitchhiking lesbian prostitute, was no longer prey; she had become a predator. She enacted the forbidden feminist longing for armed female assassins who would rescue girls and women from incestuous fathers and stepfathers, pedophiles, sexual harassers, serial rapists and from sex slavery in brothels and private dungeons.

Talk about women who run with the wolves! Wuornos navigated America with a primeval cunning, a scavenging genius, without which neither wildlife nor prostitutes could survive: Not for a day, not for an hour. She was a feral child, a Wolf-Girl, a snarling loner, and she understood early on that mutilated female corpses litter the landscape all over the country and that they remain unclaimed and un-mourned.

Once, Wuornos had discovered such a corpse herself. In a letter to a childhood friend, Wuornos wrote that in 1973, when she was seventeen, she was hitchhiking outside of Chicago along I-80 when she smelled something real bad, a "foul odor" which she followed; then, she found a woman's pitiful headless, limbless torso. Wuornos writes that, although she frantically tried, she could not get a state trooper or even a trucker to pay the slightest attention.

Wuornos "got" it a long time ago: Women are treated like garbage, whether they're alive or dead.

* * *

Oh, I had my reasons for getting involved. I wanted a jury to hear the truth about how dangerous the "working life" really is; how prostitutes are routinely infected with diseases, gang-raped, tortured, and murdered; and that Wuornos had been raped and beaten so many times that, by now, if she was at all human, she'd have to be permanently drunk and out of her mind.

I was a bit younger in 1990, the year she committed most of her murders. Would I get involved now? I doubt it. Physically, I couldn't do it. Would I still see Wuornos as a feminist folk hero of sorts? Yes, I would, or primarily as a dangerous, damaged, doomed, and demented woman—well, she was that, too.

Would I still be as sympathetic toward this volatile, trigger-tempered, foul-mouthed child-woman, and would I still risk being seen as defending, or advocating for such an unsympathetic woman?

Perhaps—for here I am, publishing the damn book.

I put whatever I'd written away in a box, kept it safe, thought about it from time to time, but mainly forgot about it. Then, in the summer of 2019, as I was renovating my apartment, that box literally fell off the shelf. I opened it and was amazed by how timely and important the issues raised by her case still are.

I resurrected my huge Wuornos archive and began reading thousands of pages of legal documents and the interviews I did with Wuornos both on the phone and in person.

I found our correspondence and am publishing some of our letters for the first time in this book.

I also organized the hundreds of interviews I did with the entire cast of colorful characters, including her biological mother, the lover who testified against her, a multitude of Florida lawyers, former prostitutes, the team of experts I'd put together and hoped would testify at her trial, and the feminists who worked at Florida's shelters for battered women and rape crisis centers.

This book is about Wuornos, but it is also about my trying to get inside her head to see it both her way and my way, and to understand us both.

I still believe that her first murder took place in a violent struggle to save her life. As a prostitute with a prison record, she could not report what had happened to the police. After this first, traumatic kill, something—maybe everything—changed. She went on a murderous "spree" which lasted about a year.

In 1980, the late, great true crime author, Ann Rule, first wrote about serial killer Ted Bundy and then again twenty-one years later in a revised and updated edition. Bundy was, literally, "the killer beside her" as they both worked on a suicide helpline.

Bundy was handsome, charming, "likable," well-spoken,

and very smart. He had an uncanny ability to say exactly what people wanted to hear—and he planned his crimes very carefully. His facade of "niceness" fooled Rule. She had a hard time believing that Bundy was the sadistic and prolific serial killer that he was. And she remained haunted by her friendship with him.

If Rule were still alive, I would tell her that Bundy's "spiritual" advisor, born-again Christian and anti-pornography crusader, John Tanner, was the very man who would prosecute Wuornos as "pure evil."

I would tell Rule that I'm also a bit haunted by my time with another famous serial killer.

* * *

Author's note: I had behind-the-scenes access to Wuornos and to those involved both in her life and in her case. Much of what I have to say and how I say it is not duplicated anywhere else. Everything I write is based on facts: Legal documents, transcripts of in-person and phone interviews, diary entries, correspondence, etc. However, what you are about to read is also a genre-blended form of fiction/non-fiction. I've gotten inside Wuornos' head, tried to see it from her point of view, and have had to imagine the conversations she held with others.

SECTION ONE

Murder in the Woods

CHAPTER ONE

The Hooker and the Whoremonger: First Man Down

GODDAMN, IT HAD taken Aileen more than twelve hours and seven rides to hitch all the way from Ft. Meyers to Tampa, and from one end of Alligator Alley to the other. She'd started when it was still light, and it was dark now, and raining. Aileen was damp, soaked, and chilled—almost sober.

Aileen was used to being on the road, on the move, one step ahead of the law. Being on the move felt safe. Aileen saw herself as a beatnik, a Merry Prankster, a Dharma Bum, a biker, a street-child: Woodstock to Altamont to Natural Born Killers. When Aileen wasn't moving from one hole-in-the-wall motel room to another, she was out on the highway hitching rides, an Anti-Johnny Appleseed, if you will.

When Aileen did finally move in somewhere, she really inhabited the space, made it her own, knew how it smelled, and how the light came in, or didn't, every hour of the day and night; as if it were her jail cell, which in a sense, it was; as if it were her lair, where she hid out, primeval.

When Aileen hitched, her M.O. was to come across as a normal civilian, an everyday woman, the kind with kids and a house, a lady just down on her luck and in distress. Aileen didn't dress like a whore. Passing for ordinary was her disguise, her working clothes.

Aileen stood at the intersection of I-75 and I-4, under an underpass, her thumb in the air. She thought she saw a car stop and start to back up. Aileen couldn't see very well, she never could. Aileen usually had to walk right up to a car, otherwise she couldn't tell if the driver was a guy or a girl. This time, it was a guy in a two-door cream-colored Cadillac with tinted windows. Not bad.

"Goin' to Orlando?" Richard Charles Mallory asked.

"No, I'm going to Daytona," Aileen Carol Wuornos told him.

"You're in luck," Richard said. "I am, too. Hop in."

Then, there they were, Aileen and Richard on the road, barreling off into the amazing American night.

Mmm, the cushions felt warm and soft, almost velvety. Aileen arranged her things and settled in for the long ride ahead. She looked Richard over. She made him for fifty, fifty-five. She saw he'd lost his bout with adolescent acne, but hey, her own forehead was still scarred from a childhood fire that she and her brother Keith had set.

Aileen was bone weary, but she had no complaints. She had $250 in her bag, and a ride straight through to Daytona. Yeah, she and Tyria had bounced around a lot. In the last year they'd lived in five different motel rooms, but their luck was changing, they were about to move into a duplex apartment—c'mon, they were practically moving into a house of their own—on Burleigh, in Holly Hill in Daytona.

Richard asked Aileen if she wanted to share his pot and some vodka. Aileen told him she didn't drink hard liquor and she didn't smoke dope. Richard was having a high old time. He was as high as the moon. Richard talked; Aileen listened, the way wives and girlfriends do. He told her he had business and love troubles. Normal stuff. Then Richard said: "I own a video store. I do special photo sessions with the girls from the topless bars. I pay 'em good money too. Maybe up to $2,000 a session. You interested?"

Aileen said she wasn't. Who knew who watched those flicks,

maybe someone who knew there was a warrant out for her arrest. Aileen wasn't an idiot. $2,000 my ass. Richard told her, if she knew someone else who might be interested, to pass the word along.

In Orlando, Richard stopped for gas and beer. He saw that Aileen drank a lot of beer for someone who didn't touch hard liquor or smoke pot. "You're a good listener, you're real helpful," Richard said. "How come you understand married men so well?"

"That's easy. I'm a hustler, a hooker," Aileen told him.

And Richard said, you mean you hustle sex? And she said, yeah. So then Richard said: "Well, God. I thought we were going to get it on, I mean eventually, but you don't do it for free. You probably do it for money, right?"

Aileen said: "That's right. I do it for money."

Richard repeated, "So you don't do it for free, right?"

Aileen said: "No, I don't. This is my job. This is what I do for a living."

* * *

Richard was used to women who charged for it. Last night, (or was it earlier that night?), he'd partied with Chastity Lee Marcus and Kimberly Guy, two topless, bottomless dancers, hookers, and real hot, too. They'd had sex with each other and then with him, made him crazy. Richard had given each of them a 19-inch color TV and a VCR as payment.

But Richard was used to stealing sex, too, or at least trying to. In 1957, when Aileen was not quite two years old, and Richard was nineteen, Richard was sentenced to four years in the Maryland Penitentiary for attempted rape and then transferred to the Patuxent Institution where he spent a total of ten years.

Richard was born in Jamestown, Pennsylvania, and moved to Maryland when he was eleven. His father was a welder who drank, his mother was a housewife. Everything was perfectly normal: Richard masturbated for the first time when he was twelve, eloped with his high school sweetheart when he was seventeen, graduated from high school when he was eighteen. By the time he was nineteen, Richard had signed up to join the Army. He was a good, working-class boy who, all through school, had held down steady part-time jobs.

One thing though: When he was sixteen, Richard was for the first time gripped by "compulsive sexual thoughts about sexual intercourse with different women." He fought these thoughts for two years, but by the time he was eighteen, no matter what he did, Richard couldn't erase the nonstop images that burned through his brain, of himself having intercourse with women he didn't know, for example, with every woman he ever met on his job making home deliveries.

He actually quit his job over this, but one delivery stayed in his mind. He'd knocked, there was no answer, he tried the door, it was open, he went in, looked around—and then he saw her, lying across the bed sleeping, and he couldn't get the image out of his mind not even after he'd quit the job. She was sleeping, and she had red hair, and she didn't know he was watching her. It was like a dream. Only real.

Richard's friends told him that redheads were "passionate and sexually responsive." He'd only been with one woman, but his urge to have intercourse with other women, the redhead in particular, was so strong he couldn't resist it, so he gave in, returned, and reentered the dream reality. This time the redhead wasn't sleeping. He tried to pull off her blouse anyway, but she fought him off, and although Richard almost instantly fled and ran straight home and changed his clothes, the police picked him up three hours later and the redhead identified him as her assailant. Richard's young wife and parents were devastated, but they stood by him. Richard said he had no future, nothing to live for.

Richard pled guilty because of insanity.

Some men are born losers. Richard had failed to fuck the redhead, and he'd failed to get away, too. Whoever heard of a white man in America in 1958 being sentenced to ten years for attempted rape? Richard must have picked on the wrong man's red-haired wife. Maybe she was the mayor's wife or daughter.

On March 14, 1961, poor Richard stole a car and escaped from prison, but he was captured the very next day near his home. Richard also verbally (and by gesturing) "molested" a prison nurse who'd reported him instantly.

Once Drs. Boslow, Dabney, Kandel, Morgenstern, and Sorongon, the prison psychiatrists, got their hands on Richard, they diagnosed him as "unstable," "emotionally immature," "sexually impulsive," and "defectively delinquent." They said he had "strong feelings of inadequacy for which he tries to compensate in his sexual acts." They said he suffered from a "Personality Pattern Disturbance" and was a "schizoid personality." The doctors reported that Richard thought he was "sexually irresistible to women." During these interviews, Richard picked at his face and squeezed his pimples anxiously, constantly.

* * *

Richard asked Aileen how much she charged. Aileen told him: "Thirty for head, thirty-five straight, forty for half and half, a hundred an hour." Aileen said: "Look, after an hour's up, I don't say you gotta give me another hundred. If a guy is alright, if I'm staying with him, if we become friends, then I'm not greedy. If I can make my rent, that's cool. A hundred is fine. I don't care about making any more."

Richard said: "So, if I give you a hundred dollars we could spend a couple of hours together?"

Aileen thought well, why the hell not, it's only 4AM, I can't go home yet, I'd wake up Maggie, she'd bark, the landlord would be on my ass, Tyria would start complaining that she can't get no sleep. Might as well hang out with him until it's light. But first, Aileen said, they'd have to buy some condoms. Richard said that he never left home without some. And they laughed.

It was still dark when they reached Daytona. Darkest before dawn, they both said. They exited the highway, went down a smaller road, then pulled into a secluded, wooded area.

Way it was, Aileen explained, the two of them oughta get undressed. Aileen thought it showed good faith on both sides.

Aileen took her clothes off, folded them real neat and put everything on the back seat. Richard went out back to the trunk to get the rubbers and a blanket. When he returned, he was still dressed. Richard turned on the dome light and said: "Not bad."

Aileen said: "Well, I don't know. I have a lot of stretch marks and a beer belly."

Richard had a smirk on his face. "You'll do." Then, he turned off the dome light.

Aileen didn't like it that Richard was still dressed. Then he said something Aileen really didn't like. "What if I told you I don't have enough money?"

Ah, shit! Aileen was gonna fuck him to pass the time but on principle, she wasn't going to fuck him for free. That was way out of line. Aileen said: "How much you got?"

Arrogantly, off-handedly, Richard said he "had just enough for breakfast and for some gas."

Aileen said: "Richard, no way. I'm not here for my health. I guess we're gonna have to call this off."

The deal was off, Richard had just reneged on it anyway, but what could Aileen do, haul his ass into court for breach of contract? As Aileen saw it, if a John didn't pay, but he still got to play—that's rape. If she and a John agree on a price and he pays up front, then it's a deal, he gets to come offa her, she gets his money, there's something in it for both of them.

* * *

Swiftly, Richard whipped a cord around Aileen's neck and pulled her toward him. Aileen heard Richard say: "Listen, you bitch, you're going to do everything I tell you to do. And if you don't, I'll kill you." Aileen had no time to sweet-talk him down. She'd done it before, plenty of times, with guys who'd freaked, she knew how to do it, but Richard was choking her and she couldn't breathe and the blood was rushing to her head and she saw spots before her eyes.

Aileen couldn't talk at all, all she could do was hope. Aileen pried her hands under the cord around her neck and kept trying to expand it so it wouldn't choke her to death in the next few, precious seconds.

Aileen heard Richard say: "It doesn't matter to me. I'll kill you and fuck you later. Just like the other sluts I've done. Your body will still be warm for my huge cock. Do you want to die, slut?"

Aileen shook her head no.

"Are you going to listen to everything I've got to say you have to do?"

Aileen nodded yes. Richard told her to raise her hands, just like she was surrendering to the cops, or like they were in a Western, only Aileen wasn't an Indian or a cowboy; she was the steer being roped. Richard tied Aileen's hands to the steering wheel and told her to lie face down on the seat with her feet near the window.

The hours of pretend-friendly conversations and compliments were all for nothing; they meant nothing. In Aileen's line of work, they never did.

Aileen heard Richard tell her to "slide up and get comfortable because I'm going to see how much meat I can pound in your ass." This was Aileen's absolute nightmare. Being fucked up the ass was definitely not for sale. No way. Aileen abhorred the idea of anal sex; she thought it was filthy, degrading.

Richard unzipped his fly, climbed into the car, lifted Aileen's legs up a little higher, then fucked her violently up the ass, for as long as it felt good to him. He could hear Aileen moaning and bawling, but from far away. When he was ready, Richard withdrew and quickly thrust his penis into Aileen's vagina and came. And kept coming. Aileen was crying her brains out. She heard Richard say he loved it when they cried, it turned him on.

Richard saw that his penis had blood all over it. He knew that sluts were full of disease. He always cleaned himself afterwards, right away. He kept water and rubbing alcohol in his car for this reason. Richard got out of the car, walked around to the trunk, opened it, took out a bottle of rubbing alcohol, soap, a toothbrush, a Visine bottle, and two soda bottles filled with water.

Aileen said: "Hey, Richard, what are you doing?" Aileen couldn't see a thing, she strained her neck trying to look back while her hands were still tied to the wheel. What the hell was he doin' out there?

Aileen heard Richard say: "Honey, I'm full of surprises for you tonight."

Aileen thought: "This guy is gonna kill me. He is going to get rid of me. He is going to dissect me or something. He is totally weird."

Richard took his Visine bottle, lifted up Aileen's legs, and squirted the rubbing alcohol in, and in, and in, to be sure that every little place he tore in her ass would burn, bad. For good measure, he squirted the Visine bottle up her cunt, too. She oughta thank him for cleaning her up. Who knew where else that cunt had been. Then, Richard squirted rubbing alcohol up Aileen's nose.

Aileen heard Richard say: "I'm saving your eyes for the grand finale."

Aileen was really pissed. As she cursed him out, Aileen heard Richard laugh. "That's what I want to hear. I want you to start crying out in pain." Aileen was still butt-naked, butt-bleeding, tied up, and freezing, too. It was cold, right around dawn. Richard was cold too; he put a jacket on over his clothes, got a radio, turned it on, sat on the hood of his car, his back to Aileen, listening to music, enjoying himself, smoking some more pot.

Aileen thought: The bastard's gonna kill me. I have to clear my head and concentrate. She got past the beer, past the fatigue, past the pain, but not past the rage, the rage cleared her head. She needed to figure out how Richard would do it, so she could be ready to fight him off. She'd done this before, survived, like the time those guys tied her down to the bed and gang raped her in Georgia, or the time that guy beat her so bad she was in bed for two months.

Aileen kept trying to free herself. She kept using her full body weight, she never stopped trying. Richard heard her, even over the music. Without turning around, Aileen heard him say: "I can feel you moving in there. Don't worry, you ain't gonna get untied until I untie you." Aileen kept trying to free herself anyway. Aileen heard Richard say: "Can you believe it, I've gotta come back in, it's getting too cold out here for me."

He looked in and sized the situation up. Aileen heard Richard say: "I'm going to untie you from the steering wheel. You better be a good girl or I'll kill you." Richard untied Aileen from the steering wheel, but quick-whipped the cord around her neck and held it there like a leash, like reins. Richard told Aileen to move over so he could move in, and to spread her legs.

So, Richard had done ten long years in the can for trying to get some free pussy but he hadn't learned his lesson; something in Richard still wanted free pussy if he could get it. Maybe Richard wanted the whore compliant, cowed, a little younger too, if you asked him. Maybe Richard didn't intend to kill Aileen, just teach her a lesson. Maybe Richard was so high he didn't know what he was doing.

Aileen thought: You gotta do something, you gotta fight, he's gonna play with you and hurt you some more, and then he's gonna kill you. You're gonna die.

Aileen decided to fight, not for her honor, but for her life.

It happened all at once in a split second: Richard was choking Aileen harder, harder, and slapping her across the face, really hard. Aileen was breaking loose, grabbing his arm, pushing him back, grabbing at the reins, grabbing for her bag. Richard quit struggling, and got up on his knees. Aileen heard him say: "You're going to be a lot of fun."

It was all the opening Aileen needed. Aileen jumped up real fast and spit in his face. Aileen heard Richard say: "You're dead bitch. You're dead." He started comin' towards her. Aileen ducked down, real quick, grabbed her bag, got her .22 out—and immediately shot him twice, as fast as she could. Richard still kept comin', so Aileen shot him again. The third bullet didn't kill him but it finally stopped him. Aileen pushed Richard away from her.

Richard couldn't fuckin' believe what had just happened. A whore with a gun? Richard was stunned not so much by the bullets as by the nerve on the cunt. Richard half-sat up in the driver's seat. Aileen moved backwards out of the car and screamed or whispered, she wasn't sure: "Don't come out. Don't come near me. I'll have to shoot you again. Don't make me have to shoot you again." Richard started comin' at her and Aileen shot him again. Four bullets, and Richard was down, face down, for good.

Aileen stood there and looked at him and thought: "I'm gonna run him over if I don't move him." She didn't know why, but she didn't want to run Richard over. She dragged his body away from the car. Then, while she was still naked, Aileen got in the car, turned the key in the ignition, started to drive the hell outta there, stopped, put the car in neutral, grabbed the carpet-mat from the floor, ran back, and covered poor Richard.

Aileen didn't want the birds to be picking at his body.

It made no sense, not even to her, but Aileen seemed to care more about Richard as a corpse.

* * *

Nearly two years later, at trial, the prosecutor insisted that Aileen had planned to kill Richard Mallory for his money. Aileen repeatedly disagreed with him. He persevered. Aileen remained adamant.

She said: "I had no choice whatsoever. I shot him and it killed him. I had no choice. I couldn't stop the clock and say, well, let's see where I can shoot him at so he will stay alive. Shoot him in the foot, shoot him in the arm. I'm not the greatest aimer. I did whatever I could do just as fast as possible. He was going to kill me. He was going to beat the living daylights out of me, choke me to death."

The prosecutor asked: "What did you get in the way of money from him?"

Aileen told him she got $38, maybe $40 out of Richard's wallet, and that she'd spent it on food.

CHAPTER TWO

Lee's Incessant War against Neighbors and Bus Drivers

THE LIGHT WAS COMING UP, maybe it had been up for a while and Aileen just hadn't noticed. She hadn't noticed a lot of things, including that she was still naked. Aileen threw her clothes back on, quick, just as she made the road. She'd have to scramble to cover this whole thing up. She couldn't go to the police; they'd never believe her version of what happened, and even if they did, they'd put her in jail once they found out about the outstanding warrant for her arrest. Aileen had better not tell Tyria anything, either.

Aileen thought: I gotta take a shower. I gotta see Ty. I'm fuckin' tired. I'm all beat up. I'm hurting all over. My crotch hurts. My ass hurts. My nose hurts. My head hurts. I'm freaking out. I need a shower.

Okay, she thought. I'll go to the car wash and wash the car off, empty the trunk, get rid of his stuff, ditch the car. Lay fuckin' low for a while.

Aileen drove Richard's two door, cream-colored Cadillac with the tinted windows and the orange-and-blue "Gator" tag straight home to Tyria in their room at the Ocean Shores Motel in Ormond Beach. Maggie heard her comin' and started barkin'. Tyria, and Tyler, the cat, both met her at the door.

27

Tyria asked Aileen about the "hickeys" on her neck.

"Hickeys?" Aileen asked. "These ain't hickeys. Listen. I gotta take a shower, but this friend of mine lent me his car. We can use it to move our stuff."

Tyria thought nothing about the Cadillac. Aileen was always bringing things home: cars, cash, things. She'd say a trick had given it to her, or an old friend. The things would all eventually disappear. Tyria never asked where they'd gone to: the pawnshop, the junkyard, back to their owners. Tyria knew how to keep her mouth shut. Or, she didn't ask because she didn't believe a word Aileen said.

Aileen picked up Tyria after work in Richard's Cadillac. By evening, they had moved into their new place at 334 ½ Burleigh, in Holly Hill.

Later that night, Aileen and Tyria were sitting on the floor— they didn't have their couch yet—watching TV. Suddenly, "Aileen just came right out of the blue" and told Tyria that she had something to tell her. Tyria thought that Aileen's voice was unusually calm. Tyria, eyes fixed on the TV, asked her what she had to say.

Aileen said: "I shot and killed a man today. I'm sorry, I'm really sorry." Then, Aileen cried.

Tyria kept watching the TV. Tyria didn't believe Aileen. That Aileen could run a line of bullshit about anything. She could be joking, pulling her leg. After a while, Tyria said: "You're shittin' me." Then, Tyria thought: Well, if Aileen wasn't lying, if she had killed a man, maybe it's the best thing that coulda happened to her. Maybe this would change her, take the hate out of her.

Aileen told Tyria that she had left the dead man out in the woods, but had covered up his body with a rug.

Tyria felt sorry for Aileen. She thought: That man musta done something to set her off, maybe he tried to force her to have sex with him. Tyria had never known Aileen to "allow anyone to get the upper hand on her."

Way Aileen saw it, the whole wide world had been waging a private, undeclared war against her for more than three decades. By now, if you messed with her, she'd go head to head and toe-to-toe with you. "You think my ass is worth only ten bucks? Listen, you fucking asshole, I'll punch your lights out. I can do it, too. You think you're so hot to look at yourself? Motherfucker, I'll kick your ass. Who're you calling a cunt, you cocksucker?"

Tyria figured that Aileen just killed the man for trying to take advantage of her. Maybe he had made some advances on her—but so what? Tyria thought, that's what Aileen does for a living, and no matter what I say, she won't stop.

Tyria didn't understand how Aileen could go out and fuck men, given how she felt about them. Aileen really hated men. It made no sense to Tyria. But then, Tyria had stopped trying to figure Aileen out long ago. Aileen had moved in right after they'd first met, so Tyria hadn't found out how Aileen made her money until months later, when it was too late, when Tyria already loved Aileen and thought they'd be together forever.

Tyria didn't like how Aileen made her money. She'd told her she oughta stop, but Aileen wouldn't hear of it. There was something about hustling that Aileen couldn't let go of. Sometimes, Tyria thought, Aileen behaved as if she'd taken a dare, or a bet, and she'd be damned if she'd be the one to chicken out. Tyria knew it was no use talking to Aileen about it. That's why Tyria never wanted to hear any of the disgusting details.

Maybe that's why Aileen did not tell Tyria that Richard Mallory had tied her to the steering wheel and raped her up the ass and poured alcohol on her, too, and threatened to squirt it into her eyes. And maybe kill her. No point in reminding Tyria that she couldn't go to the police. Tyria'd be on her ass too, blaming her for hitching and hustling to begin with. Aileen was too shook up to risk Tyria getting on her case.

A day or two later, Aileen told Tyria she'd ditched Richard's Cadillac in the woods near John Anderson Drive. However, she'd left the rear license plate intact and, for no good reason, had scattered Richard's credit cards nearby. Aileen had bicycled back home on her ten-speed bike.

Aileen didn't tell Tyria that the Cadillac had belonged to the man she killed.

* * *

Way it was, Aileen didn't work every day, she worked a cou-pla days every week. Mainly daylight hours, with an occasional overnight. After she killed Richard, Aileen didn't work for three weeks. It's not as if she stayed in bed because she couldn't look anyone in the eye. Aileen got up every day, drank her coffee, drank her beer, watched the games on TV, visited some bars. Listened to music.

When Tyria heard on the news that the police had found a man with a rug over his body, she freaked. Tyria thought: Oh my God, she really did do it!

Tyria knew that Aileen had a .22 handgun and a .45 too, she thought. Aileen took a gun to work with her, kept it in her plas-tic shopping bag, for protection, she said. But Tyria had nev-er seen Aileen cleaning, loading, or unloading her gun. Tyria couldn't imagine Aileen using a gun.

Tyria never gave it much thought.

Okay, a man was dead in the woods, covered by a rug and his name was Richard something. Hadn't Aileen shown Tyria a paper with the name "Richard" on it? Yes, she had, when she'd brought in the loot: the toolbox, the suitcase, the purple Pola-roid camera, the gray jacket, the scarf, and the box of papers. Was Aileen's Richard the dead Richard on the news? Naw, Ai-leen probably made it all up.

The day Aileen began working again, Tyria thought: See, she made it all up.

It would take Tyria a year to decide that Aileen had, in fact, probably been out there "selecting men to kill on the basis of whether she thought they had a lot of money on 'em." In her deposition on January 15, 1991, Tyria would say that Richard probably had hurt Aileen, but that Aileen probably "just got a thrill out of (killing) the first time and it was so easy for her that she just kept doing it." Tyria would also say that she "believed that if Aileen wasn't stopped she'd still be out there doing it."

It would take Tyria nearly four years to decide that Aileen was probably "wanting to die" when she told Tyria about killing Richard. "When she told me about killing Richard Mallory, she was actually saying, 'Go tell on me, I want it to end.'" Tyria remembers how Aileen kept saying: "How can you still love me after I killed somebody?"

"That's when I told her I thought it would change her. Maybe she wouldn't hate people as much as she did before. But it didn't. She was the same afterwards."

* * *

On December 1, 1989, Sergeant John Bonnevier, of the Volusia County Road Patrol, found Richard's "vehicle." It had been abandoned near I-95, the highway that runs from north to south along Florida's east coast, in a wooded area off John Anderson Drive in Ormond Beach near US 1. The car had been backed up about fifteen or twenty feet. The keys were missing, but Aileen had thrown Richard's wallet and credit cards conveniently nearby. Sgt. Bonnevier impounded the car, placed the other property into evidence, and filed a report.

A more cunning criminal would have destroyed the credit cards, ripped off the license plate, thrown her victim's wallet into the deep blue sea. Not Aileen.

It took a few days for Bonnevier's report to reach Investigator Lawrence Horzepa's desk. When it did, Horzepa contacted Detective Bonnie Richway, "from over in Pinellas County, (because) the address that we had for Mr. Mallory, on his driver's license showed that he lived over there." Horzepa asked Richway to find Richard Mallory, tell him they had his car, his license, and his credit cards. Richway checked Mallory's house, an apartment in a multi-family dwelling in Clearwater known as The Oaks, but nobody had seen him there for a few days.

Richway also checked his business, Mallory Electronics, but he hadn't shown up for work either, not for several days. People told her that wasn't unusual, from time to time Mallory would just take off for several days with no explanation and then come back.

Richway found out that Mallory had a newly ex-girlfriend,

Jackie Davis, over in Largo. Jackie's grown son, Jeffrey, turned out to have been the last person to have seen Mallory before he'd left on his trip to Daytona. Jeffrey had been working for Mallory, but Mallory had fired him as soon as he'd broken up with Jackie.

On December 6th, Cammie Greene, aka Aileen Wuornos, pawned Richard's 35mm Minolta Freedom camera and a Micronta Road Patrol Radar Detector at the O.K. Pawn Shop in Daytona Beach. Cammie got $30 for both of them. Pawning the loot in the immediate vicinity was very risky.

* * *

On December 13th, Jimmy Bonchi and James Davis were out scavenging for scrap metal in the woods. In Bonchi's words, they "were exploring throw the woods and seen a Buzzard and we smelled stink! I saw a tarp with a hand hanging out of It!"

According to Marion County Investigator Bruce Munster, who was called to the scene: "A badly decomposed body was discovered in Volusia County. The body was that of a W/M (white male) fully clothed but covered by a carpet mat."

Investigator Brian Jarvis, also of Marion County, noted that the mat had been "laid carefully atop him."

The autopsy results showed that Mallory had died as a result of gunshot wounds to the chest. Four .22 caliber copper-coated, hollow-nosed bullets with a 6 right-twist rifling were recovered from his body. Horzepa, who led the investigation in Volusia County, further noted that the police "recovered the body 12 miles from where the car was found."

Nearly two years later, at an examination before trial on October 15, 1992, Investigator Horzepa was questioned by Trish Jenkins, Aileen's public defender.

Jenkins: "Tell me the positioning of the body when you found it. Kind of describe the immediate area and then the positioning of the body."

Horzepa: "Basically what had happened was two gentlemen were out looking for scrap metal in (the) illegal dump site over there… (and they) came across a body that was covered up by a red carpet. As soon as they saw a hand sticking out from the particular carpeting, they immediately left the area and went down to the nearest phone and called us…The immediate area is a wooded area. It was large enough that cars could drive in there to dump their trash."

So, Aileen and Richard had gone to a garbage dump to have their tryst.

Horzepa: "The body was about two hundred and fifty, maybe three hundred feet off the road… I believe that the body was face down. We… had very large decomposition from the shoulders up; it was basically skeletal remains. The rest of the body was… in fairly good shape… his pockets were turned slightly inside out. He was wearing a pair of jeans and a pull-over type shirt. That was about it. Oh, and his belt buckle and pants [were] off to the side."

So it was true: Richard had never taken his clothes off.

Horzepa: "I had gotten a physical description of Mr. Mallory. I thought that there was a possibility it could be him. I had contacted Detective Richway, asked her to check on Mr. Mallory for me to see if there were any priors or criminal history over in her jurisdiction. She advised that he had been arrested in the past for DWI, and that she did have prints on him. I asked her to go ahead and send these over to me along with the booking information, which she did."

Jenkins: "So you've now identified the victim as being Richard Mallory. Where did your investigation go from that point?"

Horzepa: "… we then did some backtracking trying to get some background on Mr. Mallory… (he) was extremely suspicious of people, didn't really trust many people. He was very private, didn't really tell anybody what he did, where he was going. He employed several people. Of the employees that we were able to interview, none of them were there for a very long time…"

Horzepa confirmed that Mallory was either too drunk, too high, or too busy with topless-bottomless lap dancers and prostitutes to run an efficient business. Like Aileen, Richard worked erratically, usually for a few days at a time. However, Jackie Davis said that Richard always had large sums of cash on him, obtained in mysterious ways. Richard paid his whores in cash.

Horzepa: "We found that he appeared to be heavy in debt; he owed several thousand dollars for the rental of (his) storefront property. We found hostile notes (and calls) from customers who had dropped items to be repaired, which he apparently never did. We took a look and saw over a hundred items that were in need of repair which he hadn't even started to work on. We found correspondence from (the) IRS. Apparently he was in trouble with them, and (it) looked like he was going to be audited."

Horzepa found that Mallory owed $3,800 in back rent, consorted with known criminals, and was himself a known criminal. Mallory was also highly sexed. When Horzepa searched Mallory's apartment, he found a large collection of X-rated videos, Playboy magazines, and thousands of photographs of naked women.

Horzepa: "In speaking to Jackie Davis, which was (his) last known girlfriend, she said that he would like to drink, enjoyed the strip bars, was into some pornography, but that she didn't partake of any of that. When he decided he wanted that particular lifestyle, he would go out by himself during those times. He went to numerous strip bars in the Tampa/Clearwater area."

In the last weeks of December 1990, two years before Aileen's first trial, Jackie Davis told Horzepa that Richard Mallory had done time for burglary and for some kind of sexual offense back in Maryland, that he'd been in some kind of… experimental program for sex offenders. Horzepa didn't probe further; the unspoken specter of male castration was too unsettling.

Aileen's jury never got to hear any of this.

Horzepa asked Davis if she thought Mallory would pick up a female hitchhiker. Davis thought he would. So did Linda Nusbaum, the second ex-Mrs. Mallory, a woman with a criminal past of her own. Nusbaum confirmed that Mallory was a heavy drinker, smoked a lot of pot, was extremely paranoid, did lots of disappearing acts, and was, above all, obsessed with pornography.

Jenkins: "At the time (early in 1990), did you have any clue at all that perhaps the assailant was a female that was hitchhiking?"

Horzepa: "The possibility existed. And that was because… we had found that the driver's seat had been pulled all the way to the front, and Mr. Mallory was a little larger than that unless he liked to drive in what I would consider an uncomfortable position."

Wuornos had not bothered to cover her tracks. Was she completely rattled, or was this her standard M.O.: thoughtless, brazen, self-destructive?

Richard Mallory had lost all contact with his family. He hadn't seen his first wife, a son he reportedly had, his second wife, or his sister, in years. Although Richard and Jackie were no longer together, it was Jackie who took Richard's body and had it cremated.

She scattered his ashes in a wooded area.

* * *

Way it worked, Aileen mainly cruised the bars alone, but she sometimes took Tyria along too. Tyria had learned not to say too much, otherwise she'd never hear the end of it. Aileen would give Tyria "dirty looks" and accuse her of wanting to sleep with everyone Tyria spoke to. To keep the peace, Tyria had learned to sit nursing beer after beer, butch-silent, watchful, as if she were a bouncer, a bodyguard, a bashful girl-of-a-man.

What she really was, was Aileen's prized and only human connection/possession, on display. A "look, but don't touch" policy was in effect. Tyria was Aileen's entire family: her mother, her father, her sister, her brother, her wife, her husband, her child—hers, her property, which Aileen isolated, hoarded, guarded. Tyria was Aileen's drinking buddy and strangely placid hostage, Aileen's Other Half, Better Half, Mission Control, Ground Zero, Aileen's last link to reality.

Aileen liked to play pool. She liked beating the guys. Once,

Tyria saw her make the eight ball on a break. Tyria was impressed. Aileen didn't like darts quite as much because Tyria tended to win that game.

Way it worked, Tyria would go home right after work and wait for Aileen. When Tyria wasn't working, she would stay in the room and wait for Aileen to return. Then, they'd eat takeout, drink beer, hang out at a bar or in the room, watch *Jeopardy* and *Wheel of Fortune*, watch football or basketball, listen to music. Tyria had a hard time getting to sleep, though, since Aileen insisted on blasting the music until 2 or 3am. Didn't care if Tyria couldn't sleep, cared only about herself, Tyria thought.

* * *

Ironically, Aileen wasn't the one who'd thought about getting a gun. Aileen said that she'd always "dated" police officers, ex-officers, too, and that they were the ones who'd taught her how to shoot. Men might have understood how much danger Aileen was in. Men, not women; men, not Aileen, especially men in uniform, cops, or men who'd served in the armed forces might have understood that a man needs a gun to defend himself when he's attacked, especially when he's in a war.

Aileen respected men and listened to them even though she hated them. Sometimes, Aileen behaved as if she were a man.

Both Aileen and her tricks lived in Big Gun Country. The roads that ran through Volusia, Marion, Pasco, Citrus, and Dixie Counties bore signs that advertised guns for sale. Car stickers said: "This car is insured by Smith and Wesson." It was well known that women, especially when traveling alone, were Big Game on the highways of north-central Florida. Those women who could afford it, had car phones and guns of their own on board so they could lock themselves in, call for help—or aim, when a man tried to run them off the road, or take advantage of a lone woman's flat tire to rob, rape, or kill her.

Hey, shit happens.

Aileen couldn't stop hustling. Aileen was armed, to defend herself. Aileen knew how the gun worked, she'd used it; it had saved her life.

Way it worked, if Aileen couldn't get anybody to drive her over to the highway, she'd walk to the Votran bus stop and ride the bus to work.

There she was, a white woman alone, a white woman on foot, an apparition, walking along the sun-blazed highway, hitchhiking. The cars zoomed by, leaving her behind, as if they were from a faster, future age, and she was still trudging along, biblically. Aileen wasn't a bum, she was a working girl, but without a car in Florida, you're a real low-down, burned-out piece of shit—unless you're being crafty, hiding from the police, right there, out in the open, invisible.

Maybe Aileen didn't like having to stand around and wait for a bus. Man, it was fuckin' hot out there. Maybe Aileen didn't like her line of work anymore—but then again, maybe it was the only thing she still liked; she couldn't stand much else. Something had gone out of control, and Aileen couldn't make it stop, God knows, you can't say she wasn't trying to drown her rage in alcohol, so she could keep on truckin', but maybe there just wasn't enough beer in the universe.

Usually, Aileen didn't wait at the official bus stop. Where the hell was it at anyway? Aileen had a hard time toeing any line. She'd be walking along, she'd hear the bus, and she'd stop right where she was. Aileen expected the bus to pick her up "right where that finger was," which is how driver Dennis Metcalf put it. If not, she'd bitch and moan and complain.

Aileen hated the bus drivers and fought with almost every one of them. Reported 'em, too. They asked too many questions: Where you goin', where you from, what's in your bag, where you work at? Aileen had a hard time with men in uniforms. That included bus drivers.

The Votran bus drivers, dispatchers, and supervisors all knew Aileen personally, had heard about her, or had heard from her. She used to call the supervisors up to complain that one of their bus drivers had fuckin' passed her by, or hadn't dropped her off in the exact right spot. Once, when Votran's only female bus driver said "Good morning" to her, Aileen cursed her out.

Once Aileen boarded the bus, she kept to herself, but she'd also try to borrow coffee money from one of the other passengers, said she was broke, her car broke down. Mainly, she'd just sit there and air a steady string of complaints: The air was too cold, the bus had been late, the driver hadn't stopped in the right spot, men were bothering her. Once, as Aileen was getting off, in fact, just as her foot left the last step, she turned around and made a derogatory remark about "n----rs," her parting shot, so to speak, aimed directly at two black female passengers.

Aileen was a biker-style traditionalist who did not like "n----rs" or "queers." Aileen was a white woman who had done jail time surrounded by black women who didn't know their place any more than Aileen knew hers.

Years back, one of the black Votran bus drivers had said to Tyria: "You are looking good."

Without a word, Aileen pulled the driver out of his seat and punched him right in the mouth. The driver had sent her crashing through the glass doors of the trolley. Aileen, aka Cammie Green, took action against Votran. The driver was "terminated," and Aileen/Cammie agreed to a small settlement. See there's another example: If Aileen had a legal job (and it's not her fault, is it, that she didn't) she coulda held out for some Big Bucks.

* * *

The first time that James Albert Legary saw Aileen was about a month after she'd killed Mallory. James had just pulled into his driveway on Burleigh. Aileen was just standing there, staring at him. Glaring at him. Looking like she wanted to kick his ass. James thought well, this is a really nice way to meet your new neighbor.

Well, as James saw it, all the tenants next door had to meet certain requirements. For example, their cars couldn't have mufflers. They had to be big, noisy drinkers. They had to argue with their wives in the middle of the night. Something. This new renter looked like she fit right in. James wondered what criteria she'd met. And he laughed, just thinking about it.

Aileen was deeply offended by James' laughter. At least, that's what she told the landlady and that's what the landlady later told James.

About a month later, James was working on his car in the driveway, when he saw Aileen toss a firecracker out her window. A goddam firecracker! Then, James heard her cackle. He thought she sounded just like the Wicked Witch from *The Wizard of Oz*. James thought this was pretty strange. Stranger than all the other Good Neighbor Policies next door.

Aileen played her music very loud. Pink Floyd, Canned Heat, Country Joe and the Fish, the Miami Sound Machine, Phil Collins. James never called the police; he didn't think it would do much good. Actually, he thought the music was okay.

Aileen managed to stage some Major Incidents with James. First, Aileen accused Lenny, James' son, of stealing Tyler, her cat.

"What the hell would he want it for?" James pointed out.

Aileen started yelling at James.

James yelled right back at her. "Why in Hell don't you just go back inside your little house? That'd be a good idea."

Which Aileen did.

Tyler turned up, but that didn't stop Aileen from accusing James and Lenny of a whole buncha other things.

On January 24th, ten months before Mallory picked Aileen up, the state of Florida finally executed Ted Bundy. He had not been tried for raping and killing "more than 100 girls and women over a fifteen-year period" (Washington state investigator Robert Keppel's estimate), but for raping and killing three women in north-central Florida. Bundy's youngest victim, Kimberly Leach, of Lake City, Florida, had been twelve years old when he'd killed her in 1978.

For years, Bundy's M.O. had been to pose as a man in distress, on crutches, in a (fake) cast. Bundy would ask women to hold his briefcase, open his car door, help him, and then he'd attack them. Viciously. Three women who'd survived his attacks suffered broken jaws, broken arms, crushed fingers, severed nerves, hearing loss. Their teeth were knocked out, too.

News of Bundy's execution had dominated the media in Florida. Everyone had something to say. "It's sort of like the Super Bowl," Mayor Gerald Witt told The Associated Press the day before the execution.

"There's no question about it. It'll be a therapeutic act," said Jerry Blair, one of the state attorneys who'd prosecuted Bundy.

Attorney Chuck Leidner said: "I do think the justice system stinks. If Ted Bundy had been black or Hispanic or poor and unattractive, he would have been killed long ago."

Attorney John Tanner, Aileen Wuornos' future prosecutor, had befriended Bundy and served as Bundy's spiritual advisor. Tanner tried to delay Bundy's execution for two reasons. First, as Tanner told *The Orlando Sentinel*, when the Supreme Court turned down Bundy's appeal, Bundy began to confess; within days, Bundy had confessed to an additional 23 unsolved murders. Law enforcement officers, Tanner said, were getting verifiable, hard facts concerning unsolved murders, but it would take law enforcement up to three years to check out the details.

Two years before that, in 1987, Bundy had asked Tanner, then a newly elected state prosecutor, to arrange an interview with James C. Dobson, a psychologist and religious broadcaster. In the interview, Bundy blamed pornography for what he'd done.

On January 25, 1989, Investigator Robert Keppel told The Associated Press that "pornography is maybe one-one-thousandths of the whole problem Bundy had." Keppel viewed Bundy's interview with James C. Dobson as "totally self-serving."

On January 22, 1989, Tanner told the *Miami Herald* that "I want to emphasize that my role was to put Ted Bundy in contact with law enforcement and I've done that. It's caused the people I represent to be very angry at me."

Tanner may have learned that it was risky to befriend a serial killer in Florida.

CHAPTER THREE

Two Additional Male Corpses
and a Lap Dancer on the Run

B Y THE END OF JANUARY 1991, Volusia county investigators Horzepa and Bob Kelley had found the two
women Richard Mallory had "dated" the night before he'd met
Aileen: Kimberly Guy, aka Danielle, and Chastity Lee Marcus,
Kimberly's lap dancing partner.

Kimberly insisted that she had never had sex with Mallory,
she'd only had sex with Chastity, for Richard's greater viewing
pleasure. Chastity, Kimberly said, was the one who'd fucked
Richard. Chastity would insist that it was Kimberly who'd had
sex with Richard, not her. A classic case of Honor-among-Hook-
ers.

Kimberly was certain that she and Chastity had been with
Richard on the night of November 30th.

On October 15, 1991, more than a year and a half later, in an
Examination Before Trial (EBT), Horzepa told public defender
Jenkins that he'd toured the Tampa strip clubs, and that the manager of Club "2001 Odyssey" said she'd once seen Chastity with
a handgun. Chastity's professional photo was that of a blonde,
thin woman with large breasts, and many tattoos, including one
of a devil, a unicorn, and a dragon. She looked twenty-five years
old. Chastity had been stripping, lap dancing, and hooking in

Tampa for two years at clubs with names like The Circus, The Booby Trap, The Candy Bar.

Horzepa and Kelley persuaded Chastity's boyfriend, Michael "Dougie" Lambert, to bring Chastity to their motel for a little chat. In his EBT, Horzepa told Jenkins that Chastity "was very scared, I think basically because she had had run-ins with the law in the past. Her particular profession was not, I guess, viewed nicely by law enforcement; (she) had been hassled—her words—by the local law enforcement authorities."

Chastity told the detectives that she'd first met Richard early in November. He was always asking her to do "lap dances at the back of the club for a hundred dollars." By late November, Chastity and Kimberly had suggested that the two of them go to a corner of the bar with Richard and have a "good time," for three hundred dollars for three dances. After they had danced for Richard, they all smoked a joint and left the club, picked up some food, and went to Richard's office, where they had sex with one another, and with Richard (or at least one of them did). Each woman took away one TV set and one VCR.

Chastity had certain things in common with Mallory's killer. For example, both Aileen and Chastity had been adopted; in both cases, the adoptions hadn't worked out. Chastity had been adopted when she was nine by a couple in Texas, who, according to Michael Reynolds in the book *Dead Ends*, had "given her up after two years because of her incorrigible violence and thievery." Aileen had been formally adopted by her maternal grandparents in 1960.

At Aileen's first trial, Dr. Elizabeth McMahon testified that throughout her childhood, Aileen's grandfather/father kept saying that "they should never have adopted Aileen and her brother, that he wished (he) could take them out in the backyard and shoot them, hang them from trees, that they were more trouble than they were worth. This was the constant thing that she grew up with."

Filmmaker Nick Broomfield interviewed people from Lee's childhood who, on camera, described her adoptive father/ grandfather as "a bastard who beat the hell out of her for a good five minutes with a black belt while he had her lean over a chair."

Another childhood informant admitted that he had "treated her like dirt," called her "ugly, bitch," had thrown rocks at her but secretly also had sex with her.

Wuornos became the "local untouchable" and people "picked on her." For two years, she lived in an abandoned car in the woods and hooked at night in order to survive. No adult rescued her.

Both Aileen and Chastity had violent male relatives who had died violently.

Chastity's biological father had been a member of an outlaw biker gang known as the Warlocks. He had died in a motorcycle accident. Chastity's biker husband, the President of the Sons of Silence, had been killed in a rumble with the Outlaws, a rival biker gang in Indiana.

Aileen's biological father, Leo Pitman, was a wife beater and a child rapist, and he died in jail, a presumed suicide. Aileen's biological grandfather, Lauri, who was also her adoptive father, was a raging alcoholic, who had physically and verbally abused her quite viciously. Lauri had also killed himself. His daughter Diane, and his granddaughter Aileen, both held him responsible for his wife Britta's death.

Both Aileen and Chastity felt comfortable around outlaw bikers. Both women were hookers and had an alias for every day of the week.

Chastity was "Chastity," but she'd been known as Celeste, Robin, or Paige. Chastity's "real" first name may once have been Jaimie.

Aileen was Lee, Aileen, Cammie Greene, Cammie Marsh Greene, Lori Grody, Lynn Blahovec, Susan Blahovec, and Sandra Beatrice Kretsch.

Names like Lee or Cammie are at least normal, respectable names, not hooker names like Hot Lips, Baby Doll, Sugar, Candy, or other instant-edible sound-alikes.

With hookers, everything's a lie, an illusion, a fantasy, a fake. Maybe it's one unending Disneyland ride for adult men like Mallory, but it's the same scary or boring ride, over and

over again—for much needed money—for young adult wom-
en like Chastity or Aileen. The truth is: Hookers lie about their
names, their ages, their views-of-the-day, and they don't come
on the job, they fake coming, if that's what a John wants. Often, hookers are bisexual or lesbians, and not just in Daytona or
Tampa—but also in New York, London, Dublin, Copenhagen,
and Bangkok.

Talk to a hooker, talk to a hundred of them, and you'll soon
know that they're rarely "sexual" in their private lives. If it's not
the incest or other family abuse, then it's their fear of being beat-
en, raped, knifed, tortured, or arrested, or it's the drugs, or the
booze that does it: castrates them. Maybe it's just what happens
when, day after day, Daddy's Little Princess is reduced to ped-
dling Three-Orifices-Two-Tits-One-Ass and a shitload of lies
for money.

"I heard grim stories of violence and coercion, of rape and
murder, of non-payment and forced sex, of hunger pains, disease, and desperation," wrote Phillipa Levine, in her study of
prostitution in Florida. "Women spoke of jumping out of moving cars in preference to facing weapons, of being driven to
lonely areas against their will, of non-paying clients whose violent behavior forced them to comply with unanticipated desires.
One interviewee described one horrific night when three separate clients threatened her with a knife… the police confirmed
that they knew of no women who had not had bad experiences
with customers."

Aileen's jury was never informed of such facts.

After a while, when most hookers see a man ,all they see is
a John, not a real person. They can't afford to admit it, not even
to themselves. Bad for business.

Chastity called her Johns "dates," not "customers" or "clients." Better for business, and for her own self-esteem. Maybe
Chastity didn't want to think of herself as only a hooker, but as
a regular girl, too, one who's just hot for men. For their money.
But that's no different from all those straight women who run
around trying to get a rich man to marry them, see?

Neither Chastity nor Aileen had any legal ID, driver's licenses, or social security cards. It's as if neither woman existed, as if they belonged to no country on Earth.

Aileen also referred to her Johns as "dates," but she also referred to them as "clients" or "customers." Aileen didn't understand why society forced prostitutes to lead outlaw lives. Aileen said: "It's so petty a crime. You go to bed with your lover, it's the same thing with a prostitute. There's no difference. (For me) it was like going to bed with a male boyfriend. Where do people get off that you deserve to die for this, or be raped or beaten?"

Aileen was not ashamed that she was a prostitute. She viewed it as "an old-fashioned career," and she thought she'd cornered the market in Florida as a hitchhiking prostitute. Aileen said: "I owned the whole Florida state. The way I did prostitution, nobody else did it. It was a cool way of doing it. I mean, it was inconspicuous. I had all the men out there. I had all the executives. I had state executives, bank presidents, sales representatives, owners of stores, owners of businesses, owners of factories. I had a jet pilot, a private pilot for Johnson & Johnson, police officers, secret service guys, all kinds of people that was way up there."

This was a lie. Aileen had probably stolen these cards from the man she had married for a month, the guy who took out a restraining order against her.

Rachel Moran explained in her incredible memoir, *Paid For: My Journey Through Prostitution*, that it is much safer being on the street or on the road and without a pimp than it is being in a brothel, or belonging to an escort service. Outside, a woman can choose—or avoid the man and the car.

So, Aileen was not an idiot. She said she was a "country hooker, thumbing, hitchhiking all over the country so I didn't meet a lot of creepy men. The city always harbors all the most evil people. I never got busted because I prostituted hitchhiking, that's why I never got caught. When you stand by a lamppost in the city, you've got these crazies going by saying, 'I know her,' 'I'm going to give her some shit, I'm going to let her give me head but I'm going to treat her like dirt or whatever.'"

Phillipa Levine understood that Florida street prostitutes

"concur that their endurance is tested not just by actual customers, but also by those who shout and wave as they drive past, those who 'window shop' by driving past slowly, assessing the 'goods,' often returning four or five or even six times."

Aileen the hitchhiker was more... entrepreneurial, more enterprising, than Chastity. At least Aileen thought so. Aileen was also more anti-social, less able to understand or obey the most minor social conventions.

Aileen thought that some of her clients fell in love with her. She said that one real nice guy had wanted to marry her, but she'd turned him down because he was a thief and she thought he'd get busted one of these days. He was handsome, too. Aileen's point was that she'd turned him down even though he had money. She told the media that, when she was twenty, she'd left her seventy-year-old husband of one month because he beat her—even though *he* had money too.

No, being a prostitute didn't bother Aileen, being seen as materialistic did. On Death Row, she said: "You can take your cars, you can take your fine houses and you can take all the fine jewelry and anything this world has got to offer. I do not want it. All I want is my spirit forgiven for these crimes. All I care about is going to heaven, getting off this planet as soon as possible. People are evil, they don't look in the mirror and see what's going on around them in the fast lane. All they care about is lust, the root of evil, and money, lusting after money. They are exploiting me, killing me for money. Well, fine. I really don't care. You can destroy this flesh but you can't touch my soul."

But as I came to know Aileen, I understood how much even small sums of money meant to her.

Toward the end of March, Investigators Horzepa and Kelly returned to the Clearwater/Tampa area. This time, Chastity's boyfriend, Dougie Lambert, said he was scared of Chastity because she was part of a motorcycle gang called the Sons of Silence, that she'd been married to the president of a chapter up north. Lambert said that Chastity hung around with bikers, but that he wasn't into the particular scene and was afraid of possibly getting her mad and maybe having some retaliation.

However, Lambert also told the Volusia County detectives that Chastity had cried to him, and confessed that she'd killed Richard Mallory. Everyone who knew Chastity saw her acting skittish, weird, freaked out, as if she heard footsteps coming after her.

Chastity fled Tampa.

On April 5th, Horzepa typed up an affidavit charging Chastity with the "unlawful killing of a human being, while engaged in the perpetration of a robbery." The warrant for her arrest was signed by Circuit Judge Uriel "Bunky" Blount Jr., the man who would, one day, brusquely, almost brutishly, preside over Aileen's trial for the murder of Mallory.

On May 27th, Horzepa and Kelley traveled to New Orleans to pick up Chastity Lee Marcus. She'd been spotted and arrested in Jefferson Parish County, in New Orleans. In his EBT, Horzepa told Jenkins that "when [the Sergeant saw her at that particular time], she was naked in the bathroom."

Jenkins was taken aback, and asked: "Wait, when the officer saw her, she was naked in the bathroom?"

Horzepa explained: "She had run into the bathroom. There was an undercover officer who was in that particular motel room... he was outside, and when he came in, she had run into the bathroom... he saw the tattoos and said 'You're the person I'm looking for,' and then we flew to New Orleans and talked to her."

On June 29th, Kimberly Guy passed her polygraph test. Her sex-dancing partner, Chastity Lee Marcus, had already been extradited to Florida and stashed in the Volusia County jail.

However, Chastity's alibi checked out, and none of Mallory's belongings were ever found in her possession. By July 3rd, state attorney David Damore decided there simply wasn't enough evidence to bring Chastity to trial. He dropped all charges against her. Chastity immediately dropped out of sight.

* * *

Sometime in February 1990, mid-morning, on a weekday,

auctioneer James Delarosa saw Aileen standing by the side of the road. He stopped for her. Aileen, all friendly business, said she was on her way to Orlando but wasn't sure which road to take. James was familiar with the area, he lived in Holly Hill, so he assured Aileen that he could get her over to Interstate 4, no problem, and let her out at 11th Street.

Aileen said fine. She also told him that she owned a $125,000 home in the area.

He asked: "Where about?"

Aileen declined to say.

James wondered how, if she had a home nearby, she knew so little about the local roads. James didn't feel that "everything was as advertised." Aileen smoothly moved to allay his unspoken anxiety. She told him that her car was broke, she needed some money, and she showed him a picture of a little girl and a little boy. She said they were her kids.

James commented: "Nice looking children."

Aileen put the photos back into her purse, then pulled out another card holder and held it up. She told him she was a professional prostitute. "See," she said, "These are some of my customers—judges, attorneys, state attorneys, police officers." Aileen was a businesswoman. She was showing James her references. In a matter-of-fact business-like kind of way, she told him her rates: "$75 in the woods, $100 in a motel room, but you've got to use a condom for straight sex." He was quiet. Aileen said: "I prefer to go into the woods."

James declined her offer. He didn't know why, but he didn't want to offend her, make her mad, so James said: "Maybe some other time, I'll take a rain check."

Aileen said: "It's now or never." And then she clammed up, closed down, retreated into herself, dropped the friendly, outgoing, normal businesswoman act.

James let Aileen out on the corner of Highway 92 and 11th Street. She slammed the car door, didn't thank him for the ride. James headed west, towards Daytona. Aileen, walking, headed west, towards the Interstate.

* * *

On April 6th, another Cadillac, a 1984 model, was found abandoned, this time in Marion County, in Ocala. Investigator Bruce Munster tried to contact the owner, 46-year-old farmer Douglas Giddens, of Nashville, Georgia. However, Giddens' family was "unable to explain why the vehicle was at that location." The Marion County Sheriff's Department impounded the car.

Later that afternoon, Mr. Giddens' fully clothed body was found off NE 33rd Street in Ocala, in a wooded area. Mr. Giddens had been shot in the head by a single .38 caliber bullet. Giddens had carried a .38 caliber Smith & Wesson handgun with him and he may have been shot with his own gun. Mr. Giddens' wallet was found nearby with the money neatly removed.

Marion County Investigators, Brian Jarvis and Jay Manifold, were called to the scene by an "alert, sharp-sighted tow-truck driver who noticed what he thought was a wallet lying on the side of the rural dirt road." Jarvis discovered that Giddens had been "traveling to Ft. Lauderdale to pick up $2,000 in cash from a business associate investing in his farm."

Investigator Munster later noted that "the driver's seat was pulled up close to the steering wheel and empty cans of Budweiser were on the floor board of the car. Blond hair was visible to investigators on the seat of the automobile. The victim was inside his auto at the time he was killed… Someone had torn the trunk of the 1984 Cadillac apart, as if they were looking for something. However, the $2,000 in cash was found tucked away in a glove beneath the spare tire."

On May 19th, forty-three-year-old David Spears, a heavy-equipment operator and construction worker from Bradenton, left Universal Concrete, where he worked, in Sarasota. According to Investigator Jerry Thompson of the Citrus County Sheriff's Department, Spears was traveling north alone, in his 1983 Dodge pickup truck, on his way to Orlando. Spears did not arrive at his destination. Spears was divorced but still friendly with his ex-wife, Dee. For example, he still gave Dee his laundry to do, and she still did it. Dee told Thompson that she'd expected David later that night.

* * *

Aileen may have always lived in fear, but she made it a point not to know it, to deny it—to herself, most of all, to drown it in cases of beer each day, but ever since she'd killed Mallory, Aileen knew she was afraid: of being arrested, of being raped again, or being killed herself, in the woods.

Aileen was scared all the time. She didn't know if she'd left prints or anything, or if the cops—or Jesus—were looking for her or not. Despite her growing fears, Aileen had to keep on hitchhiking and hustling.

In her confession, and at trial, Aileen pointed out that every day she hustled, she had "vehicle contact" with at least thirty guys, and "sexual contact" with 3 to 5 guys. Aileen's point: she saw a lot of guys whom she "didn't have to kill, because none of them ever abused" her. Then David Spears came along.

On May 19th, sometime in the afternoon, Spears picked Aileen up. He wore a beard, jeans, work boots, a pullover shirt and a baseball cap. David was tall, and he loved to drink and party. It's the main reason he and his church-going wife had decided to divorce.

When David met Aileen he was drunk, he'd been drinking all day. Aileen didn't care. She was kinda drunk herself. Aileen thought David was too loud. Aileen usually felt comfortable with men who were like herself, but sometimes they also frightened her. Sometimes, she even frightened herself.

Aileen didn't bullshit David, she just told him her prices. She was ready to fuck him for money, to do what she called "an honest deed."

They went into the woods, took their clothes off, and climbed into the back of David's truck, where there was a bed. There they were, nude, and drunk, and screwin' around. Thing was, Aileen did only certain things, and in a certain way. You couldn't rush her, or push her, or physically try to get her to do something she didn't want to do.

Aileen was perfectly normal for someone with a Traumatic-Brain Injury, Post-Traumatic Stress Disorder, a possibly low IQ, and perhaps a Multiple Personality Disorder.

In her rigid, almost robotic way, Aileen was also saying: C'mon, guys, gimme a break, my nerves are shot. Aileen needed to feel in control at all times. If not, she couldn't work that high wire, she had no goddam safety net, she knew what could happen to her at any moment, it had happened before, lots of times. True, most of her tricks were friendly, wouldn't hurt a fly. True, some of her best (and only) friends were tricks. But things were different since she'd killed Mallory.

David Spears may have had a boyish face but he was a big man and he was drunk. Maybe David was used to wrestling as a form of foreplay. Maybe he thought Aileen actually liked it. Maybe he liked it rough, didn't much care what she liked, why should he, he was paying, wasn't he? Maybe David forced Aileen's head down too forcefully. Aileen may have thought: If this dude starts pushing on me, how do I know how far he'll go?

Aileen wasn't takin' any shit. Or any chances either. New Policy. Aileen saw a lead pipe back there. No telling if David would be using that lead pipe on her or not. He probably would. Aileen felt he had already "gotten vicious, gone radical on her."

In her confession, Aileen said that they both jumped outta the truck, she ran to the front of the truck, grabbed her bag, got her gun, and shot "quick as possible at the tailgate of the truck." Then, Spears ran to the driver's side trying' to get towards her, which Aileen thought was weird: towards her not away from her, and she thought: "What the hell you think you're doin', dude, you know... I am gonna kill you 'cause you were tryin' to do whatever you could with me." Then, through the door, Aileen pumped a total of six bullets into David Spears, and he fell back.

This was Aileen's own version of vigilante Affirmative Action—mess with her, and the John dies.

Aileen confessed that afterwards: "I just got in the truck and took off. I drove all over the place. There was a radio and some tools in the truck. I sold them and kept the radio. I told Ty I borrowed somebody's vehicle again." Aileen ripped the license plate off, threw it in a ditch, put some grass over it. She recalls being as "drunk as shit." Afterwards, she "just bummed" her way home.

On May 20th, according to Investigator Munster, "Spears' truck was spotted by a friend who reported this to the Marion County Sheriff's Office. The gas tank was nearly empty, its keys and license tag were removed. A blond hair was visible to investigators on the steering well. A torn prophylactic package was found on the floor of the vehicle. All personal property, which included a large amount of mechanic's tools, clothing, and a one-of-a-kind ceramic statue of a panther, was missing from the trunk. The truck seat was close to the steering wheel."

A pattern was emerging, but the Volusia County detectives didn't talk to the Marion County detectives, and Marion County didn't talk to Citrus County. Too busy. In each county, a car had been found, abandoned, with the driver's seat pushed up close to the steering wheel. In two cases, a torn prophylactic package and a blonde hair were found. Two of the cars had lost their front license plates. In two cases, the bodies of the cars' owners had been discovered some distance from their cars.

Shortly after David Spears' truck was impounded by the Citrus County Sheriff's Department, Marion County Investigator Brian Jarvis was notified that an unidentified man's body had been located in a secluded area in the southern part of Georgia. The murder weapon was a .22 caliber firearm. The sheriffs of Volusia, Marion, and Citrus counties were now joined by the Georgia Bureau of Investigation, in their independent investigations of the murders of four middle-aged white men near Interstate-75.

CHAPTER FOUR

Three More Men Murdered
"Ya Talkin' to Me?"

O N MAY 31ST, Detective Tom Musk of the Pasco County Sheriff's Office was notified that Charles Edmund
("Sonny") Carskaddon, a 39-year-old W/M, had been traveling alone in his 1975 tan and brown Cadillac going south on
I-75 from Missouri where he'd visited his mother, Florence, en
route to see his fiancé in Tampa. Carskaddon, a rodeo worker,
would have been driving through the state of Florida during
the daylight hours of May 31st. Carskaddon had not arrived at
his intended destination. His whereabouts were unknown to his
family and friends.

Another man missing, maybe down.

Was some loose screw out there, killing men to get their
older model Cadillacs off the road?

Carskaddon had picked up Aileen in Pasco County. Aileen
had admired his gray snakeskin cowboy boots, she thought he
was a handsome dude. A rodeo worker, he said. They quickly
agreed on a price and found a place in the woods. Once they
both had their clothes off, things changed.

In a letter to Tyria, written in February of 1993, Aileen
complained bitterly about how Carskaddon was her "least talked about" victim. Aileen felt the detectives had "dodged" and

lied about this case. Aileen claimed that she "shot him the most times." The cops said she'd shot him nine times, but she remembers having shot him eleven times. Aileen said she'd reloaded, and shot Carskaddon two more times, after he grabbed his .45 and tried to fire at her for the second time.

Carskaddon might have provoked Aileen in three ways. First, he cursed her. Aileen heard him call her a "fuckin' bitch."

Hey, Mister, I don't do windows anymore. Treat me with some respect or I might have to kill you. Aileen would never have put it this way. She didn't understand what was happening to her. All her life, she'd welcomed men who "wanted one thing only," and if they cursed at her, well, let them, they were paying; it didn't bother her anyway. Most of the time, it still didn't. She prided herself on that.

In a spring 1991 phone conversation, Aileen told me: "When I was at Citrus (county jail), the men were yelling to see tits and puss. I guess they needed it real bad. There was a little hole in my cell. I thought they were sending me an envelope filled with sugar (I'd asked for some), but they sent me an envelope filled with their cum in it. Another time, they squirted a whole bunch of disgusting liquid all up and down the walls of my cell. The men in Citrus drew a picture of me in the electric chair getting fried and showed it to me. The guards told the male prisoners that they'd like to electrify me themselves. Once, all thirty men banged their feet on the walls at me. The men in Citrus didn't bother me. I can take it. I'd like to go back there. We're just waiting for a bed to open up in Citrus."

Aileen would rather kill than say "Uncle."

Someone like Aileen might take being called "bitch" or "whore" as a friendly greeting, a compliment. From Aileen's point of view, if a man called her a "whore," it might mean he was hot for her, that he'd pay to get it. This meant Aileen would eat—and triumph over him. She'd get his money. "Feeling insulted" was for wives and other straight Ladies.

So what the hell was wrong with her?

Maybe Aileen's capacity to experience insults as if they were compliments was temporarily on the blink, or in the process of breaking down. Maybe the anesthetic effect of a lifetime of booze was beginning to wear off. Maybe the booze had destroyed too many of her brain cells, but what the hell gave Carskaddon the right to treat her like shit?

That's the first thing Carskaddon might have done wrong: treat Aileen contemptuously.

Second thing: Aileen heard him say he was a drug dealer. Aileen detested drugs and dealers. Drugs did terrible things to hustlers; Aileen wanted no part of them. Drugs controlled you, then men controlled you better, then the men didn't want you. When that happened, you died, one way or the other.

Third thing: Carskaddon had a .45 caliber handgun, with white grips. Aileen said she saw it on the hood of his car. Aileen also said she saw him pick it up, cock the trigger, aim it at her, and laugh. Laugh at her. Aileen didn't know the gun wasn't loaded, she wouldn't know that until she got the gun home. Aileen was already drunker than hell. She still might not have killed him, except when Carskaddon cocked the trigger at her, Aileen really saw red. Royal red. Aileen shot him. She kept shooting him. She couldn't seem to stop.

Aileen took all the cash Carskaddon had, and his gun. Why the hell not? She'd earned it.

* * *

On June 1st, a badly decomposed male body was discovered in a wooded area off U.S. 19 in Citrus County. According to Marion County's Bruce Munster, "The body was nude except for a baseball cap. On the ground near the body was a used prophylactic, a torn prophylactic package, and both Busch and Budweiser brand empty cans of beer. The body was identified as belonging to Mr. David Spears. Cause of death was six gunshot wounds to the front and back torso. The bullets recovered from his body were copper coated, .22 caliber hollow nosed bullets fired from a weapon, rifled with a 6 right twist."

On June 6th, a badly decomposed body of a nude male was found off County Road 52 near I-75 in Pasco County. The body was covered with grass and foliage and a greenish color electric blanket. No clothing, wallet, or identification were found. The cause of death was nine gunshot wounds to the torso of the victim. The nine bullets recovered were copper coated .22 caliber hollow nose bullets fired from a weapon rifled with a 6 right twist.

On June 7th, the Florida Highway Patrol found Carskaddon's Cadillac abandoned on the southbound side of I-75 just south of County Road 484 in Marion County. The license plate was missing.

It would take seven months for the investigators to tie Carskaddon's body to his abandoned Cadillac. Carskaddon's identity would remain unknown until December, when his mother Florence read a newspaper story about a possible pattern of highway killings in Florida. According to the Tampa Tribune, Florence then contacted the Marion County Sheriff's Office, and asked that the fingerprints of the unidentified body found in Pasco be matched with her son's. The fingerprints matched.

* * *

Being rejected was beginning to get on Aileen's nerves. Aileen wasn't about to kill a man for turning her down, but it wasn't lost on her that the men still got to do the choosing, not her. That didn't seem right—especially if she couldn't work as hard as before, not because she didn't want to, but because something was wrong.

Hey, what if she was too sick or too scared or too drunk to work more than a few hours a day or a few days a week—and she couldn't make enough money in that time because the guys weren't interested? In her business you hadda smile-you're-on-candid-camera all the time. Her mood wasn't good for business. She wasn't good for business.

On June 19th, Cammie Greene, using Florida driver's license G 650 113 62 799 and date of birth 8-14-62, pawned David Spears' box of tools at Bruce's Gun and Pawn Shop in Ormond Beach.

On June 22nd, Peter Siems, a 65-year-old retired merchant seaman and Christian missionary of Jupiter Florida, was reported missing. According to Investigator Munster, Siems "entered into his 1988 silver Pontiac Sunbird to travel alone north to Arkansas during the daylight hours. Neighbors observed Mr. Siems place luggage into his automobile and leave. Mr. Siems never arrived at his destination. His family contacted the Jupiter Police Department and initiated a missing person's report with that agency. Both Mr. Siems and his automobile were placed in the state-wide computer system as missing-ENDANGERED. Since his disappearance, Siems had contacted no one. His credit cards have not been used or bank monies withdrawn."

* * *

Tyria would later remember June and early July of that year as the months in which Aileen ("Hi Honey, I'm home!") drove three never-before-seen cars over to their place on Burleigh. Aileen almost immediately ditched two of the cars. On January 11, 1991, in her first statement to the police, Tyria would remember a white pickup truck; a .45 caliber automatic handgun with pearl handled grips; a large, brown older auto; and, the silver Pontiac Sunbird with a Florida Challenger tag. Aileen and Tyria used the Sunbird for nearly two weeks before they ditched it. According to Tyria, Aileen told "a couple of stories as to how she got the car." She also brought home about $700 in cash. Aileen took Tyria and her sister on a trip to SeaWorld with the money.

In her confession, Aileen said that "the missionary guy" had picked her up near 100 and I-95 and took her about 10 miles off the interstate, out into the woods, somewhere in Georgia. Aileen said she had no idea where she was, but then, she usually didn't. Aileen said she "took her handbag with her for fear the guy might try to rape her in the woods." She says they both got naked, but he "gave [her] a problem, too," and she "whipped out her gun." She said she hadn't wanted to shoot him, but when she heard him call her a 'fucking bitch,'" that's when she "told him she knew he was going to rape her." She said he came at her, and they struggled with her gun. A couple of shots were fired off into the air.

Then, Aileen said, she gained control of the .22 and "immediately" shot him. Aileen always said she shot somebody as "fast" as she could, and in the mid-section, so she'd know he was hit. She couldn't see very well, and she knew she wasn't an expert shot either. Afterwards, Aileen said, "I went through his things, found the Bibles and three or four hundred dollars in his suitcase."

During her confession, Investigator Munster queried Aileen about other Georgia homicides: "There's some other bodies up there in Georgia," he told her.

Aileen said: "I read about them. No, I didn't do those."

Munster asked: "Are you positive?"

Aileen answered: "I'm positive. The only one I left in Georgia was that missionary guy."

This is surreal. Aside from Siems, who was in his mid-sixties, these dead white men were in their forties and fifties, and they were big brawling men, men with big cars and bank accounts, men who took a stranded, car-less woman to out-of-the-way, secluded, lonely little hidden spots in the woods.

For the first time since Columbus had landed, maybe for the first time in ten thousand years, there were no bogeymen or sex-killers in the woods, there were only dead men's bodies in the woods, and a lone maid/whore was killing them, faster and faster too, like some speeded-up movie. This was not like any myth or fairy tale we'd ever heard, it was more like some kind of kinky American sick joke, a Lorena Bobbitt kind of joke, or a spoof on half a century of Hollywood Westerns, only this time it was a woman—a whore who stood up at the card table, kicked it over, and said: "Look at me the wrong way and you're dead."

Jesse James, or the Robert De Niro character in *Taxi Driver* ("You talkin' to me?")—as played by a Girl.

* * *

Aileen couldn't seem to control her rage when a man talked down to her, especially if he had a gun or a weapon of any kind, or perhaps, if he looked anything like her grandfather or reminded her in any way of any man who'd ever hurt her. Maybe being in the woods reminded her of the time when her grandfather's so-called friend raped her in the woods when she was thirteen and impregnated her too.

One rainy day, when Aileen was thirteen, a man asked her if she wanted a ride home. He said he knew Aileen's grandfather/ father, they'd just been together at the bar across the way from Clark's gas station. Aileen had gone down to the gas station to buy a pack of cigarettes. Aileen was trudging home on foot in the rain. The man had a car. In Aileen's words:

"The guy came up and he said, 'Hey, are you Aileen?' and I said, 'Yeah,' and he said, 'I know your Dad. Need a ride?' and I said, 'How do you know my Dad?' and he said 'I just came from the bar over there,' and I said, 'Yeah, I do need a ride home,' because it was raining. He said there were quails or something out in the woods there, 'Would you like to go see them? I know where a nest is at.' I was just a kid. Anyway, he gave me a beer, which by then I was drinking anyway, I mean all of us were, the whole neighborhood was."

Tyria said that Aileen never mentioned that this man had raped her. According to Tyria, Aileen said "she went with this guy cause he looked like Elvis. And she ended up getting pregnant."

Is this why Aileen preferred the woods to a motel room? Did she need to return to the woods, again and again, to re-enact it, the trauma and the excitement, the danger and the pleasure, trying to get it right, the way it happened that first time, trying to change the script, maybe stage a little revenge in the woods, too? Or did Aileen feel that she belonged in the woods and not in civilization, where she didn't fit in?

In May, Aileen accused her neighbor, James Legary's kid, Lenny, of dousing her garbage can with paint. In June, she accused Lenny of stealing the hubcaps off her gray Pontiac.

"You fuckin' bastard," Aileen yelled at James. "I'm gonna kick your ass. Gimme back my hubcaps. No, I'm gonna shoot you. Don't think I can't. I got a gun in the house. I'm gonna get it and use it on you."

"Yeah," James said, who was not impressed or afraid. "Well, you just need to go into the house, don't you?"

Aileen started to come at him, she looked like she was gonna wrestle James to the ground. Then, when she was twenty feet from him, she stopped, and went back into the house.

Later, Lenny went over and returned the hubcaps. When he got home, he said: "She's not really that bad a person, Dad."

* * *

On July 4th, Aileen and Tyria packed the Sunbird with beer and firecrackers, including the bottle rockets that were still left over from the last Fourth of July. They were on their way to the Seminole Indian Camp when, according to Tyria in her first statement to the police, she, Tyria, lost control of the car and crashed it through a fence. Aileen yelled at Tyria for going around the bend too fast. Tyria thought the car would blow up. Tyria saw that Aileen's arm was bleeding. Then, when Aileen ripped the rear plates from the car and threw out all the beer cans and told Tyria to run, Tyria knew that the car had probably been stolen. But then, Aileen changed her mind. They got back in and Aileen drove the car until the tire went flat. They finally abandoned the car, but not before Aileen ripped off the front plates and threw the keys into a field.

Six months later, Investigator Munster, in his January 1991 application for a search warrant, wrote: "Residents who reside in Orange Springs, in Marion County, observed two W/F's park a silver Pontiac Sunbird in front of their home. As they watched these females, the taller blond walked to the front of this automobile and tore a license plate from the front bumper. The shorter, heavy female withdrew (David Spears') red and white cooler from the back seat, and then they walked off together south on CR 315. These witnesses observed that upon the approach of an automobile, these females would dash into the woods and hide, only to reappear after the vehicle passed by. They continued to do this until they went out of sight."

"Another witness was driving by and observed that these females may need help and pulled over to assist. He noted that the taller blonde was bleeding on her left arm. The blonde wanted (the witness) to give them a ride and he refused, at which time she became angry and began to verbally abuse him. He drove off but contacted the Orange Springs Fire Department and notified them of an accident with injuries."

"Two Paramedics and a Rescue Unit drove south on CR 315 in search of the injured woman...While traveling north they spotted the tall blond and short, heavy female. The Paramedics offered assistance but the taller blonde, who did all the talking, said she 'didn't know anything about an accident and wanted people to stop telling lies about her and leave them alone.' The taller blond female was described as very angry and aggressive in her actions. The short, heavy female stood away from the conversations and said little or nothing."

Investigator Jarvis later wrote that "the girls had apparently gone to a closed real estate office and used the outside hose to clean the blood from their bodies."

The Marion County sheriff's office was notified and they quickly discovered that the wrecked Sunbird belonged to the missing and believed endangered Peter Siems. The Marion county police towed the vehicle, and processed it for prints and blood stains. Investigator Munster noted that the "property recovered from within the automobile included both Busch and Budweiser cans of beer as well as Marlboro brand cigarettes, and two 'Beverage Cozies' which held the beer cans. Underneath the passenger seat was a bottle of Windex spray with an Eckerd price label affixed to it."

Marion County investigators Leo Smith and Bruce Munster interviewed the local eye-witnesses. They called Beth Gee, a staff forensic artist, who completed a composite drawing of the two female suspects. Marion County officers began to circulate the drawing throughout the Florida Law Enforcement community. Maybe someone would be able to identify the suspects.

* * *

On July 30th at 6:20am, fifty-year-old truck driver Troy ("Buddy") Burress left the Gilchrist Sausage Company in Ocala, where he worked, in his dark brown 1983 Gilchrist Ford truck. He followed his regular route, and was due in Salt Spring, in Marion County, by afternoon. Sharon, his wife of sixteen years, and Johnny Mae Thompson, his employer, knew him as a steady and reliable man, although Sharon may not have known that Troy had a girlfriend elsewhere in Florida.

No man's perfect, and few family men are sexually monogamous. Doesn't mean they're not considered good family men, though. This kind of point made Aileen crazy and bitter, namely that both her tricks and their wives looked down on her. Weren't the wives also "in service," didn't they keep their eyes and their mouths shut because they needed their husbands' money, too? Like Aileen did. Same thing.

Hypocritical bitches.

Florida's street prostitutes not only had to deal with being circled and judged by men in slowly moving cars; they also had to deal with the women who drove past too. In Phillipa Levine's words, the women who drive by "look with a mixture of fear and hate and disgust as they pass."

Burress was a big, burly, virile-looking man. He picked Aileen up in the afternoon on or around July 31st, sometime after his last known delivery at 2:24PM. In her confession, Aileen said that Burress had "laughed" at her, pulled out a ten dollar bill and said, "This is all you fuckin' deserve, you fuckin' whore. He just threw the fuckin' money down."

Aileen also said that she thought the sausage truck man was gonna kill her, that he'd attacked her, physically. "He came at me. We were fighting, we went all the way into the weeds fighting. When I got away from him, I ran back to the truck. Now, we're still fighting' and he realized I got a gun. I kicked him or somethin'. He backed away or I pushed him or somethin', I pulled my gun out and I said, 'You bastard.' I shot him right in the stomach. He was gonna start runnin', so I shot him again in the back."

Aileen sounds utterly confused. When Aileen drank she often made no sense. But when she confessed, she was nine days into drying out—and very scared, mainly, of losing Tyria by getting her or her family in trouble with the cops. Still, Aileen sounded like she was also trying to say that the sausage truck man deserved to die because he'd dissed her, treated her with contempt.

Aileen often contradicted herself and changed her story many times, not only during her confession, but during her life. While confessing, Aileen was, by turns, rational, irrational, inconsistent, insistent, and completely "blank." Aileen kept mixing up cars and men, she couldn't remember which cars went with which men and she kept forgetting where she'd left the bodies too. It was awful—almost funny.

Aileen was, however, consistently clear about certain things, such as whether she or the man had been dressed or undressed and about why she'd shot each one. Aileen always invoked "self-defense." For example, Aileen said, the sausage truck man had devalued her worth as a prostitute, he'd laughed at her, and had also threatened her physically. The way Aileen put it: "The bastard, he's gonna rape me and shit." She might have meant that Burress was literally trying to rape her, or that he wasn't going to pay more than $10 for sex with her, or even that Burress didn't want to pay her for sex at all.

Fine for him, but then how was Aileen gonna eat?

Later the same day, Burress' abandoned truck was spotted on the northbound side of County Road 19 where it intersected with State Road 40. According to Munster, "The vehicle keys were missing as was Mr. Buress, his clipboard, and daily receipts and monies. Sheriffs, under the command of Marion County's Major Dan Henry were dispatched on horseback over a four-mile radius from where the sausage truck had been discovered. A helicopter flew overhead. By midnight, the search was (ended)."

The police didn't find Burress' body until August 4th, and when they did, it was badly decomposed and lying approximately seven or eight miles north of State Road 40 just off County Road 19. According to Munster, "Mr. Buress had been shot two times resulting in his death. The bullets recovered from his body were .22 caliber copper coated hollow nose ammo bearing the rifle of a 6 right twist firearm."

* * *

On August 26, 1990, the families of Sonia Larsen, 18, and Christina Powell, 17, two newly enrolled students at the University of Florida in Gainesville, became worried when they couldn't reach them for several days. The next day, Gainesville police officer Ray Barber discovered their nude and mutilated bodies. The two young women had been dead for about two days.

On August 27th, another college student, Christa Leigh, failed to arrive at her night job in the Gainesville Sheriff's Department. A deputy discovered her two-day-old nude, mutilated body in her apartment. The police kept the mutilations secret, but cautioned the public.

On August 28th, the bodies of two other Gainesville students, Tracy Paules and Manuel Taboada, were found stabbed to death in their Gatorwood apartment.

University of Florida president John Lombardi announced that students would not be penalized if they decided to leave town.

* * *

One blazing hot day in August, Aileen and Tyria stood on Nova waiting for the bus. They had a grocery cart between them. The bus driver, Richard Loomis, saw they were standing in the grass, they weren't on the curb. Aileen immediately asked Richard to put the kneeler down. He did, but that particular bus, for whatever reason, only went down one beep, meaning it did not go down very far. Most bus-kneelers would beep five times and keep going down for the elderly or the handicapped. This bus didn't. Aileen said: "Can't you put it down further?"

And Richard said: "I am sorry, but it's been doing that to me all day long."

Aileen continued to chew Richard out about it. She said that other bus drivers had been lying to her for years. When Richard pushed the button to let them off, the kneeler went beep, beep, beep, beep, beep—all the way down. And Aileen turned around and said, "You have a nice day." She meant it too. She thought that Richard had tried to put one over on her, but that she'd prevailed, and he'd stopped trying to do her in. Aileen smiled at Richard.

Richard had once tried to engage Aileen in small talk. Maybe Richard felt sorry for Aileen, maybe he didn't care one way or the other, he was just being polite. Richard said: "Are you still working in Deland?" Aileen hit the roof on that one, didn't stop hollering her head off until, wearily, Richard let her off.

Aileen wasn't used to any social niceties.

Dennis Metcalf, another Votran bus driver, had known Aileen as a passenger for five years. He thought she was as "mean as a rattlesnake." She would say: "Kneel this mother-fucking bus you asshole, n----r, cocksucker." In a deposition on May 23rd, 1991, Metcalf said he "would like to flick the switch himself if they put her in the chair."

Even Tyria, the soul of Butch, was embarrassed by Aileen's "cocky, hateful attitude" in public places, especially on the public buses. Tyria said she "couldn't even go to the grocery store with Aileen without something awful happening." According to Tyria, Aileen, "couldn't go through a day without saying she was gonna kill somebody for somethin'." Somebody could drive by, and if Aileen just didn't like the way they'd looked at her, she'd carry on.

Once, Aileen and Tyria were walking across a parking lot on their way to a grocery store. They weren't walking in the pedestrian walkway. A car came through. Instead of yielding the right of way, Aileen just started yelling at the driver. Tyria said that Aileen "thought she was the king of the road and always had the right of way."

Tyria wasn't nearly as upset as Aileen was about not having a car. Even if she was, it didn't rattle her nerves. As Aileen saw it, the least the car-owning fuckers could do would be to let them walk in peace. Aileen understood that in Florida, full humanity, even dignity, was synonymous with having a car. To be without wheels was to be less than human. Aileen said that the car insurance was too expensive, and that she couldn't get a license anyway. Tyria said that Aileen drank up all the money they had so they couldn't afford a car but, so what? As Tyria saw it, they both had the Votran bus company. Tyria had a Moped, and Aileen had a ten speed.

Gnomes on bikes.

Aileen's tricks picked her up in cars. Aileen just stood by the side of the road, her thumb in the air, completely dependent on the kindness of strangers.

Talk about finding a way to profit from one's liabilities. Aileen was a genius at it.

CHAPTER FIVE

A Former Police Chief Down

THIS HAD BEEN A BAD YEAR, a year in which people "just started cumin' like flies on shit, to mess with me," Aileen said.

Aileen was finding it hard to work. This was more frightening to her than the fear she had about being arrested or raped or rejected. Aileen dealt with this, her greatest fear, by denying it. She noted, instead, that business wasn't good because a lot of her regulars had gone off to the Gulf War.

Aileen never sat down and "planned ahead." Aileen took it day by day; tomorrow was a luxury. Aileen didn't think she was losing business because she was aging—or, she had thought about it, instinctively, long ago, when she'd decided to go after guys who were ten, twenty or thirty years older than she was. Tricks always liked young girls, or at least girls who looked a lot younger than they themselves were. Most guys over the age of thirty were into a father-daughter thing. Goody. So was Aileen.

Street hustlers—hitchhiking prostitutes, too—try to stay away from young guys. They're the ones most likely to trick you into being gang-raped; they're rough, cruel, greedy and never grateful, the way some of the older guys can sometimes be. At the trial, Aileen testified that "young guys were always high, or stoned, aggressive, with a violent attitude." She said she'd "learned not to deal with them."

* * *

On September 11th, at 4pm, fifty-six-year-old Charles Humphreys, a former Alabama police chief, retired Air Force major, and, at the time, a case worker for Florida's Health and Rehabilitative Services, was driving his "personal automobile," a 1985 maroon Oldsmobile Firenza. Humphreys called his secretary and told her he was going home. Then, he went to visit a former client, Gail Goodwins. In other words, Humphreys made a brief, personal, social visit. In his report, Investigator Munster, merely noted that Humphreys "was interviewing persons in the performance of his duties."

That's just the kind of little thing Aileen saw over and over again and hated. Men in uniform, men with badges, lying, covering for each other, allowing themselves to get away with things, punishing Aileen for trying to survive, getting a kick out of pushing her around.

According to author Michael Reynolds in *Dead Ends*, after Humphreys visited with Goodwin, he stopped at the Journey's End motel to inquire about a child whom he saw sitting alone outside in a parked car. The desk clerk, Ruth Mathieu, said that Humphreys "didn't raise his voice or anything but he acted kinda nervous, like he really had something on his mind and he was aggravated because he couldn't take care of whatever he had to take care of. Like he was looking for someone."

Was Humphreys in hot pursuit of an outlaw—or a hooker perhaps?

According to Investigator Munster, at approximately 5pm, Mr. Humphreys purchased some beer or wine from an "EMRO" store at the Speedway truck stop and convenience store located at State Road 44 and I-75 in Wildwood.

Humphreys picked Aileen up on Rt. 44. Impossible to say whether Humphreys felt sorry for her, in a fatherly kind of way, got angry at her and wanted to arrest her for sexually propositioning him, or whether he was, in fact, interested in Aileen's proposition.

Aileen's version, contained in her confession, is as follows:

When they got to the "spot on 484, Humphreys took his badge out and he said I'm gonna have you arrested for prostitution. I said: Bullshit you are. So he grabbed my hand... my arm, and he said, no, better yet, how would you like to suck my dick and I won't do anything, but you're not gettin' any money for it. If you suck my dick I won't arrest you and you can go scott free."

A classic shake-down by a police officer. No big deal: this happened every day, every hour, maybe every minute, to some working girl somewhere. In Miami, undercover male officers routinely patronize massage parlours to allay suspicion, before they entrap and arrest the women working there. To Aileen, it was rape, pure and simple, when the trick wanted to arrest you for doing the same thing he did, or when he wanted the sex without having to pay for it, and threatened to arrest you if you didn't consent to your own rape!

According to Aileen, she told Humphreys: "You're not gonna arrest me. I'm not goin' anywhere and you can't prove anything. Furthermore, I don't believe you're a cop, you can get one of those badges out of a Detective magazine."

Aileen didn't like fakers. She was a con artist herself and she didn't like being conned. Aileen didn't like it when a guy who was supposed to be representing the law, went around breaking the law. In her own way, she fancied herself a Law-and-Order type of person; she was forever giving cops advice about how to outsmart the criminals. Aileen had a righteous conservative streak.

At heart, Aileen was a cop-lover and a cop-killer. As Oscar Wilde said: Each man kills the thing he loves. Maybe each woman does, too.

Aileen said she was sitting in the front seat when Humphreys grabbed her arm and pulled her out of the car and she pushed him back and he grabbed her and she started shooting—or, she said, they were both outside, pushing and pulling at each other when she shot him. In the confession, she said she thought she'd shot him three times. "I shot him because he pissed me off. I knew what he was gonna do."

Charles Humphreys was the first man whom Aileen shot in

the head, execution-style.

Aileen said she took Humphreys' wallet and his keys and then she "hurried up and got in the car and started the car up and drove away." Aileen abandoned the car, but not before she'd "pried the letters off the car and the state troopers bumper sticker" off the windshield and wiped the car down for fingerprints.

"Mr. Humphreys did not arrive home," wrote Investigator Munster. "Humphreys' wife Shirley contacted his supervisor who contacted the Sumter County Sheriff's Office and the Wildwood Police Department. The Marion county police hunted for him all night, on horseback, by helicopter, and on foot."

The police found Humphreys' body the next day, just north of CR 484 and west of I-75, in Marion County. He had been shot seven times with a .22 caliber firearm, which resulted in his death. His automobile, wallet, and money were missing.

Tyria later told the police that sometime in mid-September, when she'd returned home from work, she'd found Aileen "in possession of a maroon, four-door Oldsmobile Firenza." Tyria said she saw Aileen "going through the papers in a maroon colored briefcase," a briefcase which belonged to Humphreys.

On September 12th, Marion County Captain Steve Binegar told Major Dan Henry that Humphreys was a former police officer who "wasn't known to be an individual who exhibited a great deal of fear." Who then, could have forced or lured someone like Humphreys to so remote a spot? According to Henry, he himself first proposed that the suspect "might be a female and perhaps the victim went to the scene willingly." Binegar found this theory "viable" and proposed it to his staff.

Marion County investigator and computer whiz, Brian Jarvis, would soon contend that his fellow investigators failed to properly interview the EMRO store clerk where Humphreys had purchased his last beer, and then failed to follow up on the information they subsequently obtained from her. Jarvis especially believed that Tyria's various alibis were never carefully checked out because Tyria was wanted, not for murder, but by the State Attorney's office as a star prosecution witness, and by his fellow-officers as the bait, the lure, for their secret media deal with CBS/Republic Pictures.

For example, Jarvis told me that Tyria must have known about some of the murders, she helped destroy some of the evidence, she helped wreck Peter Siems' car—but, most important, Tyria had been with Aileen in that EMRO store just before Aileen met Charles Humphreys. Jarvis wrote that "a check of Tyria Moore's work records showed that she was fired just days prior to the murder of Charles Humphreys. The cause for termination was a violent altercation with her supervisor."

According to Tyria, Aileen had called her at the motel job and "got nasty" with whoever had answered the phone. Tyria's boss, "a pipsqueak from some other country where they dominate women," chewed Tyria out about the call. Tyria said she told him she had no control over who called her, but yes, it happened to be a friend of hers who'd called. "And he said, well, you're fired. And I said, if you want me to give you a reason to fire me, I'll give you a reason to fire me. And I jumped over his desk and started beating the shit out of him. I just lost it."

* * *

According to her biological mother, Diane, when Aileen was nineteen, she had visited Diane in Texas, for the first and last time. According to Diane, Aileen couldn't stop complaining about how "no one had ever given her a break."

Now, for the first time in her life, Aileen actually "got a break" because she was a woman. Even though all the cops had seen the composite drawing of the two women who'd wrecked Siems' car, none of the cops thought that if—and that's a big if—they were looking for a serial killer, that the killer might be a woman.

On September 19th, Suwanee county deputies found Humphreys' car backed into a space behind an abandoned service station at the intersection of I-10 and State Road 90 near Live Oak. In Munster's words, the "vehicle keys, and bumper stickers were removed from the automobile. There was no visible property inside the vehicle. One can of Budweiser beer was found under the passenger seat. The vehicle had visible marks on it indicating that someone had wiped fingerprints from the inside and outside of the car. The vehicle was returned to Marion County for processing."

Once again, the driver's seat had been pulled up close to the wheel. Someone a good deal shorter than Charles Humphreys had been driving his car.

Investigators Jarvis and Munster had a discussion about the similarities between the deaths of Humphreys, Burress, Spears, and the two unidentified bodies, the one in Brooks county, in Georgia, the other one in Florida's Pasco county. Four of these men had been shot with a .22, the fifth, with a .38. Jarvis and Munster did not include in their discussion a sixth man, Douglas Giddens, who'd also been shot with a .38, or a seventh, Richard Mallory, whose body had been found in Volusia County.

On September 21st, investigators Tom Muck of Pasco and Larry Horzepa of Volusia met with Marion county investigators Bob Kelley, Bruce Munster, John Tilley, and Brian Jarvis in Marion County to discuss the corpses-on-the-highway. According to Jarvis, "a pattern finally emerged. Several key factors began to dominate all of the investigations. All of the victims were middle-aged white men. All were traveling alone on, or near, Florida's Interstate system. Most had been shot multiple times with a .22 caliber gun and had their bodies carelessly discarded in secluded areas."

According to Jarvis, they decided to send evidence to the Florida Department of Law Enforcement (FDLE) and to the FBI in Quantico. However, Munster, in his application for a search warrant, stated that this decision did not take place until sometime closer to October 12th, "when bullets from Humphreys were sent to the FDLE in Tallahassee for comparison to the other bullets in this investigation. Don Champagne, an examiner for FDLE, issued a report stating that the bullets from Humphreys and Burress 'have individual characteristics which leads him to believe that the same weapon may have fired these projectiles.'"

* * *

The first time Brenda McGarry laid eyes on Aileen and Tyria was on September 29th or 30th. Brenda lived in New Smyrna Beach and worked at the Speedway, a gas station and convenience store, right next to the Fairview motel. Aileen and Tyria had just checked into the Fairview motel, under Aileen's alias of "Cammie Greene." Brenda had been working at the Speedway on South Ridgeway for about four months when the two women came into the store.

"Hi," Aileen said, "I'm Lee and this is Ty."

Aileen told Brenda she wanted to apply for a job in the store.

By then, Aileen had already killed six or seven men. Maybe Aileen really was desperate for a more hassle-free kind of job. Maybe she liked it that the Speedway was connected to a gas station. On that visit to Diane in Texas, Aileen had told Diane that she'd always wanted to work in a gas station.

Maybe Aileen was conning Brenda (herself, too, a little), into thinking that she could still pass for normal, that it wasn't too late for her to turn over a new leaf, that deep down, she was a normal person, with normal needs. For example, she needed a steady job, the kind of job that Brenda had.

Maybe Aileen didn't give it much thought, maybe she just said whatever came into her head, and when she said it, she meant it, but then, the thought drifted away, like her life, or her tricks. Shoot! It didn't bother her, Aileen was built to say whatever someone else needed to hear, whatever helped her get by. Aileen was a bullshitter, a pathological liar, a con artist, but she was also a quintessential American, and felt entitled to a new beginning whenever she needed one.

The Speedway had a detailed job application. Brenda watched Aileen stop, and freeze, when she came to the 'past jobs and references' section. Brenda decided there was no way this woman could "truthfully complete" the application. The Speedway wanted at least two, maybe three references. Aileen repeatedly asked Brenda if she could "put down anybody" as a reference.

Aileen had a problem with references. She didn't have any. Whom could she put down? Her tricks? Even if she could find 'em, in what capacity could they say they knew her? The only relatives she loved were dead, the others hated her, and she hated them even more. Her old lovers? The guy who'd kept her locked up for sex, then had her arrested for forging a check? The girl, Patricia/Toni, who'd stolen her cleaning machine and supplies and had disappeared?

Aileen didn't know anybody, straight or crooked, who would say that this beer-bellied, foul-mouthed outlaw/outcast was, deep down, a straight-arrow and a law-abiding citizen, who needed just-one-break.

Aileen told Brenda she'd decided not to finish the application in the store; she said she'd finish it at home. Aileen never returned the application. Brenda never questioned her about it. Aileen always wanted to do the right thing, but some small, unfair obstacle always stopped her cold. Like when she failed the exam for the military by just a few bitty points. Or take this situation, where she wanted a job like Brenda's, but she couldn't come up with a few handy references. Man, it wasn't her fault that she had no family to help her out.

* * *

On October 12th, the Marion county police were advised that Charles Humphrey's wallet had been found. Munster traveled to a wooded field in southern Lake County near U.S. 27. In his words, "A search of the area revealed personal identification of Humphreys, ownership papers for the Oldsmobile Firenza, his pipe, tobacco... HRS paperwork, and ice scrapers from his glove box. Miller Lite beer bottles and Budweiser beer cans were also found next to his personal property. His briefcase, police badge and wallet were not found."

When the police examined Humphrey's car, they found a cash register receipt for a purchase of beer or wine from the 'EMRO' store, which is the Speedway truck stop and convenience store in Wildwood. The receipt was dated 9-11-90 at

1619 hours. This is the date and time of Mr. Humphreys' disappearance.

Munster rushed out to interview Anita Armstrong, the Speedway clerk who was on duty at that time on that day. On a hunch, Munster showed Armstrong Beth Gee's sketch of the two women who were seen wrecking Siems' Sunbird on July 4th. Armstrong "immediately stated that she recalled that one day in September these girls had entered her store through the front door, walked straight through and exited the rear door. She thought they might be prostitutes and watched them go behind the store. Thinking they left the lot, she did not call the Police. When asked to pinpoint the date and time, using a weekly work schedule, she was able to say that this occurred prior to 5:00pm on 9-11-90, the date and time of Mr. Humphreys' purchase at the store."

* * *

Way it was, the ladies kept to themselves at the Fairview. They didn't keep normal hours. When they entered the Speedway store, Tyria would stand right behind Aileen and never say anything. Aileen would do all the talking. At first, Brenda thought Tyria was shy, timid. After a while, she saw that Aileen dominated the relationship. Aileen gestured with her hands when she talked. Like she was signing for a deaf, deaf world. Brenda decided that Tyria was the "more conservative of the two, that Tyria balanced them out." Tyria seemed like an ordinary, regular person. Aileen didn't. There was something about her that was odd, frightening even.

Brenda saw Aileen and Tyria at least two or three times a day. In the morning, Aileen needed her coffee and a pack of Marlboro Lights; in the afternoon, she'd buy a 12-pack of Busch. Maybe a Mountain Dew for Tyria, a Pepsi for herself. Aileen never bought anything else from Brenda: no bread, no sandwich meat, no orange juice. Not even a can of tuna fish or a pound of processed cheese. Toward evening, Brenda would see the two of them making their way across the highway to the

"FlyN" bar.

* * *

By mid-October, the bottle of Windex from Siems' Sunbird had been traced to an Eckerd store in Atlanta. Based on the price labels, the store manager was able to place the sale as having been made sometime during the month of February 1990. Munster wrote that when police showed him "the drawings of our suspects, (the manager) remembered having these persons enter this store sometime around September of 1989. He was able to remember them, stating that there was a large difference in height and size of the females."

They "stood out" for another reason too. The clerk remembered that they'd entered his store late at night on a Friday. He said that the store is in a "bad part of town in a predominantly black area and that white people do not venture into this area after dark." Aileen was used to dangerous situations, she sought them out, she took pride in refusing to avoid them, and in surviving them. Aileen refused to be pushed around—even by her own fear.

The Eckerd clerk also recalled that (the two women) purchased "cosmetics and a black box of Trojan Prophylactics," the same brand of condoms found near Mr. Spears' body and inside his trunk.

According to Mr. Siems' family, he and his wife were missionaries. Neither of them drank alcoholic beverages, smoked tobacco, or had ever traveled to Atlanta.

* * *

As soon as they had settled in at the Fairview, Aileen went over to the Belgrade Restaurant which was right there, also on South Ridgeway.

"Vera, I am back," Aileen had said.

"Welcome home," said Vera.

Vera had known Aileen as a customer in the early 1980's,

back when Vera thought Aileen was just a regular person, with regular hours and a boyfriend. Vera, and her husband, Velimir, owned, ran, and lived next to the Belgrade restaurant. They served three meals a day, starting at dawn, and lasting until 9PM. Aileen and Tyria ate there almost every day. They preferred the chicken paprikash.

According to Velimir, at breakfast, on October 13th, Aileen told him that she couldn't afford the rent at the Fairview anymore, did he happen to know of anything cheaper? It could be a real small room, she didn't need much.

"Okay," Velimir said. "I got something cheap for you, we got room right behind restaurant. $50.00 a week. What kinda business you do?"

"I run my own pressure cleaning business," Aileen told him.

Yeah, she was pressure-cleaning men right off the Florida highways.

Aileen gave Velimir $30.00 down, and promised him the rest tomorrow. When tomorrow came, Aileen called him from the Last Resort and asked to borrow $20 from him. Velimir laughed. That Aileen was always broke.

At first, Velimir felt sorry for Aileen and Tyria, they just stayed in the tiny room all day and all night. When Aileen was away, Tyria just stayed there by herself, waiting. They had no visitors, received no mail, never asked to use the phone. They always cleaned up after themselves.

Some women are born favored and manage to retain favored positions all their lives. Not Aileen, she had to keep asking everyone for favors, no one offered her any. Other women always seemed to have everything they needed, all Aileen could do—all she'd ever done—was beg for some of what everyone else already had: pretty please, my car broke down, my boyfriend walked out on me. Aileen had to steal what she needed, con people out of it, fuck for it, fuck for food.

Aileen always paid her rent in small amounts: $10 one day, $20 the next day. Sometimes, when she'd return, Aileen would slip Vera $30 or $40. Every day, Aileen asked Vera to let her have some food on credit, because she was low on cash just now.

Aileen started to pester Velimir about giving her a ride to the Winn-Dixie, to her job. Finally, Velimir said, "Okay, get in."

First thing Aileen told him, was "don't expect any relationship between me and you, or between you and Ty."

Velimir looked at her and said, "Who ask you for relationship? I ask you to pay me on time."

Aileen made Velimir drop her off on I-95, at the southern exit, by the side of the road. Velimir decided that Aileen didn't want him to see where she worked. What kind of job could she have on the highway?

Velimir saw that Aileen took advantage of his broken English. "Anything she don't like, she say sorry, I don't understand what you are talking. I say, you understand very well, but you don't like to understand."

Aileen told Velimir that she thought he was taking advantage of her. She accused him of "making a profit off her." Velimir told Aileen, "If you think I make profit, just go buy your beer at the gas station store, don't buy beer over here."

Aileen had told Vera and Vera had told Velimir that Aileen was a lesbian. With Tyria.

Brenda-at-the-Fairview saw how Aileen operated. Aileen would wait on the porch at the Speedway, then, real quick-like, she'd approach the men as they pulled up for gas, not the young, good looking guys, only the older guys. Tyria would always say, "No, let's go home."

Aileen would always say, "No, we need the money."

Brenda never saw Aileen actually get into a car with a man, but once Aileen came right out and told Brenda that she made two to three thousand dollars a month doing it. Brenda understood that Aileen was a prostitute. Aileen always told Brenda that she had "to get over to 92 to make some money." Brenda thought Aileen was talking about a bar named 92, not about Highway 92.

Brenda thought Aileen was pretty strange, even for a prostitute. Not that Brenda would know. For example, according to Brenda, Aileen was "very aggressive," more aggressive than most women are, both verbally and physically. Aileen carried herself in a masculine kind of way. She flexed her muscles, she walked around marking off her territory, ready for a fight, looking for one, just as if she were a man, or a man in jail. Brenda had never seen anything like it.

Whenever a nice looking male customer came in, Brenda gave him the once-over, even Tyria looked, but Aileen didn't look. Or if she did, she snarled. Aileen told Brenda she was as strong as a truck driver; Brenda believed her. Brenda had the feeling that Aileen could blow someone's head off in a split second. Aileen intimidated Brenda. One day, in an off-hand but meaningful way, Brenda mentioned to Aileen that she kept a .25 Magnum at home, and that she'd definitely bring it into the store if she ever felt her life was in danger. Aileen said, well, she had a gun too.

Aileen was pretty much always drunk. She slurred her words, and smelled of beer. Tyria drank too, maybe as much as Aileen did, but Tyria could hold her liquor, Aileen couldn't.

Aileen had a way of talking around things. She told Brenda that she and Tyria had both worked as maids, and in convenience stores. But she never named a place. Aileen told Brenda that when they had nowhere else to go and money was tight, they'd stayed at a church, at least, Tyria had. Tyria had worked for the church too. Aileen didn't say which one.

Mainly, Aileen talked to Brenda about her family. "She would badmouth her father and glorify her mother. She said it was her father's fault that her mother died." When Aileen talked about her mother and her father, she frightened Brenda. She'd make sharp, cutting gestures.

Once, Aileen started yelling about "the pain." She said: "The pain, it gets so bad, the only thing that gets rid of the pain, that slams it, is the hate. You have to get rid of the pain, you gotta get rid of the pain, like this." Then, as if she were a football player, Aileen slammed a counter display, a cigarette rack, and the cooler door, with her shoulder. Without saying a word, Tyria walked her out the door.

* * *

On October 15th, according to Jarvis, Siems' vehicle was re-processed and a palm fingerprint was lifted from the rear view mirror.

* * *

Vera noticed that when anyone else came into the Belgrade, Aileen and Tyria would quickly and quietly get up and take their plates back to their room. Vera thought this was strange, but she had a soft spot for Aileen. She and Tyria were like refugees, it was something Vera could understand. It bothered Vera, though, when she saw Aileen and Tyria sneaking through the bushes to buy beer at the Speedway. This wasn't refugee behavior, this was crazy or criminal behavior. Aileen and Tyria were hiding from someone.

One day, Aileen asked Velimir if he had a gun. Velimir stared at her as if she was crazy. Velimir went a little crazy himself. He said: "Sure, we got a gun in every corner. I got one in house. I got one in garage. I got one here in restaurant." Aileen said that she had one and that she had a license to use it too.

Something didn't add up, or it added up, alright, and Velimir didn't like what he saw. Or heard. Once, Aileen's music was so loud, it woke him and Vera up at 2 AM. Velimir said, this is no bar, turn down music. Aileen agreed, but then she did the same thing the next night, and the night after that.

* * *

On November 5th, trucker Bobby Lee Copas was introduced to Aileen Wuornos on Highway 27 by another trucker who said Aileen was a "lady with car trouble on her way to Orlando." Aileen said she was in a jam, that "she had to get her two kids out of daycare by a certain time," and she needed to call her sister in Daytona, to meet up with her in Orlando.

Sure, said Bobby Lee, hop in. But first, he said, he had to

stop at a bank and cash some checks. He returned with an envelope filled with bills, and tucked it away, in full view, under the sun visor.

Bobby Lee was surprised, dumbfounded really, when Aileen propositioned him. Bobby Lee had really thought that Aileen was a "lady in distress." He said: "Well, I'm sorry, I have been married 30 years to the same woman, I'm not interested in nothing like that."

Aileen had always been outrageously assertive, but when she was younger, the Johns mainly chose her. Now, she was choosing them, whenever she needed their money, her money, just like they had, whenever they'd needed sex offa her. She'd learned from them, she was standing on their shoulders.

Aileen had her purse open, she was combing her hair with a big old comb, big old teeth in it. She propositioned Bobby Lee again. She said she "wasn't no prostitute but she needed money." Aileen kept glancing up at that sealed envelope stuffed with bills. Bobby Lee glimpsed what he thought was a small caliber gun in her purse laying on the floorboard.

Suddenly, he was scared. Something felt different. When Aileen propositioned Bobby for the third time, he could swear she wasn't the same person. Her personality was different. Aileen told him: "I'll give you the best damn blow job you ever had in your life. We can whip up into the orange grove right there and your wife would never know nothing about it." Aileen said she needed $100. Bobby Lee realized that he was in a situation that he needed to talk his way out of.

Aileen had him in a classic female position.

Bobby Lee agreed to 'whip into the orange grove' with her; he promised to drive her all the way to Daytona too. But first, he said, why don't you call your sister, and he pulled into a truck stop and gave her $5 for the phone. The minute Aileen got out, Bobby Lee hit the electric door locks.

Men in classic female positions don't behave the way women do.

When Aileen heard that door lock, she was mad as hell. She spun 'round, and roared over to the driver's side of the car. Aileen fumbled in her purse and hollered: "I'll get you, you fuckin' son of a bitch. I'll kill you like I did them other old fat sons of bitches." Bobby Lee thundered away.

After Aileen was arrested, Bobby Lee Copas' son showed him her picture in the Lakeland Ledger and Bobby Lee dutifully called the police, went down, and made a statement. More than a year later, at trial, Bobby Lee told the judge: "Ten hours after I made that statement I had all kinds of publicity on my doorstep, which wasn't supposed to be there. This is why I'll never step forward again, no matter what I seen from now on. I'm sorry, Your Honor. I know now why witnesses and people don't come forward."

CHAPTER SIX

A Second Former Police Officer Down—
And Then There Were Seven

O N NOVEMBER 15TH, when Aileen and Tyria came into the Speedway, Brenda saw that something was different. Tyria seemed happy. She was also talking quite a bit for a change. Tyria was going home for a vacation. She hadn't seen her parents in a while—her mom especially, and she'd never even met her two-year-old nephew, or the baby her youngest sister had a few months ago. This time, Aileen stood behind Tyria. Brenda saw that Aileen was withdrawn.

Brenda said she was very happy for Tyria and hoped she had a nice trip. Tyria said that her mother had sent her a round-trip airline ticket.

Aileen came back later by herself, "drunk royal." She told Brenda she was afraid Ty would never return. Brenda told her, you know, just give it time. You can't expect things to go wrong. You got to be a little optimistic. Then, Aileen opened up and told Brenda that Tyria was her lover, that she loved her, and couldn't live without her, that she'd been loving her for six years. (It was more like 4-1/2 years, but Aileen was drunk.) Brenda had figured out they were both, you know, together, but this was the first time a woman ever came out and told Brenda anything like this.

Aileen seemed very emotional. She said: "I supported her for six years and now she's leaving me. She's dumping me."

Aileen wanted more beer. Brenda said "look, there is a law to be followed here. You are quite intoxicated." Aileen said that she couldn't get to sleep, she was having problems, *they* were having problems. Brenda finally relented, and said, well, take the 12 pack, but that's it. Later, two unusual things happened: Tyria came in, alone, and was quite obviously drunk. Tyria could barely stand. Brenda refused to sell her any more beer.

Aileen kept accusing Tyria of knowing that she was leaving and never coming back. Tyria knew that she had to come back, even if she didn't want to. To pick up her stuff. "Yeah, I'll be back," Tyria assured her.

* * *

Aileen had offered Vera an electric shaver and a gold chain, in lieu of rent money at the Belgrade. Vera wanted the money and told her she'd have to move out. On October 17th, the day Tyria flew home for a vacation, Aileen moved back into Room #8 at the Fairview. She still owed Vera and Velimir $34.

Once, Velimir ran into Aileen buying her coffee at the Speedway. He said, joking: "Hey, when you bring me my money?"

Velimir told the police that Aileen said: "You are son of a bitch, you are lucky you still have life."

With Tyria gone, Aileen was absolutely alone in the universe. An enormous, crushing loneliness closed in on her. Aileen didn't know what to do except drink. In her own words, she was "constantly drunk." It was in that state that Aileen went out to make a little money.

On November 18th, 60-year-old truck driver Walter "Gino" Antonio left his home in Cocoa, Florida. He was on his way to Alabama and was traveling alone, in a two door maroon Pontiac Grand Prix. Gino picked Aileen up in Cross City, in Dixie County, near U.S. 19. Aileen remembered him as "an older feller, a little short guy."

Aileen said she asked him if she could make some money and he said sure. They went "way, way, WAY out into the woods." Aileen said they both got into the back seat, and stripped, and as Aileen was getting ready to do her "little deed," Gino removed a gold ring and a gold chain, and "took his wallet out of his back pants pocket and said he was a cop." He said he wanted it for free. Same thing as the last guy she'd had to kill. Aileen heard Gino say: "I could arrest you but if you want you can have sex with me for free."

When she confessed, Aileen said: "I told him I was sick and tired of people comin' up to me and tellin' me they're a cop." According to Aileen, she and Gino quarreled over whether he was or wasn't a cop. Aileen decided that "he was another faker, just trying to get a free piece of ass. Like that HRS guy." Aileen said she started to get out of the back seat but Gino got out of the back seat first and ran around in front of her. Aileen heard Gino say, "You are going to suck my dick or you're gonna have sex with me. You're gonna do something. I said, no I'm not."

At that point, said Aileen, they began to struggle with each other physically and verbally. Aileen "whipped out her gun and shot him." Gino fell, then tried to run away. When Aileen heard him say: "Shit… you cunt," Aileen said: "You bastard," and shot him again, for the fourth time, this time in the head.

Turns out that Antonio was telling the truth, he was a Reserve cop down in Brevard County.

From Aileen's point of view, the reason she didn't just run away after she'd had the drop on this faker-cop, or on the other guys, was, she couldn't figure out how that would work, practically. Aileen was naked, and far from the highway. Could she get dressed and still hold a gun on someone? What if she looked away, even for a minute, and one of the guys got away, or jumped into the car and tried to run her down? Aileen needed the car to make her escape. But, if they really were cops, they'd sure as hell find her and then she'd be back in jail doing a zillion years of hard time for insulting an officer, resisting arrest, car theft, illegal possession of a gun. Fuck it. Easier to kill 'em, right on the spot, then get the hell outta there.

Why did they have the right to call her a whore and a cunt and rape her too—and she couldn't do anything about it? Aileen was filled with hatred. These men were gonna rob her, rape her, maybe arrest her, maybe kill her. She knew that no one would stop them, and that they'd get away with whatever they were gonna do to her. The law was not on her side. The law was a mighty force against her.

Prostitution was the main reason women were arrested in Florida. The police entrapped and arrested the working girls, not the Johns, they slapped heavy fines on the whores, not on the Johns with money. The police didn't even take the Johns' driver's licenses away, but for the same crime they took the women's freedom away.

The Florida police jailed repeat prostitute offenders for long, mandatory periods of time, just stashed them away where there was nothing to do but go crazy and learn how to be a hairdresser or a secretary. The same police who had no trouble arresting prostitutes for selling had a much harder time finding or arresting the Johns who murdered prostitutes. The Green River Killer in Washington State killed 48 prostitutes, and, at that time, the police said they were never able to find him.

Forget Washington State. Right here in Florida, in Miami, in the years between 1986 and 1989, nineteen young prostitutes had been found murdered. Most showed signs of recently having had sex. Their remains were found in overgrown lots, abandoned houses and alleys.

On November 4, 1989, twenty-seven days before Aileen hitched a ride with Richard Mallory, Joseph Davis, the Dade County medical examiner, told the *Miami Herald*: "We've never had this many slayings that seemed to fall into a pattern." Eighteen of the women were black and cocaine-users. John Farrell, chief of Metro-Dade's police detective division, therefore emphasized that the deaths were all "associated with people in crack-house environments and that there seemed to be little or no risk to the public."

Aileen didn't keep count but she knew the score. She knew that prostitutes are outlaws, not citizens, not part of the Republic. Street prostitutes are not even considered human, but were treated as disposable filth, garbage. That's why Aileen kept to herself, tried not to look like a prostitute. Kept away from drugs, too.

Forget Miami. For years, right here in Daytona, for nearly a decade, local, low-income women: hotel maids, clerks, prostitutes, all of whom hitchhiked to and from work, had been turning up stabbed, dead, and ritually displayed. The murders had gone on for years but remained unsolved until 1980, when a local, twenty-year-old athlete, Mary Carol Maher, who was not a prostitute, but who hitchhiked everywhere, had also turned up stabbed, dead, and ritually posed.

The month after Maher's body had been found, a Daytona hitchhiking prostitute lodged a complaint with the Volusia county police in which she described being stabbed by a customer who'd picked her up in a red car. The police listened to her and arrested Gerald Stano of Daytona Beach, a man who'd been attacking local prostitutes in the area for years.

Yeah, Stano had been savagely abused and neglected before he was adopted; like Aileen, Stano was profoundly racist. He had killed a number of black prostitutes. He eventually confessed to killing 34 women, but in a plea-bargain, was sentenced to three consecutive life terms for the murders of six north-central Floridians: Nancy Heard, Ramona Neal, Toni Von Haddocks, Linda Hamilton, an unknown hitchhiker, and Mary Carol Maher.

* * *

On November 18th, investigator Jimmy Piper of Dixie County recorded that a man's nude body, wearing only tube socks, had been found in a wooded area off U.S. 19 approximately eight miles north of Cross City. The man's vehicle and personal property were missing. The autopsy revealed that the victim had been shot in the torso three times and in the head once, which resulted in his death. The recovered projectiles were .22 caliber copper-coated hollow nose bullets with the rifling of a 6 right twist firearm. Fingerprints identified the man as Gino Antonio.

On November 19th, Rose McNeil, the owner of the Fairview Motel, saw that her on-again, off-again tenant, Cammie Green, had a car. Aileen told Rose that she'd borrowed the maroon Pontiac Grand Prix from her boyfriend, that she had to park it out back so his wife wouldn't see it, because if she saw it, then Aileen would have to give it back. Within a day, Aileen told Rose that she'd had to return the car because the man's wife had seen her with it.

That's Aileen, a perpetual "other woman," always borrowing other women's men, and their husband's cars. Always the outsider, looking in. Always lying. Aileen gave Rose $90 in cash for the room. Aileen was so drunk that Rose couldn't even talk to her.

*　*　*

Contrary to myth, in Phillipa Levine's words, most street prostitutes in Florida "are ravaged by the work they do and look considerably older than they claim to be… they look unattractive… far from the stereotype of glamour. A certain defiant despair (seems) to form the high level of bodily neglect. They have visibly poor teeth, signs of nutritional inadequacy, are either overweight, or startlingly underweight. They often smell badly, of untreated venereal disease." That means that men are paying for sex with "'unattractive'… sick women."

Aileen was proud of how neat and clean she kept herself. No matter what, she never sank to this level.

But this time, Aileen hit the highway "drunker than shit." Men really didn't seem to care. You could be drunk, stoned, freaking out, in a blackout, and they'd still fuck you. Aileen thought it was funny, really. Men were supposed to have standards about how a woman hadda look, and behave, and they did, they had them, but they also didn't. Aileen was convinced that men would fuck anything. Men's sexual needs were nothing like her own.

There she was: drunk, incoherent, terrified, insane, in a

constant rage, and no one gave a shit. Aileen had been in this condition for years and no one ever cared enough to... what? Treat her like a human being? Lock her up? Shoot her to put her out of her misery?

Nothing had ever been right and things were a lot worse since she'd killed Mallory. What he did to her, what she did to him, had forced Aileen into a terrified consciousness. Now Aileen knew that each time she stuck her thumb out, she was in danger of being raped again, or robbed, or killed, or arrested for defending herself. Being forced into consciousness made Aileen angry, very angry.

They had forced her into this stinking foxhole from which there was no retreat, no rest, only unrelenting battle.

* * *

Aileen had been fighting with cops for a long, long time—even after she got out of prison.

Take January 4th, in 1986, in Miami. Aileen was driving a 1985 Chevy Blazer when she was pulled over. According to police reports, Aileen became nervous, said she had forgotten her wallet at the store and asked the officer if she could leave. Pretty please.

Aileen kept asking him if she could return to the car to get something. The officer kept saying she couldn't, so Aileen ran for it, she actually jumped into someone else's car and told the startled driver to beat it. The officer dragged Aileen from the car, handcuffed her, read her her Miranda rights. He also found the reason for Aileen' s agitation: she was driving a stolen car, and she had, in her possession, a .38 pistol and a box of special ammunition under the driver's seat.

Miraculously, the charges against her were later dropped.

But, five days later, on January 9th, Aileen was arrested again, this time in Volusia county. What drew police attention to her this time was an "altercation" Aileen was having with one Wayne Keith Frederickson in a Dodge pickup truck. It turned out that the truck they were in had also been stolen. Worse, the arresting officer found a .22-caliber revolver hidden beneath the seat.

Aileen and Wayne both claimed they knew nothing about the truck or the gun. Each accused the other of having stolen the truck. And the gun. Wayne said Aileen had pulled the gun on him, although he admitted he owed her $200.00. Aileen claimed she knew nothing about any gun. She said the gun had been planted on her. But the officer also found 19 rounds of ammunition in Aileen's bag. He arrested them both.

This was the official version, this was the "story" that the judge read at the arraignment. For people with jobs, families, legal identities, this is, indeed, exactly what happened. Of course, Aileen had a totally different, completely pathetic version of the same event.

To Aileen, what happened on January 9th didn't happen this way, and even if it did, it meant something else, at least to her. Aileen's version: She was on the road doing her "usual" for money when a young guy picked her up. As she remembers it, the guy was pretty drunk, and his vehicle was "staggering all over the road." This didn't stop Aileen from going with him, hey, she hadda eat too, people work in plutonium factories, that's just as hazardous, they also gotta eat. Anyway, Aileen was just about to get off at the next exit. The trooper pulled them over and ran Wayne Keith's name and vehicle registration through his computer. It turned out that Wayne was wanted, and the truck he was driving was stolen.

Aileen explained to the trooper that for Chrissake, she just met the guy, she was only a hitchhiker. Then, what an irony, the trooper checked the truck out and found a weapon underneath the seat, right between the driver and the passenger. Well, it wasn't hers, how could it be, the goddam truck wasn't hers either.

Aileen saw it from the trooper's point of view, though. How could the trooper figure out which one of them was telling the truth, he hadda bring them both in, didn't he? Yeah, he did, on a "concealed weapons charge."

Aileen remembered that there was a 1984 outstanding warrant out for her arrest, there hadda be, she'd left town before they could sentence her. That's why Aileen was afraid to use her real name. If she did, they'd put it in their system, find out that she'd skipped being sentenced. Great. The cops would love that. They'd have her on the phony 1984 charge, and for leaving town, and on this charge too. No. No more "unnecessary" prison time.

Aileen told the officer that she'd lost her I.D. and gave the police her sister's name: Lori Grody. That way, she'd be able to remember her parents' names and stuff if they asked. The police believed her. They also informed her that Lori Grody had an unpaid $200.00 traffic ticket.

Fuck. They took Aileen to the Volusia county jail. The next morning, Aileen explained to the judge that she'd never been arrested before and that she was only a hitchhiking passenger and that even the trooper had been "emotionally undecided" about what to do. The judge said OK, but you'll have to pay the $200.00 traffic ticket.

Back in jail, a few girls told Aileen about a bail bondsman who'd bail her out of a misdemeanor for a good head job. Aileen called him up. Within two hours, she was at a motel in Daytona with him. As she put it: "He got his head, he gave me the room, and left me with $20.00."

How else could Aileen make bail? It's not as if she had a savings account or a mother who'd come and get her when she got in trouble. Aileen had no one to call. It didn't bother her, though. Women like Aileen think they're lucky if their relatives don't kill them, or turn them in; they don't expect relatives to rescue them.

* * *

Cops had always had it in for her. At first, Aileen had only murdered boozers and whoremongers, and she'd only killed them after they'd become threatening to her. Siems was a mistake; she hadn't meant to kill him, but hell, he'd acted bad towards her too.

Aileen's last two murders were different. Humphreys was

an ex-police chief, out of Alabama, and he'd flashed his badge at her. Antonio had too. They were cops and, as Aileen saw it, cops were guilty every day of allowing the boozers and the whore-mongers to get away with murder. The cops protected the bad guys. Maybe that's why Aileen shot Humphreys and Antonio in the head. She'd executed them, gangland style. Not that she understood it in this way.

On November 7th, Curtis Reid of Titusville, Florida, disap-peared. On November 19th, his 1986 Oldsmobile was recovered by the Orlando Police Department. The automobile keys were missing and the vehicle seat was pulled forward near the steer-ing wheel. Marlboro and Camel cigarettes were found in the vehicle.

On November 24th, the police found Gino Antonio's car parked in a wooded area in northern Brevard County. The tag and keys were missing and the bumper stickers had been re-moved. Empty Budweiser beer cans were on the ground nearby. The car had been wiped down for fingerprints. Some of Anto-nio's personal identification and clothing were discovered ap-proximately 38 miles north of where his body had been located. Missing were his police reserve badge, handcuffs, nightstick, flashlight, and a gold and diamond ring.

Tyria had been gone for more than a week. The first time Aileen called her was from a pay phone in a bar, the day before Tyria was due back. Aileen called Tyria collect to "make sure that I made it up there okay," Tyria told the police. "She asked me if I was havin' fun and I said, yes, and she said that she was gonna be at the airport to pick me up 'cause it was gonna be on Sunday and there was no buses runnin' so that she would be there to pick me up when I came in. I said, okay."

The day after Thanksgiving, Donald Willingham was out driving, just catching the morning. He saw a woman walking along the highway. Determined, solitary. Donald slowed down. She looked like someone he'd once shot some pool with—where was it, oh yeah, at Geneva's Bar down on Beach Street and at the Office Bar on Ridgeway. Donald pulled over. Yeah, it was her, the woman with the pressure cleaning business in New Smyrna.

He hadn't seen her in over a year.

Donald rolled down his window. "Hey, Lee, where ya going?"

Aileen said: "I'm trying to get to the airport."

If Donald thought it was strange to be going to the airport on foot, he didn't say. He only asked: "What are you going to the airport for?" Aileen told him her girlfriend was coming in. Donald decided to drive Aileen there. What the hell, he had nothing to do, so he waited until after the plane had landed, and he drove them to pick up some beer, and then he drove them back to the Fairview motel.

Aileen, who knew she had to wipe her fingerprints off the cars, didn't think the same caution applied to the men's possessions which she tended to brandish about, use, and pawn, as if they were trophies. They were; she'd won them back in the war against her. Aileen gave Tyria an expensive-looking gold and diamond man's ring, size 10. It had belonged to Gino Antonio.

Male serial killers may mutilate women because they hate being dependent on women who are, in their view, faithless whores, women who remind them of women who've spurned them. If there is such a thing as a female serial killer, she might be angry about how dependent she was on men for money and at their mercy financially. She might feel that men had paid her too little, cheated her, robbed her, used her up, thrown her away. Those guys with their cars and their jobs and their houses and their children and their wives and their wallets stuffed with money and credit cards and shiny badges—they all deserved to die, Aileen thought. They had everything; she had nothing, and she'd been on her own and hustling since she was fourteen or fifteen years old.

* * *

On November 26th, early in the morning, Aileen came into the Speedway for a cup of coffee. Brenda had just opened; it wasn't even daylight yet. Aileen was extremely tense. She said she needed that cup of coffee. Real bad. Aileen told Brenda she had been waiting for her to open up for a while. Brenda had been there for half an hour and she hadn't seen anyone moving around outside.

The fact that somebody had been sitting there watching Brenda in her store for half an hour just hit Brenda the wrong way. It startled her. Still, she went behind the counter and got Aileen her cup of coffee. Aileen came over to the counter, put the coffee down, started leaning on the counter, real heavy-like. She had tears in her eyes. Brenda asked, what's wrong. Aileen said, it came out real fast, that Tyria had returned only to get her stuff, that she was leaving for good, going back home. Tyria's mom had promised Tyria two cars, and a good paying job. Aileen was heartbroken, helpless. Tyria was saying that she needed to get away from Aileen.

Aileen sobbed. Didn't Tyria understand that everything Aileen had been doing for the last six years was because of Tyria, because she loved her and wanted to take care of her? Aileen told Brenda that Tyria had made her do things. Things. Aileen nearly coulda gotten caught. "Yeah," Aileen said, "if I'm ever caught, Tyria's gonna pay too, for the things she's done."

Tyria was probably still sleeping, and here was Brenda, alone with someone who was going schizophrenic on her shift. Brenda felt sorry for Aileen, but she was also afraid of her. It was not lost on Brenda that when Aileen came down on the counter, Brenda's cash register moved.

* * *

Jimmy Carter, the owner-bartender of the Office Bar in South Daytona, on US 1, on Ridgeway, thought Aileen was an ordinary average person, same as everyone else who came in. Maybe this was as close to home as Aileen could get, a place where she didn't strike anyone as 'different,' a place where she was accepted. Aileen fit in with people who enjoyed a little wry humor. "Where you goin' honey? I'm going to the Office." Jokes for losers, drop-outs, buzzard-hearts, pirates.

Aileen was one of Jimmy's regulars. She might spend two

hours or she might end up spending all day and all night at the Office, and not leave until Jimmy closed up at 2am. Aileen always came in alone, ordered draft beer, or canned Budweiser, played the machines, engaged in general conversation. Like most alcoholics, Aileen could get to feeling good and when she did, she might express her feelings a little loudly. Same as everyone else. Jimmy never had to put her out, though.

On November 25th, the day after Thanksgiving, Aileen came in and told Jimmy that her boyfriend had left her. Jimmy saw that Aileen was wasted, all tore up about it. Aileen told him she had a bad case of the blues, and that she was too upset to go back to work, she just wasn't up to it, at least not until after New Year's, if even then. She told Jimmy about her pressure cleaning business, equipment and all, down in New Smyrna.

"Hey, Jimmy," Aileen said, "can you loan me some money until I get back to work? I got these items you can hold." She showed Jimmy a watch, a razor, and a gold chain. "This here's a gold razor," she told him.

"That's not a gold razor," Jimmy said, "that's an Avon razor," but he gave her $25 for the stuff anyway.

Jimmy remained mountain-moonshine loyal to Aileen, he never connected her to the police composites, he never turned her in; he only turned over the stuff she'd pawned with him when the police came up to the bar and came right out and asked him for it. Family.

* * *

Tyria wore Gino Antonio's ring for a few days, but then she returned the ring to Aileen, said she didn't want to wear it.

Meanwhile, all hell was breaking loose at police headquarters in five Florida counties. Excitement, dread, frustration, disbelief seized every cop. They now believed that two serial killers were at work in north central Florida, the one in Gainesville, and this other one, the one who'd been killing white middle-aged male motorists with a .22, who'd pulled the driver's seat up close to the steering wheel and drove the dead man's car away.

The cops were looking at the possibility of a short male killer or a female killer, or a pair of female killers, or two females who were assisting a real (male) serial killer. A female serial killer, one who was acting on her own, was unheard of, unthinkable.

Everyone in the so-called civilized world was at every moment ready to think the worst of women, and yet no one was ready to believe that women could ever be as violent as men were. Women kill intimates: husbands, who'd been abusing them, or whose insurance money they coveted; infants or children in their care; elderly patients. Women rarely kill adult male strangers.

By November 29th, if you included Douglas Giddens and Curtis Reid (who later turned up in Nevada, having embarked on a new life), and the unknown man found dead in Georgia, the Florida police were looking at 10 unsolved highway-homicide cases. Law enforcement officials decided to release Beth Gee's composite drawing of the two women seen wrecking Siems' car to the media to warn the citizens of Florida that a murderer was stalking men on the highways.

Since three of the cars had been found in Marion County, the police decided to make Marion County their central command post. Captain Steve A. Binegar stated that "in order to control false reports and minimize rumors, only one person should be speaking to the media and that person should be him." Brian Jarvis conceded that this was, initially, a "seemingly innocent" decision.

On November 30th, the police released the composite drawings of Aileen and Tyria to the media. Beth Gee's drawing resembled Aileen and Tyria, but only vaguely. Aileen was described as being 5'8"-5'10" tall, and Tyria as 5'4"-5'6".

In reality, Aileen was no more than 5'4", and Tyria no more than 5'2". This height exaggeration was not unusual—when women do anything: win the Nobel Prize or commit murder, they are often seen as taller than they really are i.e., as tall as men. Curiously, Aileen's mother Diane also remembered Aileen as being unacceptably "different" because she was taller than any of the other women on Diane's side of the family, all of whom,

Diane said, stood about 5' or 5'1"—more like Tyria's size.

Binegar told an astonished media that "the deaths of eight middle-aged men in Florida and Georgia may be linked," and that the police were looking for "two women hitchhikers."

Brian Jarvis was Marion County's only computer whiz. He quickly designed a computer program to track the leads they expected the public to supply. In response to their composite drawing, the police ultimately received more than 500 leads. Among them, the names of Tyria Moore and Lee Blahovec appeared, over and over again, beginning on the first day, when a Mr. "Billy Copeland of Homosassa Springs called in lead #5. He identified the composite as Tyria Moore whom he knew from one year ago when she and a taller woman named Lee moved inland."

Oh, how the media descended on Marion county on foot and by phone. The police were soon juggling 50-100 media requests per day in addition to all the other leads on the Ladies.

The media quickly assumed a leading role in the drama, and the role was both a heroic and a villainous one. The media commanded resources far greater than those possessed by all five rural, southern counties combined. Reporters could, would, and did, snoop things out that assisted, as well as outdid the police, and that also fatally compromised all pretense of due process. Turning to the media led the police to Aileen, but it also opened up, not the proverbial can of worms, but a large vat of extra-terrestrial dragons. Marion County police friendships, health, and careers would be damaged, even destroyed.

TV, print journalists, and filmmakers from both coasts, and from Europe and Asia, began offering money—or a moment of fame—to anyone who ever had anything to do with Aileen or Tyria.

The best story is this one: Just after the police artist's drawing of Wuornos and Tyria appeared in the local papers, the local mother of a would-be Hollywood producer allegedly spotted Wuornos in a supermarket. She gave her daughter's business card to Wuornos, saying: "I just know my daughter would like to tell your story." After Wuornos was arrested, she called the producer, Jacqueline Giroux, the supermarket woman's daughter, and, in a three-hour meeting, presumably told her all Giroux needed to know to make a movie based on Wuornos' life.

Within two months, California filmmaker Jacqui Giroux had tempted both Aileen, and Aileen's first public defender, Russell Armstrong, into allowing Aileen to sign a so-called exclusive contract with her, which, at Aileen's request, soon led to Armstrong's dismissal.

Eventually, of course, Aileen tried to sue Giroux, and although she ended up "re-negotiating" her contract with her instead, Aileen maintained that Steven Glazer, her third lawyer, and Arlene Pralle, the woman who would legally adopt her in November of 1991, had both "tricked her," and were themselves on Giroux's payroll. Aileen never stopped badmouthing Giroux, on camera and in correspondence.

Within four months, Giroux also, allegedly, tried to buy the silence of potential defense witnesses in Aileen's home state of Michigan, most of whom were never called by the defense anyway. Within a year, Giroux was threatening to sue Marion County because their sheriffs had frozen her out and given the inside scoop to one of her competitors, California filmmaker Chuck McClain, of Republic Pictures, who had opened negotiations with some of the Marion and Volusia County cops even before they'd captured their "first female serial killer."

McClain's film, *Overkill: The Aileen Wuornos Story*, aired on CBS in November of 1992, and was directly responsible for the resignations of two Marion County career cops: Brian Jarvis, in August of 1991, and Major John Henry, in November of 1992.

The eerie thing was: despite its vast resources, the media, television especially, was sadly limited. Television stations bore no local or specific responsibility for capturing killers, or for ensuring that they had fair trials. Television was by nature voyeuristic, inactive. It had only observer status in History.

The media's power to bestow money and fame upon anonymous, and therefore unhappy Americans, would soon exert a powerful effect on everyone involved in this case, but on no one more than Aileen herself. Before this was over, Aileen would be more interested in her own image in the media, and in proving that the cops had "sold her out" for media money, than in fighting for her life.

At first, I had wanted Aileen to fight for her life, but Aileen knew she was already dead: socially, civilly, legally. They'd been killing her, she'd been fighting them, but helping them too. Actually, Aileen had taken over the Kill Aileen Project a long time ago.

On a day in late November, in 1991, Tyria woke up and saw Aileen "goin' out the door with a suitcase in her hand." When Aileen returned, she told Tyria that she'd packed the .22 and some other stuff in the suitcase, and "taken it down to the bridge and threw it in." Tyria told the police, "when we went fishin' later that day or the next one, we were sittin' fishin' and she pointed toward the bridge and she said that's where I threw it."

* * *

On December 3rd, Donald Willingham, the same man who'd helped Aileen pick Tyria up at the airport, came back to help them again. Aileen had told him they were splitting up. Tyria was "catching a Greyhound bus," but Aileen was staying on. Aileen loaded some boxes and suitcases into Donald's car. Then, Aileen asked Donald to wait a minute while she dropped the boxes off at a storage place, it was right on the way to the bus station.

The three of them drove to Jack's Mini-Warehouse on North Nova Road. Aileen went in alone, told the clerk she was a Marine on her way to Saudi Arabia. She stored a tool box, a .45 caliber handgun, suitcases, clothes, odds and ends. Trophies. Aileen said her name was Cammie Greene. The Marine.

Sometimes, Aileen went all the way, transformed herself into one of her own clients, behaved as if she were a buyer, not a seller—a world traveler, not a local hitchhiker. A John, not a whore.

Aileen had no problem, not consciously, with any of the men she worked for. She liked them. They were family. She needed to believe this, even if she never saw them again. Anyway, Aileen was more comfortable with the kind of men who were only passing through her than with the kind of men who came to stay.

SECTION TWO

Feminists, Lawyers, and an Astrologer

CHAPTER SEVEN

Abolitionists Envision a Political Trial in Florida's Deep South

I N DECEMBER OF THAT SAME YEAR, I'm up north, living in Park Slope, drinking dark coffee, reading the *New York Times* and opening my mail, when I think I hear someone on TV say:

Two women are being sought as possible suspects in the shooting deaths of eight to twelve middle-aged men who were lured to their deaths on the Florida highways. These women are armed and dangerous and may be our nation's first female serial killers.

It's some kind of joke. Right?

Maybe what I've just heard is a review of a movie about a female serial killer, alright, why not, about two glamorous girl gangsters on the loose below the Mason-Dixon line. Scarlett honey: is that you and Melanie out there, hoopskirts 'aflying, guns 'ablazing?

These two suspects: one Big Blonde, one Butch Brunette, are probably a pair of hard-faced, beer-guzzling, coke-snorting Motorcycle Mamas. It was only a matter of time (and honey, they'll soon be doing lots of it), before such thoroughly American desperadoes shot their way onto television.

Or, could it be that 20,000 years of violence against women finally drove two Floridians completely stark raving mad and they became anti-terrorist commandos in the free fighting feminist forces, sworn to defend their country—which in this case, is each and every woman's body, standing shoulder to shoulder, worldwide?

Sure, and maybe these two suspects are avenging angels from outer space on a Mission of divine retribution—let's say for both the Washington State Green River killings, the Montreal Massacre, and for the countless prostitutes in Florida who've been serially tortured and murdered.

These women would have to be from outer space. Earth-women don't think of their bodies as their countries. And the idea of defending one's sovereign territory against attack, invasion, occupation, is something that *men*, but not women, understand.

Wait a minute! These two suspects are *murderers*: so why am I smiling? Do I really think that murder is heroic or revolutionary—or have these two evoked a macho, adolescent, male fantasy within me, one that embarrasses me?

Are a group of women actually locked, loaded and action-ready? I doubt that feminist freedom fighters have begun to arm themselves; other women would be the first to turn them in, no reward required. Right? Well, maybe yes, maybe no.

For example, movie-goers in America have already seen at least one good woman get her man with a gun—either in *Thelma and Louise, Sleeping with the Enemy* or *Silence of the Lambs*.

(Author's Note: And that was only the beginning. By now, we've seen thousands of films and television series which feature trained female assassins, female police officers, female soldiers, battered women who kill, mothers who avenge their daughter's rapes—and just plain badass female killers.)

In my neighborhood, people stood in line to see the latest ritual re-enactment of the Goddess Beauty, all quaking female fright, ravished, mutilated, beheaded, ritually posed, spread-eagle in some obscene gynecological position, by one of those Men-as-Beast Ladykillers, Bluebeards, Draculas, Jack the Rip-

pers, Boston Stranglers, Sons of Sam, Hillside Stranglers—
woman-hating and woman-killing men who nevertheless at-
tract hundreds of female supporters and offers of marriage once
they're jailed and convicted.

Well, someone finally changed this script and, to my sur-
prise, nearly everyone in the movie theatre cheered—some even
stood and cheered, when Beauties Julia Roberts and Jodie Fos-
ter finally shot their male Beasts. Women, not just men, daring
to cheer for man-killing women. Risky, brazen, blasphemous:
Women have been hung for far less.

Who would believe that "real" women, i.e., tamed women,
would ever cheer man-killing women on? They'd more likely
stone them to death on the spot. Wouldn't they? Just to be sure,
I went out today and asked some women to give me their reac-
tions to the news of a female serial killer:

Woman #1 (walking a dog): "Are women allowed to do
things like that?"

Woman #2 (in line at the bank, holding a baby): "Do you
happen to know their phone number? I've got a job for them.
Just kidding. Honestly."

Woman #3 (sitting next to me in the beauty parlor): "I bet
those men did something to deserve it!"

Woman #4: (soliciting signatures, door-to-door): "All I can
say is, right on!"

Something is definitely going on if "good girls" can joke
about the things that "bad girls" do. Anything short of total con-
demnation is probably newsworthy.

Of course, my more rabidly radical friends sounded more
like this: "Is it anyone we know?"

* * *

The police arrested a woman in the case yesterday. She
stands accused of being a serial murderer: of having killed sev-
en or eight, maybe ten, male motorists, one by one, in just over
a year, after luring them to wooded areas off Highway I-75 in
Florida.

The victims were all white working-class men, aged forty to sixty. The victims were strangers to each other and, presumably, to thirty-four-year-old Aileen Carol Wuornos, the lesbian prostitute accused of shooting them to death and of stealing their money and their cars.

Wuornos has been described as the "rarest of criminals, a female serial killer." But is this true? Men are still the deadliest killers of both men and women. When women murder, they almost always kill male intimates who have battered them or their children. They also murder husbands or vulnerable patients in their care for money. Women rarely massacre male strangers.

* * *

Sitting before a warm and lovely fire at the end of a day in the country, my dear friend, Merle Hoffman, says: "This case has so many of your themes: Women and madness, child abuse, a trial, the insanity defense, a woman's right to self-defense, women outlaws, women in prison. Why don't you write about it?"

I laugh. "If I get involved in this case, people will say that I'm in favor of women killing men, and that I want preferential treatment for those who do!"

Damn! Even as Merle spoke, I was already imagining a political trial and deciding whom to ask to testify for the defense.

"Merle," I say, "Maybe Wuornos killed those men in self-defense, maybe all the violence that street prostitutes routinely face finally sent her over the edge. Maybe she's our Bigger Thomas, but in real life, not just in Richard Wright's novel."

"Oh, come on!" Merle challenged. "Women are not always victims. You can't kill ten men in self-defense. It's not possible."

"It is too possible. Think of men in times of war. Wuornos' life as a prostitute was probably a bigger battleground." I smile at my own double entendre.

"You have a point," Merle concedes, "but I think it's not true in her case. I bet Wuornos is insane and a cold-blooded killer."

The news is all over America. On January 16th, she'd confessed to all the murders. Her name is Aileen (Lee) Carol Wuornos.

It's Lee, again, but it's twenty-eight years later, and it's not Lee Harvey Oswald, it's a woman who's out there shooting down a whole bunch of Authority Figures, a woman with an unusual last name: Wuornos. People had a hard time spelling it: Wuornos, Warnus, the hell with it, isn't it Carolyn Warmus, the woman who'd killed her boyfriend's wife? Suddenly, people were stumbling over the names of women killers.

The feminist grapevine is a mighty fine thing. After talking to Andrea Dworkin at length, my phone rings. "Hey, Phyllis," said L.B. in her deep, whiskey-and-cigarette voice. L.B. is as tall as a man, or a fashion model. She's an activist. "I heard you were interested in the serial killers. I am too. I think these women must be prostitutes."

"L.B.," I asked, "Did you ever know a prostitute who killed a John because he'd raped her, or tried to kill her?"

"I thought about it all the time, but I never did it. I got out. Other women must have done it, but how many prostitutes would turn themselves in?"

"Right," say I. "Nobody'd believe she'd been raped, and big deal if she was, she's a prostitute, right? Who'd defend her right to kill a man because he'd raped her?"

"Yeah," said L.B., in her best Bogie-and-Bacall voice.

"But L.B., d'ya think that two prostitutes could decide to hunt and kill men whom they don't know in hand-to hand combat?"

"Maybe the men were no stranger than most," L.B. pointed out. "Maybe they weren't strangers at all. If the men were Johns, the women sure as hell 'knew' them, at least in the Biblical sense."

* * *

I begin reading the clippings on Wuornos. Then, I re-read my copy of the Report of the Florida Supreme Court on Gender Bias in the Courtroom. This time, I underline the entire section on the Florida criminal justice system: sexual battery, rape, and prostitution. I call Meg Baldwin, the Tallahassee law professor who organized it.

"Meg, this is Phyllis Chesler. I'm interested in working on the Wuornos case. D'ya wanna help?"

"Absolutely."

"Meg," I say. "I hear Wuornos has got a new woman in her life; the girl's resourceful, it didn't take her long. It's someone named Arlene Pralle whom The Lord (!) has instructed to be-friend The Prisoner."

Dead, lawyerly silence.

I continue. "Mr. Kelly Turner of the *Ocala Star Banner* tells me that Ms. Arlene Pralle of Williston and the Prisoner talk ev-ery day from two to six hours about The Lord, Lee's poetry, and their mutual feelings of love. Pralle told Turner that: 'The mur-der case is completely irrelevant because God does not want me involved with that. He brought me into Lee's life to be her friend. She is my friend regardless of how this turns out. She'll be my friend forever.'"

Turner's article of February 26, 1991, was accompanied by a photograph of a petite, winsome, "pretty woman," shown talking to Wuornos on the phone and holding court for several members of the media. Pralle has established a "Wuornos Mu-seum in her bedroom."

"Meg, can you call Arlene Pralle and meet with her?"

"What are we dealing with?" Meg finally asks.

"New Best Friend probably wants to star in the drama," I say, "But until her lawyer, Trish Jenkins, decides to return our phone calls, Pralle's the only way we have of making contact with Wuornos."

Is Arlene Pralle, the lady who's not in jail, signaling to us that she's the real prisoner? That she, the straight married Lady, is really incarcerated and that Wuornos, The Prisoner, is here to rescue Pralle from her life of caged anonymity? Is Pralle guilty of 'murder in her heart?' Is that why she's mounting so vigorous a defense? Or is Pralle truly a good Samaritan, her sister's keeper? Or, does she view this alliance as a good business proposition?

I say: "Pralle's been telling reporters that she may mortgage her horse farm to pay for Lee's lawyer."

"Don't bet on it," says Meg.

Still, it's moving that a religious woman has chosen to befriend a female sinner. Pralle's not casting the first stone, she's not turning her back, she's standing by her woman. Okay, she's not a relative, she's never even met Wuornos, God knows what her motives truly are (and she says He does). Maybe Pralle's here to remind me, specifically, to be more respectful of organized religion, without which mental asylums would be full to overflowing. Are born-again Christian women, in their own way, fundamentally feminists? Or are they really good Christians, willing to extend a hand not only to the Madonna but also to the Magdalene?

One call leads to another: I speak to the directors of the shelters for battered women in Ocala, Daytona and St. Petersburg and to feminist activists in Gainesville, where a serial murderer is still stalking women. What might the jury pool be like? I speak to some longtime residents of Ocala and Daytona.

"You must understand," one woman says. "This is Right to Life country. They burned our abortion clinic down to the ground three times in the last three years. They just burned a black family's house down to the ground since the family hadn't moved out after they burned a cross on their lawn. I think that Wuornos will receive the backlash meant for the women who dared to join the local chapters of the National Organization for Women."

When I finally reach Trish Jenkins, one of Wuornos' public defenders, she says: "The state can only afford one expert witness for Wuornos for all seven trials. Yes, Wuornos' ex-female lover has been granted immunity to testify against her. Yes, Wuornos insists that she's innocent, that she killed in self-defense."

"Has anyone visited Aileen in jail?" I ask.

"No, now that you mention it, no one has. There was someone who came once for a few hours, who wanted Aileen's permission to make a movie. That's it though."

I learn that Wuornos' biological mother, Diane, either

abandoned her or was forced to do so and that Wuornos herself is also a birthmother. Wuornos' aunt, with whom she has been raised as if her aunt was her sister, is quoted as saying that "after being in a home for unwed mothers where her baby was taken away, Aileen always told me that all men are out to use women."

Wuornos was sent to the Florence Crittenden Unwed Mothers' Home in Detroit where she gave birth. Wuornos was not allowed to see her newborn.

So, the adoption triangle is involved as well.

I think I'm really getting hooked.

Did Wuornos' victims, potentially seven out of an estimated quarter of a million men (a reasonable number of "Johns" for a prostitute over a twenty-year period), demand something that so outraged Wuornos that she snapped? Or was it just the first of the seven, John number quarter-million-plus-one? Was it something he did, or was 250,001 simply his unlucky number?

Was a quarter-million men all Wuornos could take before she lost her mind/had a breakthrough in consciousness? Like soldiers in combat, were a quarter-million invaders all Wuornos could take before she decided that it was "them" or "her" and that, for the first time in her life, she didn't want to be the naked loser?

Did it happen like the Dutch film, *A Question of Silence*, in which seven women, strangers to each other, are shopping in the same store on the very day when each woman has finally had enough of being treated like a "woman," with contempt, by men? In a rather dream-like sequence, three of the women spontaneously kill the 250,001st man—the store clerk—who mistreats them and they do so without exchanging a word. After they're arrested, the women maintain an uncanny silence.

The prison psychiatrist, a happily married woman, hopes to save them by finding them insane. To her consternation, she can find nothing wrong with them. She asks her husband, a lawyer, whether he's ever seen "photos of war atrocities?" She has come to view the women's action as an atrocity of war, something that can neither be praised nor punished, but only understood as something human beings do within the context of war.

The psychiatrist concludes that perhaps women are only insane when they put up with the daily indignities and atrocities committed against them. The psychiatrist joins the silent, imprisoned women —none of whom expect justice or understanding.

What's *A Question of Silence* got to do with Wuornos? Every survey and study I can find confirms how routinely prostituted women are tied down, beaten, knifed, strangled, and raped by Johns and how they suffer from post-traumatic stress even more than soldiers in war zones do. Wuornos survived as a street prostitute for twenty years. What wouldn't she know about a John's capacity to hurt her?

Why did her lover/roommate, Tyria, agree to testify against her? Was Tyria involved in any of the murders? Did she help Wuornos destroy evidence? Did the police threaten and frighten Tyria into testifying?

* * *

In May of 1991, when Aileen had been in jail for four months, 35 year old Linda Goodmote, an exotic dancer and prostitute from Plantation, Florida, and 27 year old Bernadette Eady, her baseball-capped lesbian lover, embarked on a crime spree.

The two women had both escaped from very abusive households when they were pre-adolescents and had dropped out of school after the eighth grade. Goodmote stripped and whored; Bernadette stole things.

Sound familiar?

On May 19th, Bernadette shot, but did not kill, two brothers, Jay and Kevin Carroll, who happened to "freak her out," when they interrupted her as she was robbing their house. On May 23rd, Linda and Bernadette shot, but did not kill, a John named John Edward Coussa, while Linda was dancing for him, naked, straddling him, as he lay on his back enjoying the view, the music, and the two naked women.

On May 27th, Linda and Bernadette were with another John

named John Calfo, who'd paid them so he could watch some live lesbian sex up close. In the motel room, John Calfo overheard Linda and Bernadette first arguing, then laughing about what they'd done to John Coussa. The whores actually bragged to Calfo about how they'd "blown that six foot guy away, how he never saw it coming."

Calfo wasn't laughing. The whores had a gun, he saw it, he was "scared for his life." Calfo escaped. Within days, Calfo led the police to Goodmote and Eady. Once the police had them in custody, the first thing the two women did was to accuse each other of having shot John Coussa.

In court, Coussa himself insisted that Linda, not Bernadette, had shot him. However, for testifying against Bernadette, Linda received only a five-year sentence; Bernadette, who already had a long criminal record by the time she was 26, received five consecutive life sentences.

* * *

I hope that I've persuaded Wuornos' lead public defender to allow me to organize a team of pro bono experts to assist her.

I begin calling our "best and our brightest" to enlist their services on behalf of the issues raised by this case. If the world press remains mesmerized by the idea that Wuornos is a "serial killer," then we can try to seize the imagination of the world by focusing on violence against prostitutes.

Bret Easton Ellis' *American Psycho* is a novel about a male serial killer who rapes, tortures, mutilates, cannibalizes, and has sex with his dead victims. It is already Number #5 on the best-seller lists. We haven't a second to lose.

What do women in Florida have to say? They represent the potential jury pool. Some say that you can never trust what a woman says; women are liars and crazy; women who kill are more violent than male killers; homicide is never justified; women always lie about being sexually harassed or raped or beaten in order to justify their own murderous intentions. These good old gals are personally very glad that Florida believes in capital punishment.

On camera and in print, the widows of the murdered male motorists deny, flat-out, that their husbands could have been Johns; according to the wives, each victim was a family man and Good Samaritan, who had, no doubt, stopped to help a woman in distress, a stranded motorist, perhaps. They could be right but they could also be dead wrong.

The wives and girlfriends of men who travel the Florida highways between Gainesville, Tampa, Ocala, and Daytona begin warning their men not to trust strange women. Imagine men becoming physically afraid of women; it's almost unimaginable.

I start to put together a team for the political trial of the decade.

Jenkins might be the only one without plans to profit from these crimes and the upcoming public crucifixion. A judge has already removed one of the male public defenders for trying to sell what he knows to the media. Everyone is on the take, one way or the other. Makes Wuornos' prostitution tame, child-like, by comparison.

Wuornos' biological sister/aunt, whom she hasn't seen since 1976, has allegedly cut a deal; three of the male cops are allegedly trying to sell their tax-supported investigation to the media for an emergency cash fund for the victims of violent crime; Tyria has allegedly cut her cash flow deal with CBS. Years later, during an in-person interview, Tyria insisted that she'd never received any movie deal money.

* * *

Met with Andrea Dworkin for an hour yesterday to discuss possible lawyers to approach. She says:

> Flashy lawyer #1: He'll keep tight control; will probably opt for an insanity defense and/or for whatever defense will allow him to be maximally patronizing, chauvinist, the heroic rescuer of his "poor" client; he'll fight like hell for her; she's his property, you insult her, you're insulting him; he might even

be tempted into going for an acquittal. He'll cost a lot of money; will arrive with his usual incredible entourage, will use his usual experts: right-wing men—who are nevertheless pretty good on the issues from our point of view.

Flashy Lawyer #2: He's tired, loves the limelight; prefers defending black men and/or people of color (Wuornos is neither).

Flashy Lawyer #3: She's real expensive; never known to give up her fee; must support a lifestyle of luxury; may or may not have the litigation experience necessary in a homicide case; is pretty good on the issues.

Andrea asked the Oregon Council on Prostitution to write a letter to Wuornos when she (Andrea) addressed them in Portland on March 8, 1991. Their director, Susan Hunter, is also well known to Meg.

I've interested lawyers who are willing to work on her case for a minimal fee—but I have to raise their expense money.

Dean Sandra Norton and Professor Jan Hokinson of Florida Atlanta University have found me the perfect assistant, Yemaya Kauri-Alecto, who will drive me around Florida, and do some research.

The lead public defender is now Trish Jenkins, the lawyer with whom I spoke nearly a month ago. I sent her my vitae and said I'd be interested in helping; she said they only had money for one expert and they'd just hired a local one. I said I would help pro bono. She never called me again, nor has she ever responded to Meg Baldwin's calls.

By now, Meg is worried. I've been leaving messages for Jenkins, telling her that I'll be coming down and that I want to meet with her. I'm also going to ask Yemaya to bring some of my books over to the jail with a note for Lee. Then, I'll try to visit Lee on Easter Sunday.

Speaking of the Lord: Pralle has told Meg that Lee has seen the light and has accepted Jesus into her heart. Pralle's husband is accusing her of being a lesbian; Pralle insists that if Lee dies that she will too; Pralle has revealed that she, too, has attempted suicide.

Last night, I read in *Publisher's Weekly* that Bret Easton Ellis' *American Psycho* is still on the best-seller list and that the 21-year-old black mother of a four-year old had been slashed to death in her "cage" while at work in a live sex pornography palace right here in Times Square.

CHAPTER EIGHT

Biker Bars, a Horse Farm,
and Very Colorful Characters

TALLAHASSEE, WHERE MEG teaches, is at least five hours' driving time from Williston, where Arlene Pralle lives. Meg drives down and, when she arrives, Pralle is busy having her hand held, not by her manicurist, but by Mark McNamara of *Vanity Fair*, but hey: According to Pralle, Mark's the one who'd persuaded a reluctant Pralle to see Meg in the first place—and to "trust" her too.

"It's wild," is how Meg puts it. "Arlene thinks Wuornos is the sweetest, most caring woman on earth and that Wuornos'll come and live with her on her horse farm once she's acquitted—that's if the Apocalypse doesn't happen first. Arlene describes herself as a Warrior for Jesus. She says she saved her father's life when he was in the hospital by 'casting out Satan' through prayer. She's decided to like me. She thinks I'm the feminist Archangel."

"How's the married lady dealing with the fact that Wuornos is a lesbian?" I ask.

"Pralle's in some kind of love with Wuornos. She goes on and on about how womanly Lee's voice is. Anyway," says Meg, "she's certainly in love with having control over an illustrious or a notorious person. According to Arlene, Lee has seen the light and has accepted Jesus into her heart."

The Lord's little warrior had been very "inquisitional" with Meg. She'd wanted to know who Meg "really" was. "How do I know that's who you really are? How do I know if I can trust you?" she'd asked.

We have our work cut out for us. Pralle is a canny, clever taskmaster. She'd already tried to put Meg to work. ("You're a lawyer, aren't you?") Seems that Pralle-Wuornos wanted Meg to break some pre-existing contract that Wuornos had signed with Jacqui Giroux, of Twisted Pictures. (I kid you not, call information, a little south of Los Angeles, it's listed.)

"Mark McNamara told Arlene to listen to me and she decided to take his advice." Wuornos has absolutely no one but Pralle—and Pralle's a woman Wuornos has never met. Pralle seems quite alone, too; she's also relying on the kindness of strangers: Wuornos, and the passing parade of journalists.

Pralle insists that her relationship with Lee "developed through the intervention of Jesus"—I can't wait to hear this story in person, it's so American. Something in Wuornos' eyes spoke to Pralle, convinced her that they were soul sisters and that God wanted her to befriend The Prisoner. Wuornos probably needs one woman and one woman only—preferably one with a line of bullshit equal to her own— rooting for her.

"Yup," Meg says. "Arlene is very invested in having that control position. Now it's 'Lee and I have decided together that Pralle will be in complete control of who has access to Lee.'"

"Pralle is Lee's pimp," we both say simultaneously. Not her pimp, her mother.

Wuornos is in utero, helplessly mainlining love. She does exactly what Arlene, her mother-pimp, tells her to do. No, each woman is pregnant with the other, each is the fetus, each is rescuing and being rescued, neither seems to know where she ends and the other begins, it's sheer bliss, utter madness. They share haunted childhoods, each has been abandoned by her biological mother. (I knew the adoption triangle had to figure in here somewhere with this much craziness going on.) Both women have attempted suicide, probably more than once. Pralle insists that if Lee dies, she will too.

The telephone is their life support system, their umbilical cord. Aileen and Arlene are on it, every day, for hours, and are running up quite a bill. ("The Lord will provide," Arlene later assures me. "He always does. Look, he's sent you.")

On February 26, 1991, Wuornos is quoted in the *Ocala Star Banner*: "There's times I say to myself, tell Arlene to forget all this. I'm so worried about what she's going through. She's going to get tired. She'll eventually get worn out. If she does, (I hope she'll) please stop and don't worry about the outcome. I prefer her health above all things. God forbid anything should happen to her."

Pralle's comment: "Now that's a human being."

Pralle, the ecstatic missionary, prides herself on being able to separate Lee as a woman from Lee as a killer. According to Meg, Pralle wants to sign an Old-Testament "covenant," become Wuornos' blood sister by "cutting veins and mingling their blood." She wants to become Wuornos' legal guardian, too.

Meg and I are trapped in a demonic fairy tale. In order to get to Lee/Rapunzel/the real Thelma and Louise/the anti-Christ, we have to go through Arlene, her Dominatrix/stepmother/pimp/changeling child. We don't want to join the line of suitors willing to tell Arlene whatever she wants to hear, win her trust, win the jackpot: telephone interviews with Wuornos. We're feminist cowgirls, not journalists, we're not after a commercial "killing," we want action in the courtroom, not entertainment.

The plan: I'll fly down to Daytona on March 31st, try to visit Wuornos in jail, meet Meg, visit Pralle, see Jenkins—who's now refusing to take my calls. I've tried and failed to schedule a visit with Wuornos directly. Three wardens confirm that approval for any visit to Wuornos must come directly from her attorney. Jenkins has left explicit instructions that "no one is to see her client."

Meg is glum. "Well, Jenkins is behaving very defensively," she observes. "Maybe it's a good sign. Then again, Jenkins may not want to do anything out of the ordinary."

Prophetic words.

By the time my plane lands, I've become Pralle's enemy, too, and she's canceled our meeting. Pralle has decided that "Chesler is an evil ripoff artist who just wants to profit from the details of Lee's life and Meg is probably in on it, Meg's got a cut of the proceeds." According to Pralle, Wuornos is also "upset" because my first letter to her had been typed, not hand-written, and because it was brief and "cold." I hadn't signed the letter "love," or even "your friend."

What is it with women? I can understand why someone like Pralle might prize a hand-written little note on baby-blue stationery, with a spray of flowers or a white fleecy lamb running alongside one margin, but is our so-called first female serial killer also as sentimental as any housewife in America?

Pralle tells Meg that she's "leaving the house to avoid being tempted by one of us into changing her mind." Pralle then calls Mark McNamara (who's working on a story about Wuornos for *Vanity Fair*) from a payphone for advice. Allegedly, McNamara tells her that "Phyllis wants in to get a big story, but why not give Meg the benefit of the doubt."

Thanks, Mark.

Wuornos' theory: "Meg is setting Pralle up to trust Phyllis, because Meg is getting a cut of the proceeds."

Maybe it's hopeless. Wuornos has no way of understanding who we are, or in what sense we "care" about her. Yes, we have an agenda, but it isn't a commercial one, we're more ambitious, more foolhardy than that. Despite everything we know, Meg and I still believe we can persuade Wuornos to join us in mounting a defense on her behalf. Maybe we're even crazier than Pralle.

By evening, after several long conversations, I've become Pralle's potential Savior again. That's how things are around here: Biblical, borderline, and breathless, changing so fast it whips my head around, and keeps me on my toes, off balance, as it's supposed to do.

Time on my hands and nothing to do but explore Daytona, a town long known for its spring break mayhem-on-the-beach and for its biker runs, in my view frightening fascist activities, although my close friend, the anthropologist Barbara Joans, insists I am wrong. Barbara first learned to ride her own Harley when she was in her mid-fifties, and she's no fascist, she's an anarchist, a rebel girl. Barbara's been "leathered up" and hitting the American highways ever since, doing the "runs."

Barbara is a white heterosexual married lady, the mother of two grown sons, and a grandmother. Barbara insists that only bikers ride the American wind, that riding is noble, that the biker community is initiatory, tribal, in a way that "straight" society isn't. "Phyll," she said, "the guys respect anyone who rides, man or woman."

Barbara is my imaginary companion as I go out looking for Daytona's biker bars on a moonless night. Yemaya is an "older" graduate student, all of thirty-seven years old, who'd driven hundreds of miles in her neat blazer jacket to meet my plane, and to assist me on this mission. Yemaya grew up in Livonia, Michigan, not far from Wuornos' hometown of Troy, under another name (her "slave name"). Like Wuornos, she'd come to Florida many years ago.

"Oh, if her name's Yemaya, she's one of mine," says my friend Z Budapest, the woman who'd formed the Susan B. Anthony Coven #1 in Santa Monica in the early 1970s, and whose work is well known in certain circles. Z is right. Yemaya, whose eyes are as brown and steady as her hand is on the wheel, is "into the Goddess."

We drive along the ocean on Route A-1A. The sea is dark, the motels quiet, only their neon lights are noisy as they blare their fantasy names out loud against the sky: The Bamboo Inn, Treasure Island, Kon Tiki, Sea Dip, El Caribe, Catalina, Aladdin Inn and The Sun Viking. Eden, discounted.

The Zodiac Bar, where Wuornos first met Tyria Moore, no longer exists. It's still in the phone book but no longer anywhere on Earth, at least, not in Daytona. Robin Suarez, a former Florida police officer, says:

"Zodiac used to operate over in St. Pete. That Zodiac showed 'lewd' films. They had live, mainly lesbian sex performances. They allowed male customers to perform cunnilingus on the female employees. We closed them down five or six times and then for good."

"And the bikers, what are they like?"

"They're mainly white. A lot are getting old, they're in their 50's and 60's. They'd be dead if they were on drugs. They drink beer. They're each about 50-75 pounds overweight. Their skin tone is bad, like they haven't seen the light of day. Some work 9-5 jobs, some are here on vacation, some are drug dealers, mainly crack cocaine and methamphetamine."

"The women?" I ask.

"Some women sport three-tone hair and look punk and tough but they're really messed up, like they're on drugs or are being regularly beaten. Most of 'em are overweight too. The women don't usually deal, they transport, they're the 'mules.' The women work as waitresses or bartenders. The women fist fight and wrestle each other, same as the men do. A lot of 'em are lesbians. They seem able to practice that lifestyle among the bikers. It's male homosexuals and blacks that the bikers have a problem with. Anyway, the bikers tolerate the lesbians. They don't react aggressively to them. In my experience, bikers react aggressively to anything that challenges their world view."

At midnight, I walk into the Last Resort, the bar where Wuornos had been arrested. I want to see where she felt safe. I want to sit there alone, drink something vaguely alcoholic, do no interviews, just watch, listen, and take it all in.

The place is maybe 18x30 feet inside, with a juke box, a pool table, and a bar. Huge tires hang from a tree in the outside yard; inside, bras and panties, tattered and soiled, hang from the ceiling. Hundreds of color photos of bikers are on the walls: the men on their bikes, the women baring their breasts, or mooning the camera. I notice a few Harley-Davidson banners, some KKK calling cards, a flyer for a "Bikers' Benefit for Bow Wows," a model ship made of Budweiser beer cans, and a sign behind the bar which says "Die Yuppie Scum."

The place is deserted, except for the bartender and a waitress. They talk quietly about people getting in and out of jail, about sex, about television programs. When the sports news comes on, the waitress says: "I can take care of that whole football team and the baseball team too. They probably have such little pricks. Oh, the reception's bad, let me stroke that TV antenna for you."

The pot-bellied bartender, cycle boots up on a chair, emits a nonstop commentary on the TV programs. "How can anyone relate to this shit? It's all about rich kids. Maybe only the writers and producers can relate to this. They're assholes. Jerkoffs. Pansy-queer-pretty boys."

Nightlife in north central Florida.

* * *

On Monday, Yemaya and I drive three hours, from Daytona to Williston, to meet Arlene Pralle. We're driving into Big Gun country. Signs assure me I can buy a gun almost anywhere along the route. Car stickers say: "This car is insured by Smith & Wesson." I drive without fear. I don't yet know that women are Big Game on the highways here, and that those women who can afford it have car phones and guns of their own on board, so they can lock themselves in and call for help—when a man tries to run them off the road, or take advantage of a lone woman's flat tire to rape or kill her.

Suddenly, there they are: ten young black men, chained together. It's a startling, sobering sight. The men are prisoners on a chain-gang, and they're guarded by one white man with a gun. The chained men have just rested their picks and shovels in order to watch, leer, catcall, and smack their lips at one black woman for the entire time it takes her to cross the highway. The white overseer looks away with a jackal's smile on his face.

The woman, in her thirties, is wearing a plain, almost prim flowered housedress. She pretends "it's" not happening, and that she doesn't "mind" what's not happening, either. They're chained, for God's sake, think of it as grace dispensed, her contribution to their otherwise emasculated "manhood." But they're insulting, not flattering her, and for one mean moment, I'm glad the men are chained, and sorry their overseer isn't.

Florida has a way of bringing the alligator out in you. I'd

noticed how few facial muscles move when some Floridians tell you to "move on" (the police), or wish you "good night" (the hotel clerks). Their affect is sullen, heat-drugged, inexpressive, one notch down the evolutionary ladder—thick-lidded and predatory.

I'd always liked tourist-Florida, the white hot beaches, the sparkling water, the icy-cold hotel rooms, but l could never live here, there are too many shopping malls, too much flat horizon, too much sadness, the region is haunted by hurricanes, anti-Black lynchings, massacres of all-Black communities in Ocoee and Rosewood, and by treasures lost and fortunes murderously founded.

This trip feels like one into a more rural American past. Pickup trucks begin to appear, gas stations begin to advertise bags of feed. We see signs for DeLand, Blitchie, Morristown, and Zuber, before we come to Williston, a one-street town with one motel, one restaurant, a small library, and a school. I send Yemaya to look around town while I meet Arlene. Yemaya's report reads:

"I spent approximately one hour at the Williston Public Library. It is an extremely small facility, perhaps 30' X 50' and contains approximately 5,550 books. The library carries the *National Geographic*, religious publications like *Plain Truth*, religious college catalogs, singles connections for Christians, books on horses, and non-fiction books on 'Crime.' A major portion of the rear wall is dedicated to Harlequin Romances which are sold for ten cents each. The local Chiefland weeklies devote perhaps 85% of their space to articles about the County Fair. One notice in particular caught my attention: a small business ad with the silhouette of a pig and the words, 'Thanks for buying my hog.'"

"Maranatha Meadows" ("That's Greek for Jesus," Pralle explains), is way out of town. Pralle's black and white road sign portrays a lion and a lamb. The "farmhouse" is tiny and a bit seedy. Pralle herself turns out to be a tiny woman, with a tiny voice. She's a middle-aged ingénue: sunny, impish, winsome.

"I apologize for being such a beast yesterday," she laughs conspiratorially, intimately, as if we've known each other for a long time. "But if you are who you say you are, you could be the Long Shot we need. I told Lee: give it a shot. What have we got to lose?"

"But," she says, coyly, "why do you need to talk to me? People keep using me as a way to reach Lee. Why talk to me? Why not talk to her lawyers? Writers and movie producers keep calling and showing up at my door. Letters keep coming in from all over the world. I'm just one woman. I only want to be Lee's friend. When do you think this will stop? I have twenty-nine horses to feed every day. I'm so tired."

One's fans are so exhausting.

"Do you have a private lawyer who'll take Lee's case?" she asks. "We like Trish, but she's very busy. Bruce and Michael (Hauptmann), from the Georgia ACLU, did come down. We liked them a lot too and they met with Lee and with me and they said they'd take her first case, including the appeal, for $45,000 in expense money. We think they're a little wild."

"That's a very, very reasonable price," I say. (Attorney Len Weinglass would later agree to represent Wuornos for $50,000 in expense money—but only if I could raise that sum.)

"What do you mean by a little wild?" I ask, curious to know whom Pralle and Wuornos think is "wild."

"Well, they were eccentric."

"What do you mean by eccentric?" I persist.

"Well, they have long ponytails. But they wanted $20,000 in seventy-two hours. Where can someone like me get that kind of money?"

Pralle admits that the only reason they didn't "go" with the ACLU was "because of the sum of money involved." Pralle has been quoted as saying that she is ready to put up (the) farm to pay for Wuornos' lawyers, and perhaps she would if the farm wasn't already almost totally mortgaged.

I do not set eyes on Pralle's husband, Robert, but I do meet "Victor, the shotgun;" the kenneled-on-the-premises wolves (they're scary); King, the official pet-on-premise: a half-dog, half-wolf (he's also scary); and, the twenty-nine Tennessee Walkers in the fields and in the barn (they're tall, but not scary creatures).

I do meet Pralle's father, Palmerino, an eighty-two-year-old Italian widower originally from Brooklyn, my hometown. He asks, "Seriously, whaddya think, isn't my daughter crazy to do what she's doing? Huh? I understand, you're in for the money, you're a writer, writers chase the money, but Arlene, she's not a writer, what's in it for her?"

"Well, not all writers," I say.

"Look, don't bullshit me, I'm from Brooklyn. Ya hafta be crazy to do sumpthin for nothing, right?"

Maybe he's right.

"I'm a sick man, I can't support Arlene forever. She tells me you're some kinda doctor. Can you talk some sense into her?"

Pralle leaves the room to see about the horses, use the bathroom, and to answer the "private" line in the bedroom—the one she's installed to receive Wuornos' phone calls. Pralle's regular line is constantly busy with calls from the media.

I clear my throat and deliver a university lecture tailored to Ms. Arlene Pralle's every need. I cover double standards, both in the criminal justice system, and in the media, then move on to the likelihood, not only of "bad" press—which is what Arlene seems most afraid of, but of a series of death sentences, then onto what life might be like for someone like Wuornos on Death Row or in Chattahoochee, the state asylum for the criminally insane.

"Lee doesn't want to go for an insanity defense," is how Pralle puts it. I discuss the kind of experts who could testify about the consequences of trauma and about street prostitution in America. Pralle listens. She appears thoughtful.

"Okay, but why did you send Lee a copy of your book (I admit it, I did it), and not me? I need a copy too."

Pralle has just visited Wuornos for the first time. ("No, I can't tell you how I finally got permission to visit, that's my secret.") They were not allowed to touch each other.

"I think I'll die if they don't let me touch her soon," Pralle confides. "It's not right, is it, Lee's not being allowed any visitors? And no contact visitation?"

"No, it's not," I agree.

"I tried to give Lee a Ruth and Naomi medal, but they wouldn't let her have it. They said I could only give her a crucifix, that everything else was jewelry. You don't think she'll ever turn on me, do you? Like Betty Sain did?"

"Who's Betty Sain?"

"Oh, she lives in Bell Buckle, Tennessee. In 1966, one of Betty's horses won the World Arena Championship for Tennessee Walkers. The men hated her for this and so did the other women. Betty lost her farm. We met Betty about two years ago, that's about ten years after she lost her farm. My husband and I loaned her more than $12,000 to try and recover her farm.

Well, maybe Betty had a multiple personality, because suddenly, one day she turned on us and we were her friends. In a deep man's voice, she accused us of trying to poison her or kill her; she reported us to the Sheriff. The Sheriff said, 'Don't worry, Betty's elevator doesn't go to the top floor.' We never got our money back but we do own some horses in common: 'Speedy Jack,' who's in Tennessee, and 'Eighty-Niner,' who's my star stallion here. Betty drinks about a fifth of Chivas Regal a day. A few weeks ago, she began to threaten my life again."

Is Arlene attracted to female maniacs? Does she want to help them, live through them, cash in on them—a horse here, a movie deal there?

"I get so lonely here." Pralle brightens. "You can stay here with me if you want to. You can move in as soon as my dad leaves. I'll show you all Lee's letters and drawings. By the way, can you get me a prescription for Valium? I get real bad headaches, I have pains all over my body…"

I return to my motel, exhausted. The phone is ringing as I open the door. It's Pralle calling to "introduce me to Lee," whom she has on her other line.

"Phyllis, this is Lee, Lee, this is Phyllis. Say hello to each other." Pralle actually tries to initiate a three-way conversation by putting her two telephones together. It's no use, even shouting doesn't work, Wuornos and I can't hear each other.

"Lee, this is Arlene." She talks to Wuornos slowly, and in a loud voice, as if Lee is retarded, or somewhat deaf (which she is). "I want you to call Phyllis at her motel tomorrow. Yes, you can call her collect."

I'd passed muster with the mother/pimp/gatekeeper.

CHAPTER NINE

I Speak to the Serial Killer
and Meet with Her Public Defenders

LEE CALLS ME COLLECT at my motel the next morning. Her voice is Joplin-husky and surprisingly sweet, even girlish. Did I expect her to sound more mannish? Well, that was a real hefty swagger she had on TV, and the way she tossed her hair around! Most women do it out of nervousness, Wuornos seemed to do it out of defiance, or to intimidate, the way male lions toss their manes.

Lee said that jail didn't "bother" her, that she could "take it," that the daily verbal abuse was nothing: "Hey, whore, show us some tits 'n ass." "We'll put you in solitary forever if you do any weird lesbian shit in here." "Bark at the moon, bitch, if you don't like it." "I'm going to enjoy watching you fry, real nice and slowly, once for each guy you killed."

Most women would wither and die on the proverbial vine, if a group of men had launched such verbal hostility at them. I guess Wuornos was used to it.

"How are you?" I ask.

"First, they put me in medical isolation. I only got to sleep four hours at a time. I was very angry. I threatened to sue the cocksuckers. C'mon. Why put me in solitary? I did not attempt suicide. I did not attempt to escape."

"Do they let you exercise?"

"No way," she says. "I haven't been outside in three months except once, for fifteen minutes. They needed three guards to do it. One on each side of me, and one with a rifle. The one with the gun walked behind us. What do they think I'm going to do? They search us before we leave the jail. They search us before we come back into the jail. And outside there's a net wire over our heads. I wanna go back to the jail in Citrus (County). You can smoke at Citrus. You have nice coffee there. You got coloring pencils and drawing paper. When I was at Citrus, they put me in with the men."

"What a nightmare," I say.

"I can take it. The men in Citrus didn't bother me. I'd like to go back there. We're just waiting for a bed to open up in Citrus."

Here was a woman long used to abuse, a woman who takes pride in being able to go head-to-head, toe-to-toe with her tormenters. She'd be goddammed if she'd say "uncle." She'd rather kill.

"Here in Volusia, we're allowed to receive only one package every six months, which means I have three more months to wait. They say I can only have three books and three magazines. They won't let me exchange a book once I've read it. They haven't let me go to church. Ahh, I don't want to go anyway. Once, I was writing something private for my lawyer, and one of the guards said that she'd have to look at it before she sent it out. She opened it and read it right in front of me. Are they supposed to do that?"

"I don't think so."

"I don't want to stay here in Volusia. I want to go back to Citrus."

"Aileen…"

"Call me Lee."

"Okay, Lee. What do you need?"

"I need you guys real bad," she answered. "The public defender has 47 other capital cases and no time for me. I'll pay you back if you get me a lawyer who has time for me. I'll sell my life story for 30 million dollars and I'll set up a foundation for abused women. Hey man: I'm going through living hell for defending myself."

She is very specific about numbers but is almost always wrong about them. Despite all her attempts at wheeling and dealing, she understands very little about money. She deals in chump change. The night before she was arrested she had sixty dollars which she "blew" on beer, pool, cheap food, and the juke box; that's why she had to sleep outside the Last Resort—she had nothing left for a motel room.

In wonder, Wuornos said: "I can't believe there are women out there rooting for me!"

Well, not so fast. Yes, many women, actually a surprising number, have said: "It's about time women started shooting back," and "Good for her. Those men must have done something to provoke her." Some feminists (and many anti-death penalty advocates) have urged me to do everything I can for Wuornos. But most women, including feminists and lesbians, see her as too unsympathetic a victim to bother with: Unstable, uncooperative, a loser, a real pain-in-the-ass, and just plain nuts.

She had absolutely no idea who I was. How could she? While we privileged few were trying to foment a revolution, she was merely trying to survive.

"Okay, Lee. Can we talk about your case, go over your legal options?"

"Sure. I already have two public defenders: Trish Jenkins and Ed Bonnett, but they're both in Ocala, which is four to six hours away, round-trip. When I first met Trish, she was pretty mellow. Now she has an attitude. Because of me, she really thinks she's somebody. She's on a big ego trip."

"She might be a good lawyer for you," I say.

"Hey, Arlene told me about your ideas for the testifying experts. Let's go for it. Can you be one of my experts? I don't know if Trish will cooperate. She doesn't think she needs anyone's help. She doesn't care about me. Fuck it. I haven't seen Trish in six weeks, and she promised she'd come. She has about 47 other murder cases to try before mine. But hey! I got rid of Ray (Cass), my other public defender, and I can do it again. Ray was in on the deal with that bitch, Jacqui Giroux, the movie-maker. Giroux had me sign a bogus contract. She thinks I'm gonna settle for $60.00 a month for as long as I live. Or until they strap me in the Chair. She thinks she gets to become rich and I get to die, no way, it's not gonna happen."

Ah, that thorny theme.

"I'm pretty street-wise. I'm not some dumb asshole. The public defenders are gonna sell me out too. They're gonna make a deal. Man! The police will keep on falsifying evidence like the media falsifies everything about me."

Now, she was hot, angry, in anguish.

"Everyone is making money off my life. Tyria, the cops, Republican (Republic) Pictures, Jacqui Giroux. That bitch has my entire family under contract. She's paying 35 people, most of whom haven't seen me for twenty years, $5,000 apiece for what they can remember. C'mon man, I was confused. I talked to Giroux for four minutes right after they arrested me. Get outta here, I don't care what she says I signed, she don't have jackshit."

"My old lawyer, Ray (Cass), the one I got rid of, and my other old lawyer, Russell (Armstrong), they're the guys who brought me together with Giroux. They all wanna make money on me. Dig this. They wanted me to cop to being loony-tunes, so they could get me outta the way. But I refused to talk to the nutcase doctor. I was shaking in my boots, but I did it. I went into the courtroom and spoke up for myself, to get rid of Ray Cass."

"That was real impressive, Lee."

"Y'know, I counted 57 lies in the news about myself. I used to think that everything I read in the papers was the truth. Now I know it's mainly a bunch of lies."

In February, at Aileen Wuornos' and Arlene Pralle's request, Kelly Turner had printed the following "clarifications" in the *Ocala Star Banner*:

(Wuornos) is originally from Troy, Michigan, not Summer, Michigan. She was with her lover, Tyria Moore, for four and a half years, not six years. She never said she 'hates' men, she was not talking to two middle-aged guys when she was arrested at a Daytona Beach Bar in January, she was talking to two undercover officers dressed as bikers. They gave her $20.00 and said they would get her a motel. They said they needed directions and asked her to step outside, and that's when they arrested her, she was never at a doughnut shop in Sanford and said she had never been to Sanford, she never lived on the street but stayed in motels or trailers until the night before she was arrested; her mother (grandmother) was never an alcoholic but took thyroid medication that affected her liver.

Oh boy. Is Wuornos in for a rare ride with the media. She sounds heartbreakingly... concrete, literal. She also sounds paranoid, like a "recovering" incest-victim-accuracy-fanatic, but I doubt that she's "recovered" from anything.

"When the ACLU lawyers came to see me from Georgia," Wuornos continues, "they read me some stuff that the police said, and most of it was a lie. I'm sure that everybody's cutting a deal. I'm not a stupid asshole. It kills me that my family and friends are trying to sell me."

It had literally killed her—and her male victims too.

"Lee, you didn't ask me for any advice. Do you want any advice?"

"Like what? Yeah, okay, I guess so."

"Try to give away as little information as possible—this phone line is probably tapped—and be cautious about what you say to anyone in jail, no matter how friendly they seem. How are you doing on toiletries, do you have a canteen allowance? Are they letting you shower, exercise, see sunlight? Lee, do you know how to imagine yourself in a peaceful, beautiful place? Can you transport yourself there psychologically?"

"You mean use my creative imagination?"

"Yes, exactly. People who are confined in small spaces, in jail, or in their bodies, if they're sick, find that this helps ease the time."

"Man," she jeers. "I know all about that stuff." Then she says, simply, "Thank you for what you're trying to do."

So: The Lady and The Tramp have spoken—and I'm not the

Lady, I'm the one who wants to "overthrow the system." Wuornos only wants a "piece of the pie," she surrendered long ago, the way all "good girls" are supposed to. Just let the woman have her Bud, her Marlboros, her girlfriend, her motel room, and when she's goddam ready to spread 'em and sell, don't mess with her. Pay her, fuck her, and be on your way.

Lee had to straighten me out on certain points because "people do not understand that cops always get everything wrong."

According to the 1984 police report, in Plantation, Florida, Aileen had been "arrested for forging her employer's signature on two checks at the Barnett Bank in the Upper Keys." As Aileen saw it, she hadn't forged anything. She'd just tried to get what she was owed, what she'd already worked for. She'd also tried to get out of a bad situation.

See, Aileen had moved in with a shrimper who'd promised to make her his secretary only he never did, he just kept fuckin' her, and duckin' out on the $495.00 she said he owed her for her work. Aileen felt like a "sexual hostage." Every time Aileen would raise the issue of her pay, the shrimper would take her out to dinner, booze it up in a bar, "sidetrack" her completely.

Aileen didn't want to "hit the streets without a penny," and she wanted out. Aileen finally decided to pay herself and get the hell outta there, so she sat down and practiced the man's signature "49 times on 49 checks" (it didn't occur to her to practice on a napkin or a newspaper), and she took the best looking check to his bank and got herself arrested on the spot for trying to pass a bad check.

But he promised! But he owed her! But she'd worked for it! She'd fucked for it. Fucked for it? Tough shit lady. The state doesn't enforce verbal contracts between whores and Johns.

Ah, c'mon Chesler, be fair. She did her part, she delivered the bodies. Can you deliver a defense team?

* * *

After talking to Lee, I visit Arlene at Maranatha Meadows a few hours later. That's when Trish Jenkins finally calls, leaves a message. I call her back. She sounds angry. "Okay, what did you do to make my client sound like a militant feminist? She's threatening to fire me if I don't see you. I want you in my office at 3:30 sharp today."

"Oh, now you can't stay all day." Arlene is disappointed. She talks as fast as she can.

"Trish is trying to tell me, in small doses, what Death Row is like, it's a 6 x 6 cell, and you're allowed very few possessions, and if you're a woman, you can shower only once every ten days, and they censor your mail. But that's not so bad. There are no phones! How am I supposed to live without our phone calls? They might as well sentence me right along with her. Trish told me that once Lee gets her first death sentence, she stays on Death Row until they either execute her or free her."

I hope that Jenkins has spent as much time explaining matters to Wuornos. Who the hell is Pralle? How can Jenkins stop her from talking to the press or from putting Wuornos on the line with every reporter—and with me, too? It isn't possible.

Pralle keeps on talking. "Think positive, I tell Lee. I'm planning a big victory party, a big bonfire on the farm, for when she's acquitted and she comes to live with me. We have a lot in common. We didn't have our real mothers. We both tried suicide, but it didn't work. I was once a kind of a party girl too. And we both believe in Jesus Christ. He brought us together." Pralle hauls out her cache of Lee's letters to her. They are filled with Wuornos' surprisingly expert drawings and clever, sentimental, Hallmark greeting card-like poems.

WOODSTOCK DAYS
Summer of 69
14 years old was I
Raisin Hell
Getting stoned
smoking pot and drinkin wine
…
And so Woodstock went down

as a Legendary time
Back that year of 69.

PRESS HOUNDS
My life is a mess
Because of the press.

"You're a doctor," Pralle says. "Tell me what you think. You
don't think my love for Lee is perverted, do you?" Pralle brings
out a file of her letters to Lee. "Look, I signed this vow promis-
ing to stand by Lee, to pray for her. See, how the letter states that
'nothing dirty or perverted is intended with this covenant.'" The
covenant, dated March 21, 1991, states:

To my beloved Lee-

I, Arlene Pralle, do hereby vow before God and His Holy Angels to stand by Aileen Carol Wuornos from this day forth
and into eternity. I will love her, respect her, honor her and
provide for all her needs. She will be bathed in prayer on a
daily basis. Her financial needs will also be taken care of...I
am willing and eager to stand by this Covenant, knowing in
God's Eyes 'It is better not to make a vow than to make one
and break it.' (Ecc-5:5) ... This Covenant is inspired by Holy
and Godly love towards Aileen Wuornos as a Christian sister, soul-mate and best friend...I, Arlene, do pledge my love,
support and allegiance to Aileen Carol Wuornos (Lee) until
'death us do part.'
Signed in Loving Commitment,
Arlene M. Pralle.

* * *

Jenkins and her colleague, Ed Bonnett, are waiting for me
in an office that has only enough room for one battered desk,
one similarly battered file cabinet, two windows (with their
shades drawn), and three or four wooden chairs. Bonnett wears
hippie-long hair, blue jeans and cowboy boots; Jenkins' hair is
frizzy-wild, and her fingers are covered in big rings. Her voice

is tight, hard, controlled, and commanding. She is absolutely inscrutable. I'm impressed. Trial lawyers must spend years developing such inscrutability.

"I don't know who you are," Jenkins says, "but the state can only afford one expert witness for Wuornos and that's for all seven trials and I've already hired her."

When I offer to testify for the defense, pro bono, Jenkins softens, slightly.

"The media's all over this thing. I've heard from Australian reporters, German reporters, Japanese reporters, American reporters. What is it, what do they want? What's going on out there? My client's former lover reputedly sold the rights to her version of the story to CBS."

"Has anyone visited Wuornos in jail?" I ask.

"No, no one has. Wait a minute, now that you mention it, there was someone, a woman, who wanted Lee's permission to make a movie. Damn funny thing," says Jenkins, "but Lee keeps insisting that she's innocent, that she killed everyone in self-defense. You're a psychologist. What do you folks call that?"

"Wuornos is probably suffering from every psychological ailment known to woman. She'd be easy to diagnose," I say.

"Your resume's too long to read," Jenkins says. "Tell me exactly who you are and what you have in mind."

And so I tell her (or rather, them), and they seem interested, and we leave it this way: Meg and I will develop what Trish calls a "work product." Trish wants to know which experts I have in mind, whether I'd be a witness too, and what, exactly, we'd be trying to accomplish. She wants it in writing.

"Remember," she says, "there's no money. You'll have to persuade everyone to do it for no money."

"I know," I respond. "You'd better cover me with a letter. I already know too much."

"Yes, you do."

"I can be summoned by the prosecutor."

"Yes, you can."

"But I don't know what I'm gonna do with you. You're also a writer. You've said you want to write about the case. What are we going to do about that?"

There is no way I can promise not to write about it. Can a writer promise not to write about something because she thinks it's too important? What if my work hurts real people, what if Pralle loses her livelihood, and Wuornos, and others like her, all hope, and their lives too, because of something I've written?

Or failed to write?

I propose what I think might be a "good enough" solution. I say, "I'll promise, legally, in writing, never to use anything that doesn't emerge as part of the public record, I'll agree not to use any inside information until after the last appeal has been decided, even if that's twenty years from now. You decide," I tell Trish.

Jenkins moves to another topic. "My expert has already spent two full days with Lee. So, a lot of what you've been saying makes sense. My client is obviously a very traumatized woman. And she does keep insisting that she killed in self-defense. I might want you to pose an additional list of questions for Lee."

Dr. Elizabeth McMahon, Jenkins' psychologist, has published nothing on rape trauma or prostitution (at least, nothing I can find), and she isn't part of any feminist network in Florida. Like Jenkins, McMahon may be more used to testifying for men than for women. Does Trish think this is the best way to go? Well, it's what she's used to, it's tried-and-true, and she's a busy lady.

"You're tied into a movie deal, is that it?" Jenkins asks.

"No, I'm not," I say.

Why does Jenkins find it so difficult to understand that feminists might actually have a political agenda, that we might be interested in Wuornos in the same way that the Communist Party was once interested in the Scottsboro Boys, or the NAACP in *Brown V. Board of Education*, or the Center for Constitutional Rights and the Southern Poverty Law Center in Yvonne Wanrow and Joan Little? (In the 1970s, Wanrow, a Colville Indian, and Little, an African-American, had both killed violent white men in self-defense.)

What is it about whoring and writing that engender so

much mythology? Why are people more interested in reading about The Happy Hooker or The Writer Who Made a Fortune, than in hearing about the daily grind and the low wages?

For years, I tried to tell people that most writers can't afford to lead "interesting" lives, that our work is the most interesting thing about us. I've always said that when I was writing, my life was uneventful, it had to be, I had to be in the same spot every day, so that in case Inspiration chanced to strike, She'd know just where to find me. And don't bother me when I'm working, don't call, don't drop in, don't interrupt me. She won't come if anyone else is around, if I'm even thinking about anyone else but Her, I have to be Hers, and Hers alone, the Muse is one hell of a jealous Mother.

Writers are nothing like whores (but we're often, similarly, seen as losers), but we're legal, even respectable. Writers are more like long-distance runners—except, if you're a woman, there's usually no one around to cheer you on, and you've got to run anyway, you've got no choice, not if you're a writer. It's the curse of the red shoes. But this is true for whores too, they're always working, always looking for action.

I could stretch this analogy, and it might prove illuminating: writers ply their trade at all hours of the day and night, some writers drink and take drugs—but never as routinely and systematically as whores do, although there are exceptions. Maybe I'd rather compare "writing" and "whoring" than figure out whether I personally have anything in common with Wuornos.

Look: I don't want to intrude myself into this story, but I don't want to expose everyone else, and remain safely hidden myself.

My life is not like Wuornos'. She slept in abandoned cars, she did time in many jails, she always lived—not just on the edge, but way over the edge, she's a world-class Altamont style hippie. I'm not in her league. This is her story, why bring myself into it?

Because I'm your stand-in, your guide, the connection between you and the killer.

But I've lived long enough to learn some caution. By now,

I know that anything a woman tells you about herself can and will be used against her, so it's a luxury, even dangerous, for any woman, even a writing-woman, to reveal too much about herself—at least not before she comes into serious money, or dies. So: I'm a bit reluctant to tell you anything, I'd prefer to just give you my name, rank and serial number, nothing else, not yet.

Was I beaten as a child? Of course. Did I flee when I was too young to be on my own? Of course. Did I run the same gauntlet of shame that every girl and every woman has to run in terms of catcalls on the street, and harassment and rape on the job? Of course. Was I betrayed by boyfriends, girlfriends, and spouses? Of course. Prick me, will I not bleed? And yet, absolutely nothing in my life could ever compare with the abuse that Wuornos experienced.

Jenkins says: "You know, my experts were also involved in the Ted Bundy case."

"What?"

"Stay in touch. Get me your work product. Gotta go." Jenkins was done with me.

I retreat to the long, cool veranda of my motel for a very cold drink, and to savor the shade, the languorous palm trees, the defiantly decorous all-white outfits people often wear in hot climates. I turn that veranda into my office. I schedule all my appointments there. At night, the air is soft and warm and makes me wonder why I continue to live in so cold a place as New York.

After this, I'm either on the phone with Wuornos, on the open road, or at a meeting with Dr. Judy Wilson; Jim Shook, Esq.; Arlene Pralle; Trish Jenkins, Esq.; or, Prof. Meg Baldwin—and, as I remember it now, I seem to have done these things at high-speed, over and over again, so that years later, everything remains fixed in my mind, as if it were a movie, one that I can watch any time I want and the only thing that can ever change are the conclusions I draw, or what I notice: some detail I missed the first time round, but it—the week, the place, is made of more eternal stuff, and I'm but a cowled gardener, in the vineyards of memory.

CHAPTER TEN

Ocala: They Burn Crosses and Abortion Clinics Right Down to the Ground

I'M HAVING DINNER on my motel veranda with Judy Wilson and her husband, Jim Shook, who are both tall, fair-skinned, and slightly sun-burned. Jim's a semi-retired lawyer, licensed pilot, scuba diver, and computer wizard. He's a good-hearted loner, burned out from fighting the good fight.

Dr. Judy, the director of the Ocala Rape Crisis Center and the Ocala Shelter for Battered Women, tells me: "Wuornos is gonna receive the backlash meant for the rest of us steel magnolias. Women have been real uppity in Ocala and Wuornos is gonna burn for all their uppityness."

"How do they treat battered women who kill their batterers down here?" I ask.

"Honey," hooted Judy, "a woman doesn't have to kill a man to be in hot water here. There are women in this town whose jobs have been threatened because they went and joined the National Organization for Women."

"My husband was the lawyer on the Joyce Brothers/Steven Hays case. Do you know the case?"

I do. It's an incest-custody battle, filled with extraordinary charges and counter-charges, a father with money, a mother who's broke—the usual. Joyce and her mother, Evelyn, had briefly hidden Ashley, the little girl.

"Well, we'd never seen anything like what happened next," Judy's voice got Magnolia steel-steady. "First, the judge jailed Joyce and Evelyn. Evelyn worked part-time at the shelter. They began an investigation of the shelter. Our Board forced us to fire Evelyn. Then, we don't know who did it exactly, but someone poisoned my husband, right there in the courtroom. They had to rush Jim out to the hospital. Sure did. He nearly died, but the judge wouldn't delay the trial. No-sir.

"Two replacement lawyers: Garnett Harrison, you know her? The lawyer in the Crissy Foxworth custody-incest battle out of Mississippi, and Alan Rosenfeld, from Vermont, had to be flown in. They stayed with us, they slept right in our living room and all of a sudden, Garnett and Alan got real sick. Pretty mysterious if you ask me. We couldn't figure out whether they'd spiked the pitcher of water in the courtroom or used voodoo or what." Judy roared with laughter.

"You just know that the judge gave that father sole custody, no visitation to the mother. And he let that father leave Ocala for his daddy's place in Alabama. Jim started some legal actions, and the judge and his friends fined Jim, and tried to have Jim disbarred. We'll tell you about it!"

Maybe "coming down" was not such a good idea.

"Honey, Trish is *the* Marion County Public Defender." Judy says. "A course, there's only one other woman public defender in town and wouldn't you know it! The two of them just hate each other." Judy pauses, shrugs, smiles. "The other woman is pretty weird, though. She loves to represent male perverts, she hugs them in the courtroom, each and every one of 'em, after she gets 'em off. It's how she gets off, I think."

"Frances actually has a high success rate," Judy says, "Jim, remember how she got that serial rapist, Frank Cash, off? Frances insisted on keeping Frank's case even after Gene Abel, the psychiatrist involved in the case, said flat-out: 'Do not let any woman lawyer handle Frank's case, because he will try to rape and kill her.' Guess what Frank's doing now? Threatening to kill Frances."

And Judy laughs in the gargoyle's face, demonstrating the fine southern art of enjoying idiosyncratic and eccentric things.

"Trish," Judy says, "is tough in the courtroom. She's real strong-willed. She's loyal to her clients. She's not bad to rape victims, not even when she's representing the rapist, but she fights hard for her boys. I don't think she's ever had a real notorious case before."

"Now, lookit here," says Jim. "Trish is a damn fine lawyer. Her boss, Skip Babb, now he's the one the town elected. Course, he drinks too much. But people here aren't going to like a lawyer who's too good. Our prosecutors are sloppy. They depend on judges bending over backwards for them, which they do, sideways too. So, Trish oughta know better. They are really violating your friend's civil rights by not allowing her to have any visitors."

"Jim, Aileen Wuornos is not my friend," I say.

"Ah, still can't understand why you're not running to the newspapers," Jim exclaims. "Not letting her have visitors is a gross violation of her civil rights. You can call the FBI about this. Tell them that our local male serial rapists and killers are getting all the visits they want."

He may be right, but I doubt I'd get very far.

Jim leans forward. "Don't you know that every male involved in the legal system in the wild west of Florida wants Wuornos to burn?"

"Don't forget the women, Jim," Judy says. "When the police first announced that it was women out there who were shooting their men, remember how they'd order their husbands not to pick up any female hitchhikers? Tried to get 'em to stay home. Even tried to go along with 'em in their cars."

"Well, the whole town went kinda crazy," Jim remembers. "Now, about your friend." (I didn't try to correct him anymore. Maybe Jim liked having dinner with someone whose so-called friend is a so-called serial killer.) "Your friend hasn't even been convicted. She's being deprived of her civil rights before she's been convicted of any crime."

"How would you handle the case?" I ask him.

Jim says: "Insanity's not a bad way to go. They'd send that gal to Chattahoochee and there's a revolving door right outta that place."

"Wait a minute," I interrupt. "Are you telling me that they'll ever let Wuornos walk out of the Florida state loony bin?"

"Well, the State has no money to keep everybody in." And he laughs.

"We know murderers and screwballs who are back out on the streets in months or years," Judy says. "There's one stalking Jim right now, name of Michelle Cooper. Jim put her away when he was a prosecutor. She killed at least five, maybe six men about a decade back. Michelle kept falling in love with 'em, and they wouldn't leave their wives for her, Michelle warned 'em. She smeared witchcraft symbols on their front doors. But when they still wouldn't leave their wives, she killed 'em, One after the other. Michelle's out now, and she's after my husband!"

"Florida can't be this strange," I object, over their laughter.

"Strange?" Judy stops laughing. "Now, John Tanner. He's Wuornos' prosecutor. John Tanner's strange. He's the most interesting character so far. Are you ready for the details?"

I am.

"Well, John Tanner's family has a full complement on his father's side. Lots of mentally ill, plenty of suicides. His family was very poor, often went hungry. Tanner's father drank. John was always his father's favorite. Heard that his father abused the other two children, but he never laid a hand on John."

"How do you know all this?" I ask.

"Darlin', everybody knows everything, that's how," says Jim.

"John used to be a defense lawyer in private practice," Judy says. "Did very well too. Then, he turned born again. He saw the Office of the State Prosecutor as his Christian duty. John believes that women should stay home and that Christian men should protect them. He's very sympathetic to women in that sense. His wife is a Mississippi sorority girl, the perfect Southern woman. First thing John did was develop a dress code for women in the prosecutor's office."

Then Judy tells me that John Tanner's half-sister is a friend of hers and that she's dying to meet me. I think: it doesn't get any better than this, does it? I was wrong. They'd saved the best for last.

"John's the one who tried to delay Ted Bundy's execution in order to keep Bundy alive, so he and Bundy could keep exposing the evils of pornography. John's one of the guys who tried to nail Two Live Crew for their dirty lyrics. He's the one that's been personally raiding the video stores for pornography."

To Jim and Judy, Tanner's position on pornography constitutes "fighting words." They see Tanner's attempts to outlaw pornography as part of the fundamentalist attempt to repeal both the Constitution and The Bill of Rights, the First, Eighth, Thirteenth, Fourteenth, and Twentieth Amendments in particular.

"Man says he's a Christian," Jim expounds. "Yet, he closes down small stores and backs the death penalty without a hint of Christian charity."

"Jim," I say, "if you're up for it, I'd like to see the legal papers on Michelle Cooper. (I never could track down Cooper's record.) And I'd love a guided tour of Ocala. Judy, I'd like to pay my respects to the Shelter tomorrow, too."

We three'd been sitting together for hours. The after-dinner dancing in the bar seemed to draw people from another era: ladylike women with lacquered hair, chivalrous men in string ties and cowboy hats, polite and perky waitresses, the kind who dress like cheerleaders or ice skaters in short, swirly, skirts, who sport jaunty bow-ties, bondage collars, little name tags, the kind whose paychecks are more modest than their outfits.

So, we'd been in the 1950s all evening, the era had never gone away, it was still here, that time when everyone knew their place. Eisenhower was president and everything took place behind closed doors. Everything's out in the open today, both the "progress'" and the refusal to progress.

For example, within a few thousand yards of where we're sitting, highway billboards advertise "Topless Car Washes," "All Naked Waitresses," "Topless and bottomless, Go-Go Girls," and "Abortion stops a Beating Heart 4,000 Times a Day."

* * *

Morning, and Wuornos is on the line again, calling collect.

"Lee, I've been thinking. It might help your case if you begin writing about how often you've been raped or had your life threatened on the job. You might even want to write your own book."

"Well, I'm not stupid," Wuornos explodes. "I don't want anyone else to profit from my life. But I don't want to write about the murders. No way! I want to write about the dangerous life I've lived, when I was on the street as a kid, the perils of the road, yeah, the rapes and the brutal beatings. I have it all worked out. People are backing me up. I have my own publisher. I have a friend who made nine million in one year writing about the Nautilus submarine."

Wuornos is very definite about numbers. She has to be, she's in the selling business, she knows that everything is for sale and has a definite price: $30.00 for head, $35.00 for straight sex, $40.00 for half and half, $100.00 for an hour of her time. Wuornos has been quoted as saying that the media told "57" lies about her, that when she'd confessed, she'd said it was self-defense "37" times. Now, she tells me, she's going to sell her life story for exactly "30 million dollars."

"Nobody but me knows about my life!" Wuornos is outraged, proprietary. "I was a loner, I hung around with my soul. Check this out! I saw the police on TV saying that they won't let me write my own book but they're gonna write a book about me. They're gonna get the money! Fuck that shit!"

Indeed, the sheriffs whose work led to Wuornos' arrest had allegedly been negotiating some kind of media deal, possibly even before they'd arrested Wuornos. By the summer of 1991, accusations would surface that Maj. Dan Henry, Capt. Steve Binegar and Sgt. Bruce Munster of the Marion County Sheriff's Office had been exploring the possibility of selling the rights to their story to an entertainment company—but, presumably, with the intention of donating any money they made to a fund for the victims of violent crimes. Retired Ocala Detective, Brian

Jarvis, accused the three sheriffs of covering up leads that linked Tyria to one or more of the killings, for the sake of financial gain.

More than a year later, on November 11, 1992, Major Henry of the Marion County Sheriff's Department would finally resign. According to the *Ocala Star Banner*:

> Henry's resignation came after the release of a taped telephone conversation between himself and Deputy Bruce Munster. Munster taped the phone call and turned it over to his attorney. On Tuesday, his attorney gave a copy of the tape to sheriff Don Moreland and Sheriff-elect Ken Ergle. Henry, who was with the department for nineteen years, resigned. No one involved would discuss the contents of the tape.

"I'm not interested in the money," Wuornos cheerfully lies. "When I was twenty, I was married to a very rich old man. He told me I was his Egyptian slave. He beat me with his cane. Hey, I'm not a materialistic person. I got out of that marriage after sixty days, even though the man had money."

This is the husband who obtained a restraining order against Wuornos and quickly divorced her.

Wuornos moves to another topic: her ex-lover, Tyria.

"Tyria's the sweetest, she honestly is, but she emotionally abused me. She just stayed in waiting for me, drinking beer, smoking cigarettes, watching TV. She had only two jobs in the four and a half years I was with her. One as a laundry worker, the other, as the manager of a laundry place. Man, she'd stress me out. I'd be hustling two hundred miles away, she'd ask me to hitchhike back to give her cigarette money. I'd do it, of course." Here, Wuornos pauses, then slowly, and in an intimidating, sultry tone tells me. "When I love somebody, I go all the way, I love them all the way."

She almost sounds like Barbra Streisand's incest-victim call-girl in the movie *Nuts*, who's on trial for killing a violent John. On the stand, at her competency hearing, Streisand turns to the judge and, slowly and deliberately, tells him exactly what she can do for him with her hands and her mouth, exactly how it will make him feel, why it's worth every dollar she charges.

Wuornos' voice has a harder edge, and she's talking about "true love" not "love for sale," but she's also boasting, staking out the territory she'd once traveled hundreds of miles a day to protect, protecting it still. Wuornos begins to talk about love on a more global level.

"We need to reach out. We need a Jesus movement. Something's happening in the world and evil is stomping out all the good karma. Our world needs healing. If people have loved ones on the street, they know we need a sister and brotherhood movement."

"Lee, do you need stuff like toothpaste, shampoo, stamps?"

"Oh, I need some underwear, size medium. I need a bra. I want a pair of Reeboks."

The Prisoner laughs wildly, and signs off.

Wuornos has "switched voices" at least three times in this conversation. She has a soft, almost girlish voice, an angry, menacing voice, in which she issues orders, makes threats and boasts about secret schemes. When she talks about Jesus, she speaks rapidly and urgently, as if she's in a trance, or "channeling" information from Above. Wuornos' voices have this in common—they brook no interruption.

I'd talked to Gloria Steinem, someone whom I've known since the late 1960s. Gloria wanted to know whether supporting Wuornos would weaken feminist work on behalf of battered women who kill their batterers in self-defense. "After all," says Gloria, "Wuornos is rather far out, and not at all typical."

"Gloria, I think it's the other way 'round. I think it's time to expand a woman's right to self-defense to include prostituted women. It's time to argue that any woman, prostituted or not, has the right to kill in self-defense."

"Yes," Gloria says, and she promises to call around for a pro bono, Florida-based criminal attorney.

"Was Wuornos sexually abused as a child?" Gloria asks. "Do you think she's been ritually abused? Do you think Wuornos is a multiple personality?"

"Maybe she's a multiple personality," I say, "but ritual or satanic abuse, that's small potatoes compared to gonzo patriarchy—which is a much larger cult."

I don't know if Wuornos is a "multiple," but given her history of childhood abuse and neglect, I wouldn't be surprised if she is. She certainly switches voices—or moods—pretty frequently. Still, I doubt that anyone will be able to persuade Wuornos to plead "insanity," and even if she agrees to do it, I doubt a jury will much care.

Justice for Wuornos—a fair trial--would be nothing less than a fucking miracle.

So: Arlene, Meg, and I are not so far apart, we're all expecting a miracle. Meg and I have no illusions about winning, we merely want the privilege of battle. We're not attached to Wuornos "personally," God hasn't brought us together. Meg and I are deeply moved by Wuornos' plight, deeply in her debt for the opportunity she's given us, but Wuornos is not our Lifetime Mission. We'll move remorselessly on, no matter what happens, to the next battle.

* * *

Gentleman Jim Shook arrives to take me on a tour. Ocala is "horse country." People breed, board, train, and race horses here. In Ocala, men are "men," women are "women," people are either rich or poor, and if you're black, you stay back. The town is run by a group of rich white Christian men who speak in booming voices.

According to Joan, who works with Judy, Ocala's filled with "rednecks" who are "really not educated. We've got some people who've been in Ocala for four generations, but even if they've gone off to college, they haven't ever been out of Ocala. We've got a class of really wretchedly poor people from the North who came down here to be happy and aren't. They only got as far as Ocala and then their money ran out. They can't afford to move further south. They have no extended family, so when they get stressed, they start hitting their wives or their kids or they start fucking their kids."

Susan, who also works at the Shelter and whose father, Clyde, had been business partners with one of Ocala's finest, most important men, said that behind drawn shades, many of the local white wives who lunch, also drink, and have discreet, periodic "breakdowns," too.

"Some women drink all night long, and sleep all morning. My momma did. Daddy'd hide her car keys to keep her from driving drunk or creating an embarrassing scene. Momma was drunk the night she died. Daddy's new wife is the widow of another wealthy Ocala man. She drinks too, only no one will admit it."

Susan tells me that "the northwest section of Ocala is where most black folks live. Folks think this used to be an Indian graveyard, and because people built houses right over sacred land, that's why their lives are cursed. That's why, they say, when a woman comes to Ocala, even if she wants to get out, she never can."

"You don't want people from around here on Wuornos' jury," Jim says with bitter passion. "You want Trish to try and move the case to Miami. Wuornos can't get a fair trial here. The local papers have been filled with news of Wuornos for nearly half a year. It's gonna be impossible to find a juror who hasn't read or formed an opinion about her case. Even if it turns out that Wuornos didn't kill those men, they're gonna fry her." Jim is emphatic.

"First off," Jim says, "they think they have a confession. Makes no difference how they obtained it or even if it's true, her being a lesbian—that's so far off the wall it won't even count against her. They're gonna fry her because she's a prostitute. People here are real hypocritical about sex. Now, things might be different, if prostitution was legal. It's like drugs. If something's illegal, lots of undeserving people are gonna get very rich because of it. And a lot of otherwise good, honest, people are gonna be forced to become criminals. And then, they won't stand a chance in a court of law, whether they're the victims or the perps."

"Lemme tell you about the judge who sat on the Hays case,

the one where they tried to poison me. That judge used to bring a gun into the courtroom. He started waving it at the lawyers and their clients. Think he was fined or taken off the bench? No sir! He was just told to sort of act a little bit better."

"Jim," I ask. "Would you be willing to talk to Trish about Wuornos' visitation rights? Would you represent Pralle in this matter, pro bono?"

"Sure, don't mind if I do," says Gentleman Jim. "But I don't exactly practice law anymore. Ah've had it with the judges and the lawyers round here who won't practice law."

* * *

"Will you accept a collect call from Miss Aileen Wuornos?"

"Sure will, operator."

"Hey, Arlene tells me she met with a lawyer-friend of yours. That's great. But lissen. I don't want any visitors if can't have Arlene. I gotta have contact visits with her. That's the main thing. That's what I'm holding out for."

"I made a list of all the rapes."

Lee tells me about being tied down, spread-eagle, and gang raped any number of times at parties even before she was raped and impregnated. Once she began hitchhiking out West, some of the truckers who picked her up demanded sex for the ride, robbed her, held guns to her head, threatened her with knives. Lee learned to be quick to flee, and even quicker to hit back— and to hit first if possible.

She said: "I had a lot of willing sex before I was 13. But I was also tied down and forced into it a lot too. Maybe eight times. Then, I was raped when I was thirteen, that's how I got pregnant. When I was fourteen, an elderly man, he was around fifty-eight years old, he ran the nudie theater in town, he raped me. That same year, a guy in the next town, he was around twenty-eight, he raped me too. When I was sixteen, two bikers from a group called 'The Renegades' raped me. Then, maybe two months later, two guys who claimed to be in the Mafia raped me."

"Then, when I hitchhiked out of Detroit, lots of truckers,

cops, and guys I was partying with raped me."

I interrupt her. "Lee, maybe this is too hard to do when you're in jail and alone..."

"Nah. Lemme tell you. Ya asked, didn't ya? So, as I was saying, when I was sixteen and a half, five guys at a party tied me to the bed and raped me. I passed out. When I was sixteen and three quarters, three guys dragged me out of another party and carried me into the woods. I passed out. When I was seventeen, I wasn't raped, but it was close. It happened in Jeffersonville, Indiana. This guy was a child molester. Maybe he murdered kids, too. He beat me severely. The cops could not tell if I was a man or a woman, my face was so swollen. It took two months to heal. When I was eighteen, a police officer in Lauderdale raped me in an abandoned house and he brought his buddies along. About six months later, I wasn't raped, but two guys tried. I was beat and left on the side of the road. When I was nineteen, I needed a place to stay, the guy who put me up forced me to have sex with him."

Wuornos takes a breath—I can't—and continues. "Now, these here rapes comin' up are from my hustling career. A lotta guys beat me out of money. They beat me all over my body. They used pain. It's like they liked to hurt you. They called me every name in the book. Some threatened to kill me. Choke me to death. Stab me to death. Mutilate me. Cut off my head. Crazy jazz. What saved me was my calmness. That, and not rejecting them. Talking to them kindly changed their hearts. That's why I survived. When I could, I ran the fuck outta there, or I took control by yelling."

Run like hell and yell, Lee, yell.

In a matter-of-fact voice, Wuornos continues. "When I was twenty-nine, a truck driver raped me. He took my money, too. This took place in a motel. That same year, two black guys raped me at a party in Macon, Georgia. When I was thirty, a guy took me to a motel, where another guy was waiting. They both raped me. They robbed my money too. There were three more rapes, but I can't picture seeing them. They happened in wooded areas when I was thirty, thirty-one, thirty-two. I was hitchhiking and hustling. Each time, the guys took my money. But it's vague. When I was thirty-two, a guy tried to rape me but I talked him out of it. He dropped me off. From when I was thirty-three, I had eight rape attempts. (She is now talking about 1990, the year she'd committed most of the murders.) One UPS driver did not go through with it. He ran away when I defended myself with a gun."

How many times has Wuornos been raped, gang-raped, nearly raped? Twenty times? Thirty times? Fifty times? More? What does Wuornos think rape is? To Wuornos, is having sex with a man only "rape" when he refuses to pay, or when he forces her to do something she finds repulsive, like anal sex, something she didn't agree to do beforehand?

Maybe it's "rape" only when the man threatens to kill her, when he ties her hands to the steering wheel of his car and she knows she's no longer "in control," that something is happening to her that's a lot more than what she'd come to accept as something she could live through again without dying or jumping out of her mind.

In a 1992 letter to her childhood friend Dawn, she writes: "Let me tell you what can happen in a rape. Your hair gets pulled out, he shoves his penis fully erected down your throat and bruises your esophagus, as well as the roof and sides of the (inside cheeks) of your mouth....Also, telling you if you scratch my cock with your teeth your dead. Then he pulls your pussy hairs out, for additional pain, grabbs your ass real hard like (kneading dough) as he's cramming his cock in you, same thing in anal screwing. Bites nipples, to also, nearly cutting them off... as he's screwing you viciously, pounding as fast and as hard as he can...And also while this is going on, threats are being made, and dirty talk at the most provockativist provanity you could imagine. So rape is not just get on and get off. Society doesn't understand this, nor cares, especially if you're a hooker. There allowed to treat you like this, and also kill you."

The experts have just begun to understand how one rape can affect a rape victim. What can we say about forty or fifty or a hundred rapes? After one rape, a woman can get on with her life, but inside, in her head, in her heart, she's suddenly afraid of half the human race, she's afraid of her own apartment, the street where it happened, but she's also afraid of other apartments and other streets too; she doesn't feel safe anywhere, and she puts a lot of energy into denying that she's slipping away—until the insomnia, the nightmares, the flashbacks start to happen, and anxiety dissolves her personality, and depression buries what's left of her under a glass, darkly, and she has no energy left to pretend that "everything's just fine."

One rape can trigger buried memories of childhood abuse, and if the victim's loved ones don't handle the situation compassionately, it may subtly, but deeply, alter their relationship to her forever. If she has no "loved ones," and even if she does, our victim/survivor might still take to drink and drugs, prescription or otherwise, to stop what's happening, but it won't stop, and she might just lose her job as well as her mind.

Okay, not all women have this view of rape; an American female soldier was raped by her captors during the Gulf war, they broke both her arms too. Admirably, she says that this is what war is, and that worse things can happen. Maybe her training as a soldier, her clarity about rape being an act of war is, indeed, a redemptive point of view.

If Wuornos can "half-ass remember" so many rapes—how many has she "forgotten?" Ah, Chesler, give it up. The jury won't sympathize with her, no matter how many rapes she can remember or document. If Wuornos argues that she's suffering from (a well-earned) diagnosis of Post-Traumatic Stress Syndrome, jurors will think: "So she admits she's deranged! Maybe her victims weren't trying to rape her, maybe she only *thought* they were."

This is entirely possible and yet, this means that awful things had happened to her before. A woman doesn't have to be crazy in order to kill a man in self-defense.

But here's the rub, the fly in the ointment. For a woman raised in this culture to actually kill a man, even in self-defense, it means that she's gone over the wall, fled the cage of all she's been taught, namely, that a man's life is worth more than hers.

In a 1995 letter to her childhood friend, Dawn, Lee writes that she once chose a boyfriend whom she thought would protect her, but "I was wrong. The gang rapes continued. I was now very experienced in the field of sexual assaults." She suggests to Dawn that we need: "a Nationwide Law for Women of Self-Defense. Every woman should learn Self-Defense. Also carry guns and know how to use them."

She has a point.

"That book you thought I should write," Wuornos says. "It's been taken care of. I got a publisher. It's all worked out. The money will go to Arlene and to another friend of mine, nayma Dawn."

The girl's fast.

"I'm somebody," Wuornos says matter-of-factly.

She's right. Wuornos is no longer an unknown prostitute. She's the first (so-called) female serial killer. The world is filled with women who've been bloodied and battered, they're a dime a dozen, but Wuornos is no longer in this category, she's entered a previously all-male profession: that of serial killer. She's made headlines for what she's done, not for what's been done to her.

Major magazines on at least four continents have already commissioned articles about her; four books, and at least three movies are underway; three or four networks have already inquired about renting rooms in the courthouse to film the first trial.

All this notoriety, and she's still in a cage, destined to be executed.

"Lee, look at it this way," I say. "Christ was really somebody too, and look what they did to him…"

"Hey man, that was before he was famous," Wuornos says instantly.

In *Live from Golgotha*, Gore Vidal imagines twentieth-century TV networks competing for exclusive world and video rights to the crucifixion. Vidal would have enjoyed this moment in the conversation.

Wuornos, like most Americans, sees celebrity as the antidote to the human condition.

"I want *you* to write about the crooked cops," Wuornos demands, in her Marine-sergeant voice. "You get me a private lawyer. You get the testifying experts, I'm not telling you about my life. Not yet. Maybe later. When we see how things work out."

So: I had Wuornos' permission to write about The Case, but not about her life. Does she think that her life or what she's done "belongs" to her and not to the universe-at-large? Does Wuornos think she can sell pieces of her story, or the same piece, over and over again? Does she think being on trial for murder is an asset she can merchandise?

So I say: "Oh, you're gonna wait and see what I can do for you before you'll show me more."

"Yeah, it's like that." And Wuornos laughs, because even she thinks it's funny. I do too. But it also makes me uneasy that Wuornos has absolutely no capacity to trust anyone who isn't prepared to "fuck" her. What headway can I make against such a jinxed mentality? In time, which is where all things happen, I begin to understand that to someone like Wuornos, the entire universe is a John, whom she's always "hustling"—Wuornos' word for what she did for money.

Aileen had been on the ropes for more than three decades. She was tired of hurting so much. She felt as if someone was beating her up all the time, choking her, drowning her, and she had to fight against it, over and over again: that was Aileen's normal, everyday life. Even when the pressure let up, if the booze was so good that Aileen could take a pain-free breath for a minute, for five minutes, maybe even for five hours, Aileen still understood that this was it, all there was, and it was never gonna get any better, only worse. For years, Aileen thought she'd rather be dead.

In the last year, Aileen discovered that she hadda slam the pain in a really big way.

Aileen needed survival money, too, but she didn't want to fuck for it, at least, not always. She didn't mind fucking, she just didn't want to have to fuck everyone all the time, especially not if it meant being raped. Not if she could get the money some other way. Sure, Aileen would have rather been a cop, but if the only way she could get survival money was to kill for it, then she'd do what she had to. To survive.

There was a war going on, and Aileen was Cammie Greene. The Marine.

* * *

I did not yet understand Wuornos' relationship to money. It took time before I understood, really understood, that Wuornos' entire world consists of only money and Johns, that her short-leash trajectory, her dialectical stroll, was whether she was taking them, or being taken. 'Hey, Mister!' I could hear her saying inside my head, 'I'm in this business for the money, that's all that matters, that's all there is, everything's for sale, everything has a price, nothing's free, but, hey, you know that. You taught me everything I know.' Wuornos has no quarrel with how things are, she hangs tough, it's a point of pride, just give her the money and move on.

What Wuornos "cares" about is money, it's all she can count on, but she's only interested in peanuts, loose change. It took me some time to understand that to Wuornos, I'm a John, too. Maybe Wuornos thinks that writers "get off" on talking to prostitutes, or that writers are the richest, dumbest Johns around. Well, here I am, acting like I need her real bad. What I need is for her to work with me to try and save her life.

Fuck her, who does she think she is? She's the whore; I'm her superior/savior/John. Unsentimental educations are always expensive. For someone like Wuornos to trust me, even for a moment, would be revolutionary.

CHAPTER ELEVEN

Raping and Battering in the Deep South

"**W**ILL YOU ACCEPT a collect call from Miss Arlene Pralle?"

"She's calling me collect from the next town over? Okay."

"Phyllis, it's Arlene. I'm freaking out, I'm a real basket case. Lee didn't call me today at 5AM, our usual time. Do you think something bad's happened? I'm paying another inmate to keep an eye on her for me. I haven't heard anything from her either. Could something bad have happened to both of them?" Arlene is moaning and gasping for breath.

Within a few hours, Arlene calls back.

"Oh, it was nothing," she laughs. "There was just something wrong with the jail phones this morning. Maybe you think I'm crazy, but Lee means so much to me. Phyllis, Lee and I need your help. She's very upset. Jacqui Giroux (Pralle always repeated Giroux's entire name) sent her an evil letter. Lee is entitled to a lot more money than Jacqui Giroux agreed to pay her. Lee made me tape record our conversation today. She wants me to play it for you. She wants you to get her a private lawyer. Trish hasn't visited her for six weeks and she's not doing anything to get rid of Jacqui Giroux. Trish is not fighting to get us any contact visitation either. Lee said 'If I don't get to touch you soon, I'll do something. Why are they treating me like I'm an animal? I'm a human being.'"

"I'm pretty upset too," Arlene says redundantly. "When my father leaves next week, I'll be all alone on the farm. My husband's still in Illinois." She laughs. "My own husband just accused me of being a lesbian because I'm so obsessed with Lee!" She sounds a little nervous. "You're a doctor. Do you think I'm a lesbian?"

Reader, dear: I didn't touch this one.

That night, I visit the Ocala shelter for battered women. I am, as ever, impressed by grassroots doggedness and savvy, by the kindness and friendliness of those who've been battered, and who are willing to climb out of bed or shut the TV off in order to talk to a visitor about their lives. I can hear Judy Wilson a mile away, she never goes anywhere without at least twenty keys on a ring: keys to supply closets, back doors, front doors, cars, vans, office equipment. She's like the abbess of a monastery, firmly in charge of many lives.

It's late and dark and quiet. The littlest residents are asleep and their mothers look too young to be mothers. The shelter furniture is spare, spartan, donated, but signs of female care are all around: Iron beds have been painted, coverlets have been knitted, soft, stuffed animals are everywhere. If you're a child, all you need is a peanut butter and jelly sandwich and a working television set, and you're safe in America, at least for one more day.

Joan, one of the shelter workers, says, "There is still a real strong mentality in Ocala that women are property, children are property, men own them. When you counsel a woman who's been abused, you are seen as interfering with a man's family and he is likely to come after you and shoot you or run over you with his pick-up truck."

"We have a joke," Judy says. "It's called a radical lesbian whore. The batterers say—oh, you're with those women, you know, those radical women. Then the next thing is, they accuse us of all being lesbians. Then the third thing is we're all whores."

"When I worked on the weekends," Joan continues, "I had men come to the door and demand their wives back. I always explained to them that the women don't live where our office is.

We have six shelters in Ocala. I'll give your wife a message if I can find her. Then I get accused of interfering: 'You're breaking up my family. You're interfering in my life.'"

"When's the last time you were confronted with a man coming by for his female property?" I ask.

"Yesterday," Joan says. "Some of 'em are drunk. Most of 'em aren't. Some of 'em are armed too. We had one episode a few years ago where this guy in a blue pick-up truck said he was coming to our place at 4 p.m. to blow his brains out. At 3:30, I was downtown with two police officers trying to find the blue truck so they could search and arrest him because we knew he was carrying a firearm. Meantime, it's 3:45 and he's at the mental health center threatening a counselor over there. She calls the cops. He was gonna wipe out whoever was helping his wife first. At four o'clock, just like he said, he was at our place."

"Did he get arrested?" I ask.

"Yeah," Joan says. "But you can't 'Baker Act' somebody for longer than 72 hours in Florida. That's to preserve the rights of the mentally ill. Unfortunately, this means there are really dangerous people out on the street. They try to kill somebody, they shoot six people, get adjudicated insane, not guilty, go to the state hospital, stay two years, get on medication. They're great, they're under control, they're released. As soon as they walk out the door, they quit their meds and then they shoot somebody else."

"There's a law in Florida," says Judy, "that you have to be sane before you can die in the electric chair. If you're insane, you can't die in the electric chair."

"But in Florida," Joan says, "if you are insane at the time you commit a crime, you are adjudicated insane or not guilty. Tell her about the case where a man said his diabetes made him insane."

"Oh yeah," Judy smiles. "A woman psychologist testified for him, too. A divorce was going on. The judge ordered Holly Griner and her parents to stay in the house. The husband got one bedroom, Holly got the other bedroom. He got one bathroom, she got the other one."

"The judge ordered him not to mess with her," Joan chimed in. "So he murdered her and he murdered her parents. He threatened her on tape ahead of time. He shot them all as they crawled across the lawn right in front of the neighbors. He got away. He disappeared, went to Key West and got amnesia."

"He was sane enough to run," says Judy. "He had an article in his car trunk about a man who did exactly the same thing and who also got amnesia. After a couple of years, he turned himself in to a priest in Daytona, and hired Earl DiCarlos, the best criminal defense attorney in Gainesville. In the meantime, Holly's relatives up north are calling us. They're saying they had to hire bodyguards because this man had threatened to kill them, too. And if he ever was brought to trial and got out, they would have to have bodyguards for the rest of their lives. Well, he stood trial."

"The male psychologist," continues Judy, "said he wasn't crazy, he was only fakin' it. The female psychologist, first case she's ever had like this, she looks like Cinderella. She got totally fooled by this man. She testifies that he went into a psychotic episode caused by a lack of insulin and stress, and didn't know what he was doing. Forget that he'd threatened to kill his wife before, when he wasn't diabetically insane. It so happens that this psychologist looked just like the judge's ex-wife. He's a sucker for every blonde that shows up."

"He got off. Man's living in Texas now with his daughter."

"You know," Judy says, "one of the interesting things that went on in town was, 'Well you know, Holly was a bitch anyway.'"

Joan says: "The laws here are pretty bad too. If you get arrested for beating your wife, the bail is $500. If you get arrested for killing a cat, the bail is usually $5,000."

"Can I tell her about the woman who died because of this?" Judy says. "It's a matter of public record."

Joan says, "She was the first woman who died while she was a resident of our shelter. Her husband had threatened to kill her. He beat her up. He went to jail. But there was a nice young woman who believed everything he said and went and made his $500 bail. Man tracked his wife down at her job, she worked for a doctor in town, he tracked her down and followed her to her car. He found where she was parking her car and then a few days later, he disabled the car. When she tried to start the car, she couldn't, and there he was, waiting for her. He pulled her head through the window by her hair and shot her. Twice. He blew her face away. This happened in 1990. He's the one who got out on $500 bail."

"He killed himself later that afternoon. He was an engineer. Turns out, he was on probation from California for burning his second wife's house down while she was still in it. This was his third marriage."

Joan says: "A guy's collecting turtle eggs in town. He had to make $100,000 bail."

"Guess we have to become an endangered species, then we'll be alright," says Judy. "My paralegal's husband is in jail right now," Judy tells me, "because he threatened to kill his little boy. He held the kid hostage for two days. He's been in jail three months now. The trial's coming up."

"They're doing this one right," says Joan.

"Yeah, but they're only doing it right because she's got three lawyers behind her. And because she works for me. And because she's a legal aide. And because it's all being paid for by a Florida Bar Grant. Woman took her man back into her house because he was saying all the right things. He'd give her these speeches, 'I used to be a batterer but I know better now.' But then he got upset because she made more money than he did and because she's got lots of friends among the lawyer community. One day, he just went berserk and did the same old thing he'd been doing for ten years. He'd behaved himself for about ten months"

"It makes me so sad," Joan says. "The worst thing about women staying with an abuser is these men are the perfect role model for their son to grow up to be an abuser and for their daughter to grow up and find somebody just like Daddy. It just drives me nuts, it's so sad."

Me too, me too.

"Judy," I ask afterwards, "You're running the local rape crisis center here too. Theoretically, could you testify about rape in Florida for the Wuornos defense?"

Judy says flat out that she'd probably lose her funding if she was a witness for Wuornos but that she'd think about it anyway.

"Ah, Judy, your funding is safe. Trish's secretary's just left a message that Trish wants me to know that she's not yet prepared to write a letter retaining me. She hasn't had time to think it through yet. Sounds like Trish already has cold feet."

"Hey honey," says Judy, "when your lawyer friend from Tallahassee comes down, why don't we all go over to Peter Dinkel's? That's where the local judges and lawyers unwind on Friday nights. It'll be a hoot. Trish is usually there. Trish sometimes asks me for advice. You're offering her an incredible gift. Will you allow me to tell her that?"

It's a risk—I don't know what Judy's relationship to Trish is, and I don't want to scare Trish off, but lead-time is beginning to slip away.

"Are you free for lunch tomorrow?" Judy asks. "A reporter from the *Ocala Star-Banner* is following me around for the day."

"Judy, I believe I'm meeting with your husband tomorrow."

* * *

"Jim, here's what Wuornos says she wants." I hand over a memo I'd typed, with a list of Wuornos' requests for regular contact visits, and for more than the same three books and magazines.

"Wuornos says she's only been allowed outdoors once since she was arrested, and then only for fifteen minutes. She doesn't want the guards to read the letters she writes to her lawyers. She says she hasn't seen Trish for six weeks. She wants a lawyer who'll spend time with her, a lawyer who'll help her break her contract with Jacqui Giroux."

Jim looks up. "If Trish is overworked," he says, "she can ask for additional assistance. My old partner could help her. He's usually called upon when an indigent prisoner has good reason to change his public defender. He's very methodical, has a mind like a steel trap. Whoever's in charge ought to consolidate all the trials, move 'em down to Miami, and plead insanity. Otherwise, they'll kill her."

"Jim, how does a capital case proceed in Florida?" I ask.

"First, a jury decides whether you're guilty or not. Then, it decides what your punishment will be. This is Florida's way of getting around the accusation that we kill more black people than white people. This way, it's not the judge who decides to kill you, it's a jury of your peers. But no matter who you are, they are never your peers. But it gives the facade of justice."

"Now, you can only get the chair for first-degree premeditated murder; otherwise, the maximum you can get is thirty years, and that's for second-degree murder. The maximum for manslaughter, or for third-degree murder, is fifteen years. But, technically, you're eligible for parole six months after you begin to serve your sentence. With time off for good behavior, someone could serve a thirty-year sentence in ten years, and be out scot-free, no parole, no probation. We have people who refuse parole. 'I'll serve my time and then I'm outta here. Piss on you people.'"

* * *

Peter Dinkel's restaurant is like every other modern-Victorian restaurant I've ever been in, all aswirl with beveled mirrors, stained glass, boisterously gleaming polished brass, huge hanging greenery. By 6 p.m., the human herd is at full cry, the decibel level easily that of any trendy watering hole in San Francisco or New York. The place is wall-to-wall lawyers, judges, smoke, alcohol, conversation, laughter.

Trish is here, and so is Ed. They're sitting with someone I don't recognize, a man with a ponytail who turns out to be Don Sanchez, their private investigator. Trish is surprised to see me and Gentleman Jim together, but she's friendly, in a wide-eyed and vigilant kind of way. Trish drinks rapidly and steadily. She's definitely in charge of her men. Trish tells me that she's Mississippi-born, and once lived in Charleston, until her husband, a research optometrist, died of leukemia.

"Understand this," Trish says, looking straight at me. "I love two things. The South. And the law. I went to law school later on in life. I'm a public defender on principle, not for profit. I don't need the money. They couldn't pay me for what I do."

Maybe Trish is the right lawyer for the case; if so, I don't want to ruffle any one of her many, bristling feathers. Meg's late, where's Meg? A lawyer only trusts another lawyer. With Meg-by-my-side, whatever I propose will seem plausible, not out-landish. True, Jim's also a lawyer, and he's already at my side, but maybe Jim's a threat, maybe Trish and Jim have a "history," may-be I shouldn't have asked him to broker visitation for Wuornos and Pralle…

I'm right. Trish nearly jumps out of her nervous system when Jim brings up the question of visitation. Trish becomes so guarded, and heavy-lidded, that I immediately lead the retreat.

"Trish, if you think it's not a good idea for Pralle to have any more contact with Wuornos than she already has…"

"That's it, sugar. My client tells that Pralle woman (she pro-nounces it 'Pray-lee') what brand of cigarettes she smokes, what kind of beer she drinks, and in one minute flat it's on the air-waves, the prosecutor's got it, and then the police just happen to "find" that very brand at one of the crime scenes. Tell you what I think, I think Pralle is in it for the money. I think Pralle's taping every conversation she has with Lee. I think she's going to sell it to the highest bidder. Just watch."

Trish, of course, turns out to be right. Trish is tough, but I like tough women. Then Meg, another tough woman, arrives, and then there are three tough women talking, and then four, when Judy Wilson joins us. Jim Shook, Ed Bonnett, Don Sanchez and Bill Miller are here, too. They may also be tough, but for now, they're four relatively quiet tough guys.

Meg and Trish are talking in lawyer-ese, they're rapidly calling out statute numbers and what's pending, at each other. I don't understand what any of it has to do with the Wuornos case, but I keep smiling. If they get along, I'm happy.

Calmly, smoothly, Meg presents some facts about prostitution in Florida. She knows the studies, the researchers, the vice squads, the women, the legislators. Trish seems impressed. Meg and I then launch into a low-key performance about how often prostituted women are raped, beaten and killed, nation-wide, and that under such circumstances, a prostitute might reasonably conclude that she is about to be raped or killed as soon as any John threatens to hurt or kill her.

Meg is opposed to doing anything that could be construed as a "psychiatric cop-out." Meg is a hard-liner on this, and in her view, unless I prove otherwise, I'm not to be trusted. She prefers the "political" approach, which argues, simply, that women are entitled to defend themselves, just like men. What's seen as an open-and-shut case of self-defense for a man is seen as an act of political insurrection or insanity, when it's a woman who's defended herself. Unless, of course, the man is black and she's white, or the man is impoverished, and she's not. Meg may be right to insist on no "cop-outs," certainly not of the psychiatric variety. Meg reminds me of myself when I was younger.

"Okay," Trish says for the second time in four days. "We're on, you're mine, but I get to call the shots. I control what we do."

Meg and I hadn't a clue if Wuornos had killed anyone other than the first John in self-defense. I had my theories, Meg had hers, but we had no chance of getting our various hunches confirmed unless we were 'insiders.'

Here we are, begging the state of Florida to "please, pretty please," accept all our volunteer labor. We're in trouble. We need Trish more than she thinks she needs us, the handwriting is already *off* the wall, but Meg and I are busy celebrating, not fund-raising like hell for a private lawyer.

* * *

"Will you accept a collect call from Miss Aileen Wuornos?"

"Ya gotta get me a lawyer. I gotta see Arlene. If I can't see Arlene, I don't know what I'll do."

Wuornos' ass is in a major wringer and she's mainly worried about whether she can hug the new lady in her life.

"Lee, Meg and I think Trish's okay, we think she's more than okay. Trish seems interested in our strategy. She'll try to visit you soon. I have a feeling that you're going to see Arlene soon, too."

"I don't know how to thank you guys."

"Lee, tell me. How much money are you allowed in your commissary every month?"

"I need about $120.00 a month."

"For…?"

"For drawing paper and cigarettes and for presents for the other girls, the ones who got no one. I need money for my phone calls to Arlene. I don't have a bra. I only have one pair of panties, one pair of socks, a robe, and my same three books and magazines. Guess I need postage, too."

"I can't make any promises. But I'll try."

The next day, Meg and I spend four hours with Arlene Pralle on her farm. We try to "get her to focus," but she keeps wriggling away and we can't always follow her rapid, zigzags of thought. Meg and I try to persuade Pralle not to talk to the media, not to focus on her own needs, but on Wuornos' needs. In return, we promise to try and focus on some of Pralle's needs. I give Pralle some money for the phone calls and for some of her other immediate needs. I promise to try and find her a low-cost, trustworthy, local psychiatrist. (She's been requesting "help with anxiety, nightmares, insomnia," and general "pains all over her body.")

At Peter Dinkel's, when we were with Trish, Meg had been all hunkered-down and poker-faced. Pralle brought out her other, more grassroots side. Meg has the admirable capacity to be there totally: she's an active listener. She listens with all she's got: body, soul, mind and heart.

If I were Pralle, I would have caved in. Pralle didn't. She didn't need to. She was already "spoken for:" she had Jesus, and if that wasn't enough, she also had Wuornos.

Afterwards, Meg and I drive north to Tallahassee, with the windows open and the hot breeze at our ears. Meg drives with one hand on the wheel, she loves the open road, she'd drive for hours, alone, just to think, she says, and we drive that way right on through the bright, innocent colors of afternoon and we're still in the car when evening comes in, scarlet and sultry and enchanting.

We decide that "only in America," can someone like Pralle choose to champion a serial killer to avoid dealing with her own life—and get away with it.

"Arlene has absolutely no shame about assuming the starring role in someone else's life," I observe. "She doesn't think she's doing anything wrong. She thinks she's a saint, sacrificing herself for The Prisoner, not a deranged fan. D'ya think there's a chance she'll do what she promised us she'd do?"

"Nah!" We both laugh.

Three days later, when I'm back in New York, I call Pralle. She's not her usual effusive self, she's reserved, something's different. On an impulse, I ask: "Have you seen Jacqui Giroux?"

After a long pause, Pralle carefully says: "Well, Mark (McNamara of *Vanity Fair*) kept telling me that I really ought to give her a chance. So I did. She came and spent a few days with me. Oh, Phyllis! She's a wonderful woman. Her only interest is in saving little girls from abuse. She has her own seven-year-old daughter. She's not interested in the money. She only wants to help Lee in order to help other little girls in Lee's position, I know she's sincere. She's been misquoted and misunderstood. Just like Lee has. She's a beautiful person. She told me I could call her day or night. She's going to stand by us during the trial."

"How will that help Lee's case?" I ask.

"Oh, Phyllis, she's shown me some of the scenes that she's already written. It was just like seeing Lee's life. It's just how it happened. I know she's going to be able to sell it to television. It'll be a docu-drama or a mini-series. I had to apologize to her. I thought she was a vampire. I had Trish's blessings to meet with her."

I just bet you did, girlie.

Giroux is rumored to have ten million dollars from a German producer for a film about Wuornos. If this is true, and I have no way of knowing if it is, I wonder how much of it she's offered to Pralle? What's in it for McNamara to broker this match? Maybe Trish Jenkins is right, maybe Pralle has sold Lee's letters and taped conversations to Giroux.

"Phyllis, don't be disappointed in me," says Arlene. "Trish even said she was glad to 'see that I'd finally understood.' So I told Trish: 'If you say jump, tell me how high.' And that's when I explained that Jacqui's a friend. And that's when Trish said: 'Okay, we'll reserve judgement.'"

"So," Pralle concludes, "Trish knows I'm talking to Jacqui and she thinks it's alright! Anyway, Jacqui's not a newspaper reporter, she's a movie-maker. And she only wants to help. So don't worry."

* * *

"Will you accept a collect call from Robert Pralle?"

"Who? Robert Pralle? Okay, operator." So Arlene's husband really does exist.

"Arlene wanted you to know that she's in the intensive care unit in North Central Hospital in Gainesville."

"What?"

"One of the horses kicked her. Three of her ribs are broken. A rib may have traveled into her liver." He pauses. "She tells me that you're gonna pay the phone bill, is that right?"

Well, not exactly. I've failed miserably to raise more than a pittance for Wuornos' defense. The most sympathetic of philanthropists are puzzled by my fervor and urgency. Maybe philanthropists need round-the-clock conferences on the subject of violence against prostitutes. Everyone needs round-the-clock books on the subject, and I'm not writing one, not yet, how can I? I'm trying to get a team together for the defense.

I need some money, bad. Where do women get money-in-a-hurry? Oh, you dimwit: Mainly from men.

Fundraising really does take time, and it was already long past midnight in terms of Wuornos' life. None of us have the kind of money-in-a-hurry that Wuornos' case required, none of us had any way of getting it—at least not legally.

Chesler, give it up, no one will ever be able to abolish the traffic in women, that endless, moving, human caravan of whores and wives, mistresses and courtesans, showgirls and girlfriends. Abolishing this requires a military solution, and a way of thinking that's foreign to most women.

Something's happening to me. I've gotten sadder since I started reading about prostitution and about the women who've killed in self-defense and who sit growing older in jail cells the world over. I don't share what's on my mind as much, not even with the people I love. Whatever I say to them won't ring as true as what I can say here on this page.

How can I understand someone like Wuornos? Some say it's written in the stars, and so I've made an appointment to consult an astrologer about Wuornos' horoscope. Her birthday is February 29, 1956, and she was born between 11:56-11:58 PM. Maybe he can tell me who she is, to me, and to you, too.

CHAPTER TWELVE

In the Closet of the Zodiac:
An Astrologer Casts Wuornos' Chart

"**W**ELL, SHE'S GOT A CHART a psychic would kill for,"
the astrologer says. "Her Moon conjunct Neptune
is the most powerful mediumistic conjunction you can find.
She's psychically more sensitive than 95% of the population."

It's late afternoon and people are consulting astrologers
all over America. Charles House, astrologer, clears his throat,
slightly. "She's a double Scorpio. She's got Scorpio rising, and her
moon's in Scorpio."

I interrupt him. "Don't assume I understand what that
means. What *does* it mean?"

"Scorpio is the most creative sign, but it's also the most ex-
treme, because of all the highs and lows, the ups and downs.
Scorpio's the strongest sign. Pluto, which rules Scorpio, is the
most elevated and powerful of the planets. Scorpio's basically
the sexual sign. There's a powerful libido here. A Scorpio can
put up with a lot. She's very, very bright. She's got Mercury in
Aquarius, and that's genius to crazy. This is a woman, right?"

"Oh yes," say I.

"She's someone totally out of control. She has incredible
sensitivity. I would say she is a sensitive, a natural receiver. She
can be taken over. She's a psychic receptacle, a magnet. She has

power, but it's very primitive. She's beset by obsessions and compulsions. She's fearful, she has always been in prison emotionally, so she may feel relieved to be in a real prison now. She is in prison, isn't she?"

"Definitely," I say.

"She's probably better off in solitary. She'll get in trouble otherwise. She's got a lot of resentment. Scorpio is going to want to get even." Charles looks up. "This is a classical chart for someone who goes to extremes, or who's involved in a murder. There's violence involved because of Scorpio rising and Pluto exactly at mid-heaven.

Scorpio Rising is the title of one of Kenneth Anger's 1960's films, his love poem really, to butch gay men. As I remember it, the camera made slow love to each man, as he slowly and deliberately leathered up to rock n' roll music—slow and stirring and flagrantly sexual—and, in less than three minutes, took all of us over the edge of desire. As I remember it, Anger's Men of Leather mounted their iron horses and thundered off-screen. Finis. Credits. I'd never before seen the male gaze sexually objectify men, not women, and, for a moment, it freed me.

Wuornos is also a rider on the imaginary wind, but she's not just Leather. Like Stevie Nicks' song, *Leather and Lace*, she's both leather and lace.

"What happened in 1989 and 1990?" I ask the astrologer. Casually, too casually.

There's tension in the air now and Charles is concentrating and slightly annoyed. "A tremendous power struggle occurred."

"A power struggle," I say. "With whom?"

"With herself. Or with anyone who'd get her attention and then resist her, or oppose her. With anyone who physically struggled with her. The threat of losing her life is what got her started."

Primly, Charles adjusts his glasses. "There are three times I see as highly destructive. The first is in December of 1989. The midpoint was in May and June of 1990. The third time was after a very powerful lunar eclipse took place, around the time of the invasion of Kuwait, say, from early August to the end of October. That blew out the lamp of her mind."

I was quiet. Respectful. The body of Wuornos' first victim was discovered early in December of 1989. Two more bodies were found in May and June of 1990. Wuornos' last three victims were killed in July, September, and November of 1990.

"Who is she?" I ask.

"She's Pisces. She's in the shadows. She's tremendously secretive. She's so sensitive, if you look at her the wrong way... but she's a tough cookie. Pisces is the mystery sign. It's the kaleidoscope, the top or the bottom of society. One minute she wants to hide, the next minute, she wants plenty of attention. There's a real need for attention here. But she's more Scorpio than Pisces."

Charles is telling me that Wuornos won't want me—or anyone else, to "get her," spy her out, know what she's done or what she's doing. She's secretive, but she also wants to be seen, wants credit for what she's done, wants to remain in control—even as she's out of control.

"There's a lot of confusion about women," Charles tells me.

"Meaning what?"

"Most likely, it's fear having to do with her mother. Her biological mother is the cause of the whole thing. What do you know about her mother?"

It's a waste of time to withhold such information. I had to work with Charles, not against him. I tell him: "Her mother abandoned her or was driven away early in childhood."

"She is not likely to have any identity, emotionally. She's very weak, unbalanced, impressionable. She can easily be taken over by spiritual entities."

"Are you saying she needs an exorcist?"

"An exorcist? Oh, don't be silly," says Charles. "But she'd likely be taken over by something negative. She probably carries the guilt of her mother running off. 'I'm no good, that's why she left, I ran her off.'"

"Okay." Charles is stern. "Now tell me who this woman is. I don't like to walk in the dark. I'd rather know what the story is."

And so I tell him, briefly.

"She really can be taken over," he says, more decisively than before. "She's an actual receiver."

I once consulted a trance-channeler about my "voices"—not real voices, but an intuitive, almost morbid awareness of human suffering, people jailed, crying out. I wanted to know: was I hearing real people's voices, had I myself once been imprisoned, or beheaded in a previous life?

Calmly, the channeler assured me that yes, I had been executed many times and always for my knowledge of the sacred. "But don't worry," she said, "this won't happen to you in your current life. You're here to bring new ideas into the world. You're bringing ideals from the Piscean into the Aquarian Age."

Is that it, am I here to interpret Pisces-Wuornos? Pisces is very literal, concrete. Pisces commits acts, not analyses. In a flash, Pisces reverses everything. For a split second, the "bottom" becomes the "top," the world splits open, and then, dark waters cover the Earth once more.

I use words to dive into the (watery) wreck. I descend; I am lost among the murky, monstrous shadows. Years later, I may surface—on a page like this one, holding aloft something I've spirited out of bondage, chaos, materiality. Is this my connection to Wuornos? Am I the village alchemist, transforming base elements into gold, Caliban into Ariel?

Who's Wuornos? She's the one in jail, the one without sunlight or privacy, the one in leg-shackles, the one the guards taunt, the one facing the electric chair. But she's also flown the coop and is here with me in New York, in my thoughts. Whenever I stop thinking about her, her unbidden, imprisoned self appears to me: a wretched Avenging Angel, a lunatic-child, a killer.

"She is extremely emotionally ill," Charles says. "People have been abusing her from the time she was born. They took away her faith. Faith is hard to come by when you've come through this many years of betrayal by your intimates."

So, is it all determined by the stars? Or do genetics also play a role? Lee's biological father, Leo Pittman, was a batterer, an alcoholic, and a small-time thief. He was finally jailed for life for having raped a seven-year-old girl—and he committed suicide in prison. Her maternal mother/grandmother, Britta, drank herself to death. Her maternal grandfather/father, Lauri, also drank, had a violent temper, and ended up killing himself. Her biological mother, Diane, abandoned her. When I spoke to Diane, she told me that she was afraid of Lee, that her temper was fierce, and beyond control, that she had always been belligerent and that the daughter she'd left behind frightened her.

"What are her strengths?" I ask Charles.

"She's much brighter than most of her family, but emotional betrayal is her problem. It's hard for her to get any satisfaction. I'm seeing that there's no fulfillment for her emotionally, not even in lesbian relationships. She's got the passive planets in aggressive signs so there's a tendency to be aggressive rather than passive when it comes to affection. It's so unfortunate, having the moon in the 12th house. It's called the closet of the zodiac."

"I see no future for her," Charles says flatly.

"Are you saying she'll kill herself or that the state will execute her?"

"She doesn't have the will to exist so you kill yourself off either by killing other people or by suicide. She doesn't fit into the world." Then, without warning, and with flat-out finality, Charles says: "I think if there were killings after July (of 1990), they were very deliberate and intentional and they probably relieved her."

"Are you saying she planned these murders?" I ask.

"The thing about her chart is there's a potential for a lot of resentment and for spontaneous action too. She's been in a psychological pressure cooker for the past few years, having to do with power: me versus them, that kind of thing. Scorpio is going to want to get even."

"Was she drunk or high when she committed the murders?"

"She's got Mars in Capricorn. She's into money. Money-making was her addiction."

I say: "I think she's a fool for love, too. Even now, she refuses to speak badly of the woman who testified against her."

Charles looks up. "I'd want to ask her why her ex-friend turned on her. It's very important to hear what she'd have to say about that." Now, Charles is grave, even urgent. "I think you need to keep your involvement as simple as you can. I would give it six months. Don't make a long-term commitment. It's a valuable thing to do, if you can do it and be done with it. Otherwise, you may have to live with it for a long time."

"If it's valuable, why shouldn't I make a long-term commitment?"

"Your nervous system can handle this now at the outset, but this is very unsettling. You just haven't noticed it yet."

Ah, he was too late. Whatever this case was about had already got me, and got me bad.

Charles asked me to turn off my tape recorder. "You know, this chart is very similar to Robert Chambers' chart." (He's the one who killed Jennifer Levin in Central Park after a night of drinking at Dorrian's Red Hand bar.)

A chill, a terror, a sadness swept over me.

"That's about all."

Our session was over. I rose, and was out on the street. Was I going to defend a cold and crazy serial killer—just in order to shed light on the issues her case raises? Okay, Libra, my astrological sign is pictured as a Lady balancing the Scales of Justice, and I'm a double Libra. But, even if I believe that Wuornos fired some shots heard 'round the world—so what?

There she stands: a prostitute, killing Johns, killing men, a dazzling fantasy, an almost perfect symbol of what it might look like if someone on the "bottom" of the social heap exchanged places with someone at the "top."

Wuornos is out of control; Charles and other astrologers insist that, astrologically speaking, the state of Florida is also totally out of control.

"Florida's a wild and dangerous place," said Don Papon, astrologer and homeopath. "When I go down there, I do my business quickly and then I get out. I leave the same day, if can."

"Pisces is Florida's ruling planet," clairvoyant Sonia Nusenbaum pointed out. "The planet Neptune rules Pisces. Neptune is about melting, or transcending the boundary of current time. It's about boundaries merging."

Is Wuornos what Florida's about: all pirate and bloody deed, Old-Time hurricanes and Old-Time religion—and a terrible lonesomeness? Is Pisces-Wuornos karmically representing all of Florida?

I'm no astrologer, but I think the whole world's out of control. Nah, I have to think literally, that's the key. Florida is out of control, that's what I need to understand, so I'm in the air again, on my way back to Ocala.

* * *

It's May, and Meg and I are sitting with Trish and Ed in Trish's office in the Sovereign Building on North Magnolia in Ocala. For the next four hours, no one leaves, not for coffee, not to use the phone or the bathroom. They're all smoking, taking turns at it, and even though I'm allergic to cigarette smoke, I don't leave, not for a minute; I'm riveted to my chair.

The tension's thick, and it gets worse before it gets better. Trish and Meg can't help themselves, they're lawyers, they have to mark their territory, engage in a verbal pissing contest, say things that only lawyers understand. The ball's sure in play.

Out of left field (or so it seems to me), Trish says: "David's a screamer and a humiliator. If he demeans me sexually, I'll file a motion." Who's David? Hush, honey, David (Damore) is one of the prosecutors.

Meg says: "I wasn't certain I was really against the death penalty until I found myself not wanting them to execute Ted Bundy."

I think Meg's hit a home run. Trish is nodding, and so is Ed, and suddenly, the atmosphere is more relaxed. They've found something "more important" (than women) to agree on. All the lawyers are anti-death penalty absolutists.

Trish says: "I went to Bundy's execution. The crowd was unbelievable. Drinking beer in their pickup trucks, partying, real ghoulish. I doubt that the white hearse bearing Bundy's body got to the morgue without parts missing from the corpse. That kind of crowd would want souvenirs."

Meg's done it, the tension's gone. We get to work.

"My client won't plead temporary insanity," Trish announces. "She keeps insisting it was self-defense." (Trish refers to Wuornos either as "my client" or "Lee.")

"Trish," I say, "we're begging you to look into Richard Mallory's past. He's got to have a record. Guy his age just doesn't start doing what he did to Wuornos out of nowhere."

"The dead man's not on trial," Trish says.

"Yeah, it's her word against that of a dead man," says Meg. "Since there are no witnesses, we have to educate the jury about how often prostitutes are attacked and killed. Prostitutes are the women most often targeted for murder."

"Can't admit the victims' past crimes," says Trish.

"At least, give me a chance to work on it," Meg demands.

"Meg's right," I say. "You'll have to educate the jury about how prevalent violence towards prostitutes is, and, if you can, about Richard Mallory's history of violence towards women. At the same time, you'll also have to try to persuade the jury that Wuornos is not evil incarnate, just because she's killed a violent man, or because she's a prostitute and a lesbian."

Dream on, Chesler.

"And how're ya gonna do that?" Trish asks.

"Yeah, how are you gonna make Lee sympathetic?" Ed asks. "She swears like a drunken sailor. She can't get a sentence out without saying fuck this, fuck that, fuck you, at least ten times."

Oh, we had our work cut out for us, alright. We'd have to import our best talent, feminists who'd experienced or seen the damage first-hand, who'd understand how hard it is for someone like Wuornos to trust anyone, or to take anyone's advice on how to behave in the straight world.

I try to make eye-contact with Ed-of-the-long-hair, who's mainly been silent. I say: "We may need eight to ten different experts. Definitely on rape trauma, but also on the adoption triangle..."

"Y'all think the adoption is important?" Trish asks.

"Definitely," I answer. "Wuornos was abandoned by her mother and forced to surrender a child-of-rape for adoption when she was only a child herself. Some studies suggest that adoption constitutes a major trauma, for both adoptees and birthmothers. Most people don't want to hear about it."

"But our experts will not be arguing insanity." I continue. "I think we need to admit that Wuornos is severely traumatized. What that means is that she'd be likely to put up with more, not less, abuse."

"Okay," Meg says. "I agree. We do need to un-demonize Wuornos, otherwise no juror will be willing to put herself in Wuornos' place, willing to see, through Wuornos' eyes, that Mallory was about to kill her."

"I like it," Trish says. "We'll be listing so many different kinds of trauma experts, the prosecution's gonna think we're arguing insanity. They won't know we're sticking to self-defense until we're in the courtroom."

Trish is a professional soldier: long on instinct, short on long-range planning, addicted to last-minute decisions. She's been in the trenches for nearly a decade, she's risen in the ranks, she's "Skipp" Babb's most experienced fighter, she's one of his best "men."

As we figure it, Trish has nothing to lose. We're wrong. Trish will lose nothing if she loses—and everything if she wins. She'll become known, locally, internationally, in history, in her home town, as the woman who'd helped the killer-lesbo-whore get off. She'd have a hard time being "one of the boys" after that.

And here Trish sits, sizing us up, not knowing whether to trust us, wondering what we're really after, wondering who we really are: do we come from money, are we secretly working for a movie company? Trish has been advised that Court-TV, CNN, NBC and CBS have all already made inquiries about booking rooms in the courthouse.

Trish is actually as worried about her own relationship to the media as her client is. Trish Hard-Boiled is outraged that her time—she has no time—is being eaten up by calls from report-ers, script-writers, book-writers, magazine writers, television producers, and film directors, but Trish Over Light and Slightly Flamboyant (the Trish who flaunts old movie posters on her walls), is talking about attending a for-lawyers only workshop in Miami which promises to teach lawyers how to "hold press conferences and use the media to their clients' advantage."

Trish sees those fifteen minutes of fame barreling down on her, hard, but she has no time for vanity, she only has time to work, sleep, work again.

Indeed, three months later, on August 19, 1991, in a pre-trial hearing before Judge Gayle Graziano, in Volusia County, Trish will say that she's "worked every night and every weekend for the last six months. Do I spend all my time on Ms. Wuornos' case and let (my many) other (capital cases) slide? Or do I do it in reverse? I am very seriously telling the Court that I cannot effectively represent Ms. Wuornos if I am forced to go to trial September 9th."

Trish will describe herself as a "serial defender."

SECTION THREE

Sunshine, yes, but ain't no justice here

CHAPTER THIRTEEN

Do Prostitutes Have the Right to Defend Themselves Against Rape?

"**M**OST PEOPLE DON'T THINK a woman has a right to self-defense," I tell Trish and Ed. "But are you familiar with the Yvonne Wanrow, Inez Garcia, and Joan Little cases?" I ask.

They're not.

"I'll get you the cases," I say. "What's relevant is that all three women killed male non-intimates in self-defense. Garcia and Little had been raped. William Wesler, a white man, had a reputation as a mentally ill child sex-offender—and he was drunk, and coming towards Wanrow while she was babysitting."

"Did the women argue insanity?" asks Trish.

"No, none of them did," I answer. "That's why their cases are so important. Wanrow and Garcia were both initially convicted, but their convictions were reversed, Wanrow's by the Supreme Court of Washington State. The Court held that Wanrow's actions were to be judged against Wanrow's own 'subjective' impressions of danger as a woman."

Garcia had been convicted after she argued rape-self-defense in California, in 1974. I'd been called by one of her supporters: Maria del Drago, who was Kate Millett's part-Italian and part-Spanish friend and lover. Maria was also an academic administrator who was anguishing over the struggle between the (homophobic) Hispanic and Black communities and the (allegedly racist) white lesbian feminists for control of Inez Garcia's "narrative."

The young, mainly white, mainly lesbian "Inez Garcia Defense Committee" wanted Garcia to make it clear that a woman has the right to kill her rapist, or in this case, the man who held her down while she was being raped, even if over an hour had passed—and not because she was temporarily insane, but because rape is a form of torture that has lifelong consequences, and because rapists don't stop raping until they're dead, or someone stops them, permanently.

"Phyllis," said Maria, "Inez is scared and confused. She may have a learning disorder. She doesn't want to be seen as a killer, or as a mentally deficient person. The feminists, and I'm one, well, the *other* feminists seem more interested in what's good for women, long-range, than in what's good for Inez right now. The ethnic communities are not interested in what's good for women now or later. There's even some hostility towards Inez because she shot a 'brother.'"

Garcia did argue rape self-defense and she lost. Her lawyer was Charles Gary, who'd defended many a Black Panther on a variety of charges without ever resorting to an insanity defense. Afterwards, one of the white male jurors told a member of the press: "What's the big deal? Inez should have enjoyed the rape, not killed someone over it."

In 1977, feminist lawyer Susan Jordan represented Garcia in a new trial. This time, jurors were carefully polled on their attitudes about rape and were educated, at trial, on the subject. Garcia still argued rape self-defense, but this time, she was not convicted.

If only Wuornos' jury could be similarly polled and educated about prostitution.

Five months after Garcia had been raped, Joan Little, a black prisoner in a jail in North Carolina, killed Clarence Alligood, her white jailor, after he'd entered her cell brandishing an icepick, and threatening to kill her if she didn't let him 'have some.' Alligood raped her. Little killed Alligood with his own weapon, when he dropped it as he came. Jerry Paul and Morris Dees represented Little who, on December 17, 1975, obtained an acquittal on the grounds of rape self-defense.

"Are you saying that none of these women argued insanity? And that all three got off?" Trish asks again.

"Why are you so interested in whether these three women argued insanity or not?" Meg asks.

"I don't think my client's all that sane," Trish says. "An insanity defense might be closer to the truth. It would probably save my client's life and the taxpayers' dollar too."

She's no doubt right, but I bet Wuornos won't do it. She's stubborn, she wants to reveal as little as possible about her impairments, or about what was done to her and what she, in turn, became and did.

"Let's not forget," Meg says. "These three cases speak to the question: How would a reasonable woman perceive the danger Mallory posed? The jury needs to understand that Wuornos was used to putting up with shit. In a sense, that was her job description. Someone like Wuornos would only shoot a man if she was literally fighting for her life. She wouldn't do it because a John was taunting her or even hitting her."

I do not share what Charles House said about the last three or four murders being "deliberate and intentional." I say nothing about my own, growing hunch that, post-Mallory, Wuornos might have killed because the violence had, finally, driven her out of her mind/into her mind.

I only say: "Given the kind of violence Wuornos was up against, it made perfect sense for her to be carrying a gun."

An armed prostitute is an outlaw many times over: She's selling her services illegally—and, if she's armed, she's also carrying an illegal weapon. She's an outlaw because she's said yes to sex for money with many men. An armed lesbian prostitute who gains the upper hand against a paying male customer is beyond the pale.

Trish admits: "Look, we're under some pressure here not to establish a precedent defense for Lee that male serial killers can use. If we develop a new approach for her, then male serial rapists and killers can use it too."

Meg flashes me an anguished look. She quickly says: "Men who kill prostitutes, or who kill women because they think they're prostitutes, get off anyway. They don't need feminist legal strategies to beat the rap."

Meg's right. Sympathy for the men who destroy women and prurient disgust for the women they annihilate is what passes for neutrality in our culture. No one stops men from sexually harassing, beating, raping, or murdering women. The law rarely holds them accountable; lawyers defend their right to get away with it. People are only outraged when a woman accuses a man of a crime against her, or stops him herself.

If a man's on trial, chances are the jury will never get to hear about his past history of violence toward the woman he's killed, it's so incriminating you can't let the jury hear it, and anyway, he's entitled to a fair trial; he's innocent until proven guilty. Ah, but if it's a woman who's done the killing, even if she's the battered victim, even if she's killed in self-defense, she's already guilty, her gender conformity *and* her gender non-conformity convict her. Juries are psychologically primed to distrust/dislike any woman even before they've heard the facts of her case.

A man who's killed a woman can usually find at least one juror who'll sympathize with him when he describes how the dead woman led him on and then rejected him or how she'd cheated on him and he'd caught her in the act, how she'd walked out on him, and he did what any red-blooded man would do under the circumstances. Few jurors understand that those men who kill women have not lost control, they've exerted final control over those who were supposed to obey them.

And yes, Trish is right: the same juror who'd let a man go for such old-fashioned reasons might also let him go for some new-fangled reasons.

We're having this conversation in the "Deep South" of Ocala. The slave-owning South is precisely where the first-ever case of rape self-defense was argued—and it was argued on behalf of a black slave woman.

In 1850, a widower in his fifties, the farmer, Robert Newsom, purchased a fourteen-year old slave child, known only as Celia. Newsom raped Celia on the way to her new home; by the time Celia was nineteen, she had given birth to two of Newsom's children.

Eventually, Celia married another slave—a jealous man who threatened her about Newsom's rape-visits. Celia begged, then warned Newsom to keep away. When he advanced upon her anyway—amazingly she killed him, burned his body in her fireplace, crushed his bones, and hid some of the ashes. Celia did not flee.

Boldly, Celia denied everything. Faced with evidence, Celia finally confessed. Newspaper reports claimed that the murder had been committed "without any sufficient cause."

Celia was tried by an all-white, all-male judge and jury. Four of the jurors owned slaves. Although the judge remained hostile, Celia's highly experienced white defense attorney, John Jameson, argued that Celia had the moral, and possibly the legal, right to kill in defense of her honor and her life. According to historian Melton A. McLaurin, this argument was both "as bold as it was brilliant." Jameson wanted Celia acquitted. The jury found her guilty and she was sentenced to hang.

On December 21st, 1855, Celia was "marched to the gallows... the trap was sprung and Celia fell to her death."

The jury, what about Wuornos' jury?

Says Trish: "I think white women are our best bet. So many women are battered in the south. I think women jurors will understand certain things here more than men ever will."

Meg and I look at each other. Trish may be 'tough,' but from our (feminist) point of view, she's a babe-in-arms.

Sure, some things are changing, but most things haven't changed so much that a woman who kills a man can count on other women to support her—just because they, too, have been beaten or raped.

"Ah, Trish," I say, "women have to be specially educated before they'll run the risk of publicly siding with another woman against a man, especially if the woman in question is a prostitute and a lesbian. Even if she's not, if she's just an ordinary woman who's been raped, she can't count on support from other women. Between Meg and I, you have easy access to every major expert on rape and battery in the country. But, what about asking someone closer to home, someone like Judy Wilson, for example? She can testify about the rape and battery that's gone on for the last twenty years, right here in Ocala."

Trish nearly jumps out of her chair.

"Is there a problem here?" I ask.

Then, very, very carefully, Trish says: "What I'm about to tell you in no way reflects on Judy or on my relationship to Judy. Trust me. She'd be death in the courtroom."

In 1972, when Judy first arrived in Ocala, Marion County rarely prosecuted the rapes of non-prostituted women. Wilson estimates that, from 1972 to 1975, about "four rapes per year were prosecuted."

"Back then," Judy told me, "emergency room nurses would yell out: 'Who's the rape victim here?' And the 'victim' would have to get up and walk across a big room with all these people, strangers, staring at her. Her name would be all over the breakfast tables the next morning. If a judge's wife got raped, or had a psychotic break, they'd fly her right out of here and into Gainesville. Back then, officers at the scene of the crime would routinely ask rape victims: 'Did you have a climax?' 'Did you like it?' 'Were you at a bar, were you drinking? What did you say to him to lead him on?'"

In 1975, when Wilson founded Ocala's first rape crisis center, the police fought her "tooth and nail for about six months," Judy says. "Then Jim, who was with the state attorney's office, got a hold of one of the key detectives and said 'Listen, goddammit! You've got to start cooperating with my wife. She's not trying to hurt you. She's trying to help you do your job.'

"But the chief of detectives kept asking: 'What about all those false reports? What about all those women who just want to get their boyfriends in trouble?' He and his men refused to look me in the eye, but they did hear me out, and after a couple of months they stopped asking all their cruel and ugly questions and started doing proper rape investigations.

"Today, we don't have much trouble with the older officers. But there's a whole new bunch of Young Turk police officers coming in, the 21-year-olds, and they're Macho City all over again. The prosecutors are prosecuting fewer rapes. In 1985, Marion County prosecuted 179 rapes. In 1990, they prosecuted 39 rapes. This is real peculiar, because we know that rapes aren't going down. Just prosecutions. We must have counseled almost 1,000 victims of rape that same year and we know that those 1,000 are about only 1-5% of all the rapes that really occurred. Part of the problem is cuts in funding. But it's also due to the prosecutors who are real woman haters, and who won't go after the rapists."

Judy paused. "And then there's the women. Women in this community are tougher on women than the men are. I can give you hundreds of examples. In 1981, a nurse from Canada was raped. She was Jewish. Man broke into her home and held her at knifepoint. He was a really scuzzy-looking guy and he had a record a mile long, which the jury couldn't hear about. He'd raped her three different ways and then he went to sleep with his arm around her, still holding the knife. She managed to escape. She ran out into the street, naked, and onto the highway, screaming for help. The police believed her story. The jury came back with 'Breaking and Entering.' She was an excellent witness but the fact that she was Jewish was used against her."

"What's this to do with women being tough on women?" I ask.

"You could hear the women jurors and the women spectators talking out in the hall. They did a job on her, the old fashioned way. 'Did you see her nails? They're so red. Did you see the eye makeup she had on? She must have asked for it. She's one of 'those' (a Jew), you know how them kind of women are, they lie.' Now, men also say that women lie, but women really go into how a woman looks. They're very catty, they use a woman's looks to demolish her reputation."

I know what Judy's talking about. She's describing how women-in-groups can destroy an individual woman, break her heart, drive her out of town, or out of her mind, simply by excluding and badmouthing her. I've also studied how much women-in-groups seem to enjoy their power over a lone, targeted woman.

Judy continues. "It's not just one class or race against another class or race. I've seen Christian women do it to Christian women. I've seen women do it to women from their own neighborhood. Here's one example. A Mormon woman was raped by her husband's best friend at knifepoint. The women on the jury seemed to hold it against her that she dressed a certain way to show off for the trial. They said she shouldn't have let her husband's best friend in the house. No matter that he'd been coming to the house for years."

"What happens when a black woman charges rape in Ocala?" I ask.

"In 1987, I shared the elevator with the jurors who'd just been sitting on a rape case. The rapist and his victim were both black. He was the woman's ex-boyfriend. He'd been stalking her. He wouldn't leave her alone. The jury didn't convict him. Even though there were pools of blood all over, and she was a mess, physically, the jurors were convinced that 'black people like rough sex.'"

"Were there any black people on the jury?" I ask.

"I don't remember," Judy answers. "Probably not. About five, six years ago in 1986, there was a fifteen or sixteen-year-old black boy who had raped five different black teenage girls. He managed to get three or four of them pregnant too. It was always the same M.O. He'd pick the girl up at a bowling alley or a skating rink, invite her to go outside for a cigarette and a walk through the woods, then suddenly slam her to the ground, literally tear her clothes off, rape her, stand up, usher her out of the woods, and split. We finally got one of the girls to testify, but the judge said that she had just gone into the woods with this boy willingly, and he tore her clothes trying to get them off her not because he was raping her, but because they were in a hurry."

"So her problem was the judge, not other women, not even the women on the jury."

"Hey, you're right. What was interesting was that the judge stopped me in the hall several times, and kind of half apologized. 'Well you know Judy, we just can't be sure' and I said 'Let me tell you something, Hale.' His name was Hale. 'When you have five young women calling in and they're not all friends, and they don't all go to the same school, and they don't all know each other, and they're describing this boy going around and he has the same M.O. each time, and three or four of them are pregnant—what do you think is going on?'"

Maybe Trish should try to get as many black jurors as possible on Wuornos' jury.

Meg says: "Black jurors might understand something about why a person might not feel safe enough to go to the police."

"Do you feel the same way about the experts?" Ed demands. "Are they all gonna be black women?"

Says Meg, caught off guard: "They should all be women. I feel very strongly about this."

Say I: "No. Here's where we need some men, preferably men who are also white and Southern and middle-aged, just like the dead men. I have someone in mind, a child psychiatrist, Dr. Paul Adams, who is both a fine feminist and a Southerner.

"Okay," says Trish. "I want work products as soon as possible. I want the names of every potential expert witness, and where I can find 'em. I wanna know exactly what they're experts in. Call 'em, tell 'em they'll be hearing from me. Don't promise anyone anything." She pauses, then says: "Phyllis, can you work with these witnesses? And, if we can't get them all in, can you take the stand and give an overview? My asking you to do all this doesn't mean I'm hiring you. It means we'll see how it works out. One more thing. I don't want you talking to Arlene Pralle anymore."

"I have a check for her," I say, "to help cover her phone bill..."

"I don't want to hear this," Trish cuts me off. "I don't want the prosecutor admitting a check with your signature into evidence."

Oh dear, she is so right.

"Meg," Trish says, "I'll need you to hit those law books. If

Richard Mallory has a criminal record, and I'm not saying he does, I wanna know what grounds you think exist to argue that such information should be admitted into evidence. I want a memo on all the studies on violence against prostitutes. And a copy of that legislation you said you drafted for Florida."

"You don't think the trial will start on September 9th, do you?" asks Meg worriedly.

"Not a chance," says Trish.

Trish Jenkins is sister to all those male public defenders out of the 1960s, who wore their hair long, smoked dope, loved black music and black (male) clients, but not as much as they loved the law, which allowed them to fight the Good Fight as if they were not merely bookish, but wild and lonesome cowboys. (Many wore cowboy boots too.)

I knew a few public defenders myself, but that was long ago, in the 1960s. Some still labor on, but most became extinct. They had families to support; they became judges, politicians, law professors, or they went into private practice and ended up defending drug dealers, pornographers, wife-killers—on principle—and for the money, because hey, baby, we're all whores, and everyone's entitled to a defense, and this money is what allows us to take those high-profile "political" cases. They have a point.

I'm sure Trish is spending more time on Wuornos' case than on all her other pending cases—a sobering view of how expensive justice in America really is, and therefore, how little there is of it, even in America.

The criminal lawyers insist: No one who's poor is entitled to a competent or to the best defense—only to a public or state-subsidized defense. There's justice in America alright, but it's rare, and while America may be better than Turkey, Iran or Saudi Arabia, you still have to be very rich, very male, very white, or very famous, in order to be able to play by the rules, or to bend them, when you're on trial.

Deck's stacked, and most women don't understand that putting their money down only entitles them to play, not to win. Men understand this better, they can afford to, they're allowed to get away with more, and when they lose, their jail-time's not as hard as women's: they have educational programs, libraries, access to gyms; they have women on the outside who watch their kids for them, write to them, visit them, even marry them.

In our bones, women understand that once they get us, we lose everyone, everything, we're as good as dead, buried alive; so, as our grandmothers said: Look busy, keep your opinions to yourself, let him think he's smarter than you. Like most women, cold wind 'cross my grave, I'm not comfortable breaking the law, I'd rather go by the book, seems safer—even though it's not.

Here's the truth: All women are outlaws, simply because we're not men. (I know it's crazy, but I'm just pointing it out, I'm not agreeing with it.) A whore knows this, and while it makes her bitter, it also frees her from certain illusions.

Trish Jenkins never did hire me, and she never did use our pro bono experts either. For a while, I kept hoping that Trish had decided to argue the case poorly, as the only thing she could do for her client. I kept hoping that the trial transcript would yield countless grounds for appeal.

But it gnawed at me, how things turned out. I finally gave up trying to figure out whether it was Trish's ego or ours, Trish's lack of vision, or our foolish, girlish expectation that we could count on the state to provide Wuornos with a "political" trial. How could Meg and I have expected to "play" without paying, without putting down at least a million dollars?

CHAPTER FOURTEEN

The Fool for Love Confesses Is Tried and Convicted and We Meet on Death Row

I WAS VERY ILL with undiagnosed Lyme Disease and in bed when Wuornos was tried, but I watched it on Court-TV. I also viewed the video of her confession and studied the transcript. Wuornos does not seem to understand why she might need a lawyer. She says:

"The reason I'm confessin' is there's not another girl. She was not involved in any of this. She was my...my...my...room-mate."

Wuornos does not seem to know what the word "counsel" means and does not understand what an attorney "can do" for her since "there's not gonna be no help for me."

At one point, she asks the cops if they're her attorneys. She does not know why it would "hurt her case" if (she's) telling the cops "the truth."

Wuornos sounds like a child, mentally, or like a woman who has lived off the grid and so far underground for so long that she knows nothing about how "straight" society works.

The cops obtained Wuornos' confession through trickery. Either they picked Tyria up, frightened her, kept her confined in a motel room, and gave her a script to follow when she called

Lee—or, as Tyria told me, years later, she was there of her own free will—because she was guilty about not having come forward after Lee told her she'd killed a man. Ty said that had she done so "maybe six innocent men would still be alive."

In any event, Ty calls Lee eleven times. Lee is suspicious and keeps asking if the calls are being taped. She cannot understand how Ty can afford to come back down to Florida, pay for an expensive motel room, and for all the calls. "What is this shit, you got somebody sitting in there listening?" Ty denies it and says:

"Lee, they're coming after me...they are talking to my family, they are a nervous wreck up there...I'm scared shitless, they're harassing my family."

Lee takes the bait. She responds: "I'm not going to let you go to jail. If I have to confess, I will. I am so in love with you...I love you right next to God."

Lee confessed in order to save Ty. She was a fool for love.

Interestingly, Lee also says: "Now I will probably die of a broken heart... My life is a wreck. I'm going downhill. By the way, I'm going to go down in history."

Ty is surrounded by cops as she speaks to Lee. Perhaps this is why when Lee repeatedly says: "I love you," Ty merely responds with: "Okay," or "I know you do," or "Alright." Or, maybe Ty is truly done with Lee, done with her vulgar, violent temper, done with her hooking life, done with living on the edge.

Wuornos' videotaped confession should have ended the moment Wuornos said she wanted a lawyer. It did not. There she was, surrounded by men in uniform who were treating her gently, offering her coffee and cigarettes as if they were Johns, and all she had to do was talk softly, "nicely," and she'd be able to save Ty and keep Ty's love.

"I'm confessing what I did and go ahead and put the electric chair to me." And she sobs. "I shoulda never done it. See, most of the times I was drunk as hell and I was a professional hooker... and when they started gettin' rough with me, I just like opened up and fired at 'em. ... I had to defend myself because if I didn't he probably woulda hurt me, killed me, raped me... I've gone through (millions) of guys in my life. And never hurt any of 'em. I became very good friends with 'em."

When she asks for a lawyer, the cops take their own sweet time about providing one. And Wuornos just keeps on talking. After all, she's the center of attention, and the cops are acting like friends. She says some heartbreaking things such as:

"Really deep down inside when I was a little girl I always wanted to be a nun. And then when I got older, I wanted to be a missionary. I'm a good person inside, but not when I get drunk. I don't know what happens when somebody messes with me."

Was she appealing to their supposed male protectiveness by lying about how good a girl she really was? Tyria told me that Lee lied continually, that you could not trust one thing she said—but, Wuornos was also detoxing from a lifetime of alcohol. Did she even know what she was saying, other than wanting to exonerate Tyria?

Wuornos claimed "self-defense" sixteen times. Yes, sixteen times. She also said that she was confessing to save Tyria fifteen times.

* * *

Is a jury ever truly a "jury of our peers?" Hardly ever. In Wuornos' case, the jury pool consisted of church goers, True Believers, many of whom had relatives who were police chiefs, sheriffs, and state troopers. Not an outlaw or a prostitute among them. Her jury consisted of a pharmacist, a bookkeeper, a power company worker, a restaurant manager, a sales representative for a cheese company, and retirees. Those who did not make the cut include a beautician who "viewed prostitution positively"—and all those who "opposed the death penalty."

Many jurors also viewed prostitution as a woman's "choice." The male jurors bantered and joked about prostitution. One man said: "Some of my best friends are prostitutes—I've been around the world in the Navy." Another man said: "It should be legalized."

The defense failed to persuade the judge to allow them to question jurors individually. Thus, each batch of prospective jurors got to hear what everyone else in the group had to say. And, whatever each juror said was heard by the others.

The judge? He's a colorful character. One potential juror tells Judge Uriel "Bunky" Blount that "he has a prostate problem." Judge Blount responds: "I don't have any problem with that. I've been reamed out twice. You're going to get along just fine with me."

At one point, Wuornos challenged the Judge in open court about the correct pronunciation of her name. He shot back: "You oughta see what they can do with 'Uriel.'"

Do we treat male serial killers differently than we treat female serial killers? Although one really cannot compare trials, let's try to see what doing so might reveal.

Both trials took place in Florida, both defendants were serial killers, one was a man (Ted Bundy), the other a woman (our own Aileen Wuornos).

Given the enormous pre-trial publicity, which included Wuornos' confession to seven murders, and given the probable biases of the Ocala jury pool, her defense requested a change of venue.

Judge Blount—the very man whom Prosecutor John Tanner had chosen to swear him in as a Prosecutor—refused to grant it. Blount felt that he could seat an "impartial" jury even if they'd seen or heard about the confession—and he did so in a day and a half!

Bundy received a change of venue, from Tallahassee to Miami, for the same reason.

Wuornos' jury was shown a videotape in which someone had carefully edited out her repeated claims that she had killed "in self-defense."

Yes, the sixteen times she had claimed "self-defense" were edited out.

Bundy's jury did not hear about his 30—100 previous murders. They were focused only on the three murders that he'd committed in Florida.

In Wuornos' case, who testified for the Defense?

Mallory's ex-girlfriend, Jackie Davis, was ready to testify

about how violent Mallory had been towards women, that he was into pornography, and had been institutionalized for his sex addiction. Judge Blount did not allow her to testify.

None of my expert witnesses were ever called, even though Wuornos said she wanted them. This fact became one of the grounds of the appeal to the Florida Supreme Court and I was thrilled to work with Chris Quarles, one of the appeal lawyers, who joined me on a panel in New York City.

Wuornos was the sole witness for the defense. Although her lawyers had not wanted her to risk testifying, her description of Mallory's murderous behavior was, in my opinion, credible and very moving. It did not matter. The jury found her guilty.

In the penalty phase of the trial, Wuornos' jury heard from two psychologists: Drs. Elizabeth McMahon and Harry Krop, who diagnosed Wuornos as a "borderline personality" suffering from "organic brain syndrome." McMahon described Wuornos as "impulsive, unstable, emotionally labile, angry, self-destructive, (as having) problems with gender identity, alienation, 'aloneness', alcoholism, head trauma, a mild degree of cortical dysfunction."

Sounds about right for a childhood victim of sexual violence and a prostituted woman.

McMahon added: "Miss Wuornos is one of the most primitive people I've seen outside of an institution... she functions at the level of small child needs... food, shelter, and clothing. Her whole life is one of constantly being in a state of living on the edge. It's a state of potential danger...her judgement is impaired. She has no normal adult insight. In my clinical opinion, Miss Wuornos believed she was in a life-threatening situation."

This also sounds about right—except that Miss Wuornos often was in a life-threatening situation. She lived in a foxhole and only came out to consort with Johns or to sit in a bar and drink hard. She ran daily raids behind enemy lines; she had to stay drunk in order to be able to "enjoy" her life. Most prostitutes never kiss or hold hands with Johns. Wuornos did. Only an abused and cognitively impaired child might do so, as a way of pretending that a John was a real relationship, that the affection was real.

Well, maybe sometimes it was.

At trial, Dr. Elizabeth McMahon told the jury that Aileen was an unusual prostitute, not because she was physically aggressive or menacing, but because she'd held hands with, kissed, sought and found affection with her Johns. Like a child, a teenager, or a slightly retarded woman might do.

Given her profound limitations, Aileen really was bright. She drew beautifully and had perfected a very neat handwriting.

But, in that courtroom, and in the media, she was seen as the lesbian prostitute criminal who hated men. But this was a Big Fat Lie.

Goddammit! Men had broken her heart again and again. When Aileen was 25 years old, she'd recently broken up with a guy named Mark, with whom she was "dearly in love." Mark's departure "took a large part of (her) heart out." But then, she met Ray in a bar, who persuaded her to come live with him—and when she did—she became Ray's "whipping post" and "human punching bag." Aileen couldn't understand why every man she loved beat her, left her, hurt her. Why did love have to hurt so much?

Aileen decided to kill herself—again. In 1978, she'd shot herself in the stomach and ended up in the hospital for 2 weeks. Aileen told the state psychiatrist, Dr. George W. Barnard, that she'd made "six suicide attempts between the ages of 14 and 22," and that she'd had "shakes and blackouts since she was 19 but no DTs, and no treatment for alcohol abuse except in 1975 when she stayed in a place for alcoholic treatment for three days and left."

Aileen was such a royal screw-up that she couldn't even try to kill herself without going to jail.

Way it happened: Devastated, disconsolate, bummed out over Ray, Aileen put on her G-string black bikini, downed a bottle of Ray's Southern Comfort that she found lying around the house, popped 100 milligrams of Librium, and headed for an empty stretch of beach to "commence her death." Aileen gulped beer after beer, as fast as she could. In a while, Aileen noticed that she wasn't dead yet but she was definitely out of beer.

In 1981, when Aileen walked into the Magic Market in Edgewater, she didn't even bother to put her shorts on over her bikini. "So the world or whoever was looking, could see my ass for the last time. Like a final farewell…'kiss my ass.'"

Aileen parked and grabbed her purse, which held $118.00 and a .22 Saturday night special in the middle compartment that Aileen had completely forgotten about. Aileen was in a hurry, she needed a bag of chips, a six pack. Slim Jims. Lemme have a carton of cigarettes, she said. The clerk, a woman, got the carton from the upper shelf behind her. As she turned around, she saw the butt of Aileen's gun sticking out of her bag—and started screaming. "You're gonna rob me!"

Aileen tried to calm her down, then gave up. Fuck it, even though she hadn't done anything wrong, Aileen decided she might as well rob her, she's gonna call the law on her anyway for attempted robbery. It didn't matter, nothing did anymore. By the time they found her, Aileen would be dead. Piss on you.

So Aileen said: "If you want a robbery, lady, then you've got one!" According to Aileen she never took the gun out, she didn't have to, the clerk was already taking cash out of the drawer and putting it on the counter. Aileen "picked up all (her) stuff nonchalantly, walked out of the store, and said: "Lady, you're an asshole! It's a good thing I'm off to kill myself today!"

Aileen got back in her car, headed down the road, and then her radiator blew. Aileen passed a cop car, going in the opposite direction. How lousy can someone's luck be? She couldn't even make it to the beach to blow her brains out.

The half-naked blonde-in-distress on the highway caused a car to screech to a halt. Immediately, two guys climbed out and helped Aileen push her car to a nearby gas station. Aileen was so involved in talking to the gas station attendant about her radiator that she forgot about killing herself and about the "unintentional" robbery.

But then, from out of the corner of her eye, Aileen saw a sheriff's car go slowly by. Then, she saw the cop standing there with his gun drawn. He was holding it "two-handed," in the air.

Almost conversationally, Aileen asked him what he was doing. The sheriff shouted: "Up against the car, keep your hands in the air! Spread your legs." He frisked her, he looked for that gun in her goddamn bikini. Did he think she had a gun in her pussy? The woman from the store identified her. Aileen was booked, finger-printed, and stashed in the tank for drunks.

For this complete misunderstanding which wasn't her fault, Aileen did 13 months at Broward.

At trial, Defense Attorney Trish Jenkins did refer to Wuornos' hard childhood and hard life as well as to her neurological difficulties and to her hearing and visual impairments. It elicited no sympathy in that courtroom.

I doubt that Wuornos was able to hear, see, or follow the trial proceedings very well. She said as much. The Judge did not care.

Talk about misguided! The lead Prosecutor, John Tanner, portrayed Wuornos as a "predatory prostitute" whose "appetite for lust and control had taken a lethal turn;" as someone who "had been exercising control for years over men" and who "killed for power, for full and ultimate control."

Please recall: Tanner was also Ted Bundy's death-row "minister" and a campaigner against pornography. Bundy—the smoothest of psychopaths, said that his addiction to pornography was partly to blame for his having become a serial killer. If Tanner really understood the relationship between pornography and prostitution, he could not have portrayed Wuornos in this way.

Clearly, Tanner understood nothing about prostitution or about who was really in control: Johns were. In 1987, four years before this trial, Tanner had published a piece about prostitution in the *Orlando Sentinel*. He wrote that "prostitution is not a victimless crime...that the children of prostitutes often are physically abused by the men who 'use' prostitutes. The AIDS epidemic adds a lethal element to prostitution. Prostitutes are prime carriers of the AIDS virus...and may infect as many as 40 men in a night."

Agreed—prostitution is not a "victimless crime"—prostitutes are the victims and Johns spread AIDS and other STDs to prostitutes, not the other way round. Would it have made any difference if Jenkins had called for Tanner's removal given his blighted, ignorant views of prostitution? I doubt it.

Tanner actually said that Lee could have made another choice, "she could have worked at legal work." Clearly, he has no idea of how hard it is for any prostituted woman to re-enter society.

In another death penalty case, Tanner told the jury that the Bible mandated capital punishment and he cited the Book of Romans in the New Testament. Oddly, in Wuornos' case, both he and the defense did try to avoid the death penalty in return for 14 consecutive life sentences, seven for each murder and seven for each robbery, with no chance of parole. The plea agreement effort failed because one of the state attorneys refused to sign on to the deal.

When men are accused of heinous crimes, even terrible crimes, their families almost invariably back them. For example, Bundy had enormous emotional, secretarial and public relations support from his mother, Louise, and his 32-year-old "fiancée," Carol Lee Boone, whom he married while in jail, impregnated (via a smuggled-out sperm donation) and who had his child. Both women testified for him. Scores of pretty young women attended the trial and openly flirted with him in court.

My people (women) are sometimes crazy—but Bundy was handsome, charming, and well spoken.

Did Wuornos have anyone in her family on her side? Nah. Wuornos' uncle/brother Barry, twelve years her senior, whom she hadn't seen for at least 20 years, testified for the prosecution. He claimed that Wuornos had never been "abused" at home and therefore had no "reason to kill anyone." He said that he himself had thrown Lee out because she "stole things from his wife" and "refused to clean up after herself." He insisted that his father (Lee's grandfather) was "not the kind of man who would beat a child" and that his family was "not dysfunctional."

He was there to cast some stones and thus restore his family's reputation in the neighborhood.

Arlene Pralle, Aileen's second adoptive mother, was in the courtroom but (thankfully) did not testify. Wuornos also had feminist political support which played no role in her trial and had no influence over whom she chose to trust.

Wuornos' jury of five men and seven women needed only one hour and 31 minutes to find her guilty, and one hour and 48 minutes to recommend the death penalty.

In Bundy's case, unbelievably, the jury took seven hours to find him guilty and seven and a half hours to sentence him to death.

The state of Florida offered Bundy a life sentence without parole; Bundy himself refused the plea bargain.

At 9 a.m. on January 31, 1992, Blount, who could override the jury's recommendation, ordered that Wuornos was to die in the electric chair—"and may God have mercy on your corpse."

Corpse, not soul.

She was immediately taken to death row at the Broward County Correctional Facility for Women.

In 1995, in a letter to Dawn Botkins, Lee wrote: "O.J. Is being given the greatest in history of favoritism I've ever seen as far as a trial on murder is concerned. Now I believe mine was the Quickest in History of trying a case, which lasted only 13 days...So obviously you can see I was Extremely railroaded with a "Rush to Judgement."

* * *

I'm still very weak but I'm finally able to walk. I want to visit Wuornos. I've been advised that I have to call her lawyer, Steven Glazer. On the phone, he tells me that "Lee won't grant an interview with anyone unless she's been paid for it," but since she cannot profit from her alleged crimes, the money goes to him and to Arlene. In turn, they can dole out money for Lee's commissary expenses. Glazer explained: "I have not been paid for doing work and I don't care...what I get out of it is...free publicity." When I press to know the exact sum that an interview costs, he responds:

"There's one person who's already given us $10,000.00 plus

4% and 33% of serializations. I don't think Lee would give me permission unless at least $10,000.00 was paid up front and other conditions were made and it would be a license, not a copyright."

I tell him that I will never pay a penny to see Lee. And I don't.

It's a 35-minute drive from the Ft. Lauderdale airport to death row at the Broward Correctional Institute. I drive up to the last building on the property. A male guard-in-uniform, armed with a gun and a walkie-talkie, is sitting in an open-doored van, observing whatever there is to observe. Me. I start walking over to ask for directions.

"Stand back," he orders. I freeze in my tracks. He calls my name in on his walkie-talkie. "You're a half hour early," he says accusingly.

"I was advised to arrive at 12:30 to allow a half hour to be processed. Can I wait inside?"

He stares straight ahead and, after a while, shrugs as if to say "guess you can."

A receptionist tells me that her only escort is busy. Eventually Sergeant "X," a woman wearing a brown uniform and heavy black men's shoes, is buzzed into the waiting room. She says: "Well, Lee is being difficult. Moody as hell. That's how she got with the BBC crew. She just didn't want to see them."

Sergeant X and I wait. And then, suddenly, she says: "Well, c'mon, let's go. I told you she changes her mind. She'll see you now."

Sergeant X leads me to a very small room with two chairs, no desk.

Lee is led into the room by two guards. She is unsteady on her feet, a bit ungainly, not that tall. The swagger and the smirk are gone, she is gaunt, not an ounce of flesh on her bones, more ghost than human.

Still, I do not completely close the door. I'm not sure what I'm dealing with.

Lee's blonde hair is pale, and pulled back into a thin pony tail. Her face is taut, her features bony, inexpressive: No energy to waste on "expressiveness." Survival in prison demands that you contract everything in order to conserve energy, and call as little attention to yourself as possible. She has great dignity. She has come from some truly faraway place to meet me, she is jerky in her motions, but gamely, she's trying to smile. As if it's a social occasion. We hug hello, briefly, carefully.

Lee's been in jail since January 1991, much of the time in isolation.

"I was railroaded," she says, "because I'm a prostitute and expendable." Lee insists: "I'd rather die and go home to Jesus than keep living in a world filled with lust and corruption." Lee doesn't want to stay on death row; she's decided to die.

You don't have to be crazy to come to this conclusion.

Suddenly, Lee is emphatic and growing louder by the second. She points her trigger finger at me and orders me to "Forget it. All I want you to do is help me expose the corruption, the crooked cops, the crooked lawyers, the media deals, the capital gains off a capital crime. Tell the world what's going on. That's all. I'm not concerned about any more trials."

I ask her if anyone ever helped her when she was a child, sleeping in an abandoned car and living in the woods or on the street. She says:

"I raised myself. I did a pretty good job. I taught myself my own handwriting, and I studied theology, psychology, books on self-enhancement. I taught myself how to draw. I have been through battles out there raising myself. I'm like a Marine, you can't hurt me. If you hurt me, I can wipe it out of my mind and keep on truckin'. I took every day on a day-by-day basis. I never let things dwell inside me to damage my pride because I knew what that felt like when I was young..."

A child is being beaten... what to do when no one ever stopped it and now it's much too late, the damage is done, the child is a woman, and the woman only knows how to sell—her body, her life story, her death. She's all used up and out of luck. Now, she means to finish what her family and what We, the People, have started: Her utter destruction.

Wuornos still kept working with Glazer and Pralle—even

as she still continued to ask me to find her new lawyers and to reassemble my team of experts, especially now that she was "famous and in demand." Yes, she understood that Arlene and Steve were only interested in the money, but she could not let go of them. She tells me that she's agreed to a new contract with Giroux, that Steve "enticed her to believe that this is the best thing to do."

Although Lee was a quick study in figuring out what someone wants to hear (she tried to sound like a feminist in her early phone calls and letters to me), eventually she decided that every feminist, including myself, who had approached her to work on her case was also either in it for money or for fame. She bad-mouthed each one of us to whoever was next up.

Lee kept asking me and L.B. and Meg to help her write a book. Her book, our book—it was never clear. Then, she placed restrictions on what it could be about. We would not be allowed to cover her childhood or the murders but must only focus on the "crooked cops." She wants no money, she only wants to expose them. But in another letter, (sometimes in the same letter), she writes that she still wants a "50-50 split." Then this:

The book she had in mind would be a "sure fire best seller on the truth… its needed to be done by someone who knows knowledge in writting." She asks me to "take on this project" so that she can "see these scum balls loose their jobs and possibly even see prison time. That is why, I reorganized my thoughts and am asking if you would take on this project. As far as (a) new agent for interviews. I'm looking for one! Are you interested! We could work out on a 50/50 basis. (No problem.) I just need Steve out of the picture."

Maybe the astrologer was right about her being obsessed with money. She may always have been money-hungry and money-conscious, but she only dealt in small coins. For example, in 1976, when she was twenty years old, Lee inherited ten thousand dollars from her brother Keith's life insurance policy. She blew it all within three months on a down payment for a car (which was soon repossessed), on stereophonic equipment, music, beer, and food. She didn't save it or invest it, or use it as a down payment for a home or to further her education. At one point, L.B. tried hard to explain to her that my writing a law review article about her case might, in the long run, be more important than making a deal with a film company. She wrote: "Phyllis's law review article is very important because the legal community will have access to real information on your case in a forum that they respect and will read."

L.B. also bemoaned the "games," lies, and frequent changes of mind that Wuornos put us through. She wrote:

"Your case is important to me because... I have very strong convictions about a woman's right to defend herself and this includes women in prostitution who run some of the highest risks. Your case is important because of you, the individual, but it is equally important for all the other women who are at risk for their lives and safety."

But Wuornos did not have the enormous luxury of leading a life of ideas. She could not envision helping "all" women. She only knew that she had to take care of the one woman who was in her life and who she'd have to pay to keep. She didn't think anyone would stick by her if she was not paying for it. She was a petty grifter. She had to be. No one else was looking out for her. She ended a letter to me trying to hustle me for money for her new/old best friend—Dawn Botkins.

I wrote back to her:

"Lee: When people like myself and L.B. and Meg work to find expert witnesses to assist your lawyers... there is no monetary profit in it, there is no marketable product (like a film) that we can create to sell over and over again. Our main and only 'profit' is justice for you and for other women in your situation. And we care about this the way people who care about money care about money. So: We also have a selfish 'motive.' It's freedom from violence for prostitutes and justice for them when they kill in self-defense."

Lee is the petit-bourgeois capitalist and Meg, L.B. and I are the revolutionary abolitionists. Wuornos doesn't want to overthrow patriarchy. She only wants her very small slice of the pie.

In retrospect, like Lee, I was also a fool, but not for love—

for radical feminist dreams. Her case was irresistible. I simply could not resist trying to use Wuornos' case to further our own abolitionist politics.

That's how I became pen pals with a serial killer.

CHAPTER FIFTEEN

Love Letters

November 24, 1991

Dear Lee:

Hello! And greetings again from the feminist movement.

I've sent you some money for stamps, paper, food, and toiletries. I hope that you've somehow managed to keep both body and spirit strong.

I don't know what you've been told about my "disappearance" from your case but you have a right to know what happened. I worked very hard on your behalf. By the end of May, I had commitments from 11 feminists (myself included), both men and women, from around the country to serve as expert witnesses at your trial and as resource people for you in general.

Maybe Trish has strategized a thoughtful and creative game plan for your defense without using any of the witnesses I found, and without resorting to any of the strategizing we've discussed. She's very smart. If she has the time and the resources she's more than capable of defending you. But if you want her to pursue any or all of the experts I found, please ask her for the list. She's got it.

In sisterhood,

Phyllis

(Author's Comment: I am writing to her before her first trial.)

February 21, 1992

Dear Phyllis:

I know your thinking Aileen you wrote! Finally! And maybe also thinking, dam you I ought to tear this letter up right now. But wait! Please don't! I've got so much to tell you and hopefully resolve a terrible situation that has occured. Please read on.

One of the major reasons for our contrast that has collapsed a possible bona fide friendship here that could of developed is basically because of my attorneys. They have decieved me, and I also believe to Arlene of you as well. Right now they were not clear as to what really is going on. But my crucifixion in court diffenately proved a possible conspiracy play on there part as well......I'm writing you to ask for your forgiveness and your support if it still available.....

I'm tired of the truth not being told. I am searching for some honest hearted people out there. And if you can help me..Then I am willing to help you in your research. I cannot help you in a book about my life. But I will help you on other matters. I am willing to help you on your book. But I cannot on a life story. For that is my project....

I know you wondering where did I mess up in the media that didn't state the truth. Easy. One I've never pursued drugs after the age of 17. You stated that I had a 25 year habit. WRONG! by a very long shot. I just tryed like everyone else did in the early 70s mescaline, acid, and marijuana. From 15-16 one year. Then from 16-17, I smoked pot, but after I quit at 17 I never went back to it. Only drank. Not much mix either. It has been beer basically all along. Also I was raped, and am not telling a bunch of wild fairy taling. The confessions speak for themselves....

I've got other stuff I need to talk to you about. I need a

bunch of caring women professionally to help me in this case. Trisha said You don't want to get into a feminist issue here. It'll look bad in court, and now I see where she's been lying to me. This is a feminist issue.

If you are interested still, I would be uttmostly gratefull. I am truely sorry about all the misunderstandings. Its my stinkin lawyers fault. I would like for us to grow closer in friendship if we could. I would love for National Organization for Women to help picket and support. Any woman's group for that matter, and if you could connect me please do. I've informed Trisha in a letter that if you wish to help me, that she best let you. As her as my defense, I demand it. She cannot deny it... what I am asking of you is for a woman's group support in picketing on raped women at my trial outside of the courthouse and sponsoring me in my defense with rape counselors, the people you contacted before. I need a bunch of caring women proffessionally (sic). I would love for the National Organization for Women to help picket and support.

I am a female who has been raped and the male dominant world is laughing. They've succeeded to putting me in the chair to prove that men can and will do as they want to us women of America. And we are not going to stand for this anymore. If you know anything about a prostitute life then you know this number (of rapes) is not big at all.

There would be hundreds dead if I were a real, callous, hateful Serial Killer over men...

I am scarrd. I'm really getting railroaded here. Thank you. See ya hopefully.

Lee.

(Author's Comment: She is asking for my help when it's far too late.)

March 2, 1992

Dear Phillis:

Hi hows things going? Thank you so much from all of you for the cards for thinking about me on my birthday. It brought sunshine to my lonely soul, in a dark cell.

I still can't believe I'm here. Especially that the confession state over and over self defense. And there intent to bodily harm me, as well as rape. Shoot! They found a prostitute in Daytona handcuffed, raped, and dead. A couple of years back. Probably was humphrey, who knows. Anyway if you sent a letter with the cards, I'd like to let ya know. There wasn't one. If not. Things that make you go hum! is all I can say. Hope I hear from you. Sorry my attorneys messed up my whole thinkin, So much decieving (sic) and deception. Just makes me sick, sick, sick. There are people who where involved most definately in a crime, but are just as innocent by justifiable cercumstances as one could ever preciene. Not all crimes committed are guilty. Even the worst of the worst. There's always a double standard. Well, do hope to here from ya soon. Thank-you again for the cards. Brough a smile to me. Warmed my soul.

Take Care 4-now, Lee

(Author's Comment: Lee knows how to "talk feminist" when she's talking to me. She is a quick study.)

March 3, 1992

Dear Lee:

...I hope you received the three birthday cards we sent. I agree with what you've written: that you were "crucified" in the courtroom, that you've been "railroaded."

I've also asked other feminists to write about your case.

I hope you begin receiving the medical care you urgently require...I look forward to working with you.

In sympathy and sisterhood,
Phyllis

June 29, 1992

Dear Phyllis:

I received a xeroxed copy of your recent Article of Sex, Death and the Double Standard. But I did not get out of which magazine it was printed in. Would you please fill me in on this, as otherwise I would like to greatly thank you so very kindly for telling teh world, just how it has been and is. Yes! You spoke the truth. There was one time while I was in the testimonial box explaining what had happened, that I expressed myself about Mallorys concern over looking for girls to do pornography filming with him. That he had the equipment. And also that he told me he was on his way to the topless bars in Daytona. The Single Shake and the Red Gardner, or somethin like that he said. So according to Jacky Davis's report. There was noway I was making up stuff in that there stand. There is only a few things you left out on the Rubbing alcohol. He also put it in my vagina, and down my nose. But the anas, is enough anyway to let them know what an Animal this creep was. I do not deserve being here. This is so wrong of the people and the cops. They merely killed me by my perfession I chose. Otherwise what I did was hair line self defense. Nothing more. Anyway. Now before my demise, I am looking for a true Gut reporter, and a private investigator. Both interested in investigating the whole conspiracy of the cops framing me for these monie they were working on 4 weeks even before my arrest the monie "overkill." I've got all the information and leads. But can't do jack shit here on Death Row. So I need help. The undercover investigation once it proves fruitfull. Is really going to blow the American people's minds at how "Sickly unjust and crooked our cops and courts are today." I'll be searching for these reporters. And an investigator willing to do the job under gratis only for the mean time. Surely eventually the money for a job well done will find its way to paying them for it, sooner of later.

If you know of any. Interested in blowing the lid off some royal deception. Let em know, I'd like for them to contact me please. It could make a reporter and any P.i,. F.B.i, (or) detective become a Notorious celebrity from the exposure. It would be well worth the efforts. I want them scummy cops put in prison before I die. If I were given a million dollars and my acquittal to keep a lid on it all. I wouldn't except it! What there doing is so DAM! WRONG! It just needs attention brought to it, my crimes redefined to what really truely happened, and their butts charged and in court for there pre moeditated conspiracy with murder of a criminal who was under a justified act of self defense use while husseling.

Again Thank You Phillis for the article. It really told it like it was. If you knew of all the deception. You'd have the whole magazine needed to place it's contents conserning in. Grant you. There is alot of heavy crookedness that took place. I want the whole world to learn of it Before I die. Take good care of yourself now.

I do hope I hear from you soon. You are a "Good Woman". Here's a hug. Emmmmmmmph!

Thank you 4 now.
Love Lee

(Author's Note: It is interesting that even though she appreciates my article she still needs to criticize it e.g. "a few things left out on the Rubbing alcohol.")

Undated letter

Dear Phyllis:

...The male dominated world is laughing over the fact they've succeeded to putting her in the chair to prove men can and will do as they want to us women of america. And I want to help change this, with my case and prove there wrong. And we are not going to stand for this anymore....
I "do not" hate men. Never have. Many many many of my clients became very close to me....Please write if your interested. Again I'm sorry. If you want to write please about me, Get the information from me first. Please no 2nd guessing. See ya hopefully. Thanks for your time.

Lee

July 28, 1992

Dear Phyllis

Thank you for taking the time to come down and interview me, in reference to your magazine issues. I enjoyed your company. You were very comfortable to converse with. Only thing that was hectic, was the lack of time. So much can be said "Concerning all the crookedness." But it could really take perhaps a good week at 6 hours a day to fill in all the dirty they carried on in. For the purposes of the money "overkill, political and promotional reasons, etc. It is a shame to realize our system does not care about you. They only care what they can gain off of you and your crime. There is no real interest to get to the matter of truth. And from all I've experienced and seen, will distort the truth, in any way they can in order to reap for their own injustice against humanity. You looked great. Health wise. I couldn't see why your having problems. You looked fit for a 5 mile jog. If your still having illness's (I'm) praying for you. For quick deliverance of. Please inform me, on your writings, your underway on now. O.K. I do hope to hear from you soon. Keep me posted. This is just a short one. I'll be sending you info on why I husseled. What sparked the startr. Take care now.

Best of Luck on your Articles.
Love Lee

August 5, 1992

Dear Lee:

Hello again! I received your letters. It's all important information about all the times you tried to escape from a rape or a gang rape, a beating, and from severe verbal humiliation. What you've begun to write is heartbreaking.

Are you sure you do not want to plead insanity? That's the way to avoid being executed. Are you willing to fight to save your own life?

Whatever you decide, I still remain committed to writing and visiting you.

Love,
Phyllis

(Author's Note: Once she began signing her letters to me "love," I knew I'd have to respond in kind.)

August 15, 1992

Dear Lee:

A little humor is called for here. I think that when you meet "the Lord," you'll be mistrustful of Her/him as your life has taught you to mistrust everyone, especially those who mean you well.

You have a knack, a genius, for "trusting" and "loving" precisely those people who are most capable of failing and hurting you, but who, along the way, are willing to get in real close, and feed the "two of us against the world" mentality that has allowed you to survive this long....

I, too, am very glad that we met. As always,

Yours in sisterhood,
Phyllis

October 2, 1992

Dear Phyllis:

Arlene and Steve have been all along, as I've always suspected, under contract with Jackie Girous, like the conspiracy of the cops and Overkill. Well not anymore. I'm taking the next 2 up coming cases to court. And so now is the time I would like to ask for your assistance. I'm also willing to allow you to help me produce my book Sound Off. But not my childhood. Maybe later but not now. Please! Phyllis want I need next to ask is, would you be helping me with the pro bono experts you had prepared for Mallory's trial. And could you get me a dam good capital defense lawyer. Also I would like to know if you've made up any articles lately on me.

I need you and trust you now, and in tears as I sit and write. If you knew how they framed, and tampered with the case... thank you for caring. It feels great considering the manifolds of hatred I've been through. Steve's been sending me suicidal books, and lastly at a visit with him...He said he had another solution to my self murder if I wished it. Cyanide, 30 seconds he said. And said he would supply it to me as well! Arlene also tried coaxing me to take my life! I wrote to him yesterday to tell him to throw the waiver papers out the window.

Lee

October 15, 1992

Dear Lee:

Hadda happen, Mallory had to have done some evil shit, there had to have been a record somewhere, it was only a matter of time before someone found something...When I first met Trish and Don Sanchez more than a year and a half ago, early in April of 1991, I urged them to do a background check on Mallory.....

Lee: I am begging you now to undertake a fight for your life. Let me come down and talk with you in person....Tell me how you're feeling, whether you ever got any of the medical attention you've been needing.

I'm enclosing individual stamps. Hope they don't stick together.

In sisterhood,
Phyllis

October 20, 1992

Dear Phyllis:

Hi long time no hear I know. But I've been really busy keeping myself on a shelf to let everything ride by, as I wait for more proof. Someone to tell me something that could. Be with proof if Arlene and Steve have been all along as I've always suspected under contract with Jacklyn Girous, like the conspiracy of the cops and overkill. And I got it! And they are. And this is why they've been coaxing me all this time to waive out and take the chair, enticing me to lay down my glove, its not worth fighting for and give up. They've done to much damage you'll never be able to prove and pull out of.

Well not anymore. I'm taking the next 2 upcoming cases to court. And so now is the time I would like to ask for your assistance....I would also like to know if you've read Delores Kennedys book, of which I never authorized her title..and I've never read it yet. Well this is my question. I am dying to read this book. But having someone send it through to me is a hard thing to do. If you could Xerox the book, and send to me. I'm home free, and will of finally had a chance to read it. I myself had nothing to do with the book. Her and Arlene did. And Arlene is "NOT" on my side what so ever. One last thing before I go. I do need stamps. Could you please send a good batch like you did last time.

I'm sorry of the cold shoulder but I needed to sort things out. Such a mess. Such a bunch of framings for monies. Killing a now ex-hooker who was raped....And of my God! here I am writing to you, and I was depressed as hell as how to explain to you, I need you now, and in tears as I sit and write. I received a letter from you! Just now! Great! And stamps! Far out. Thanks!

Well on Dead End wheather I get pissed or not, send it all Xeroxed if you can afford to do this. I'd greatly appreciate it...

The reason Steve's not interested is because all along he's been under contract with Jackie...He's been sending me suicidal books. He said he had another solution to my self-murder if I wished it. Cyanide, 30 seconds he said. And he said he would supply it to me as well. Arlene tried coaxing me to take my life! and said she's read Jack Kovarian's book from Michigan, Die Lethal.

P.S. Steve's lieing about wanting to take the cases to const. (court). He had it all planned for me to wait out (waive) Pasco and Dixion. (Dixie)..the cops conspired all their plans before my arrest...I was coarsed (coerced) to confess by tie lines (Tyria's lies) over the 11 phone conversations in jail....I was withdrawing from alcohol pretty bad. And also very much in a traumatic frame of mind...I was merely withdrawing from a whole lotta toxic poisoning and chemical imbalance that had me incoherent and incompetent as hell.

And yet I need to see you. Let me know if you are coming.

I love you women! Thank you a Million for still sticking with me. The women out there are in for a royal surpize. And finally will see how men have no regards nor respect for us. But still do not dislike all of them. Just ravishing pigs. I just received a letter from L.B. Could you call and let her know there's a green light blinking for Sound Off!

Thank you again Phyllis.

Lee

(Author's Comment: She is asking me to help her write her book, ensure that both she and Dawn get percentages, reconstitute my pro bono experts, get her a new lawyer, xerox Kennedy's book, send her stamps, etc. She is exhausting.)

October 21, 1992

Dear Phyllis

I want to thank you so much for your concern, your caring, your support. I am very happy that things are starting to roll. Look's like it's time for the cops to get busted. I want to see this so bad, before I die...And like I said to L.B. in her letter could you imagine these kinds of creeps, ladderin up to chief of Police or mayor. OK! Man, no way. What they deserve is some dam good time, and the key dropped in the deepest ocean.

I still must tell you. My life story is my thing. I may ask if you'd like to help in it later. But please don't try prying into this. Let's get down to the system's dirt...crimes cops have falsely labled for self-gratificational and monatarial seach for. Stepping all over a human life and killing it even if innocent stared them straight in the face. Just so they could prosper. Its so dam wrong. So grossly sick to allow creeps like this to have power to enforce and continue in this social environmental deception...All I ask out of this book besides the truth is the name of it, remains the same. For I've addressed its label on T.V. Many times. People are anxious for it to come out.

So please leave it as Sound Off. Anything you need. I'm here for you and meg and L.B. Willing to assist in this, all the way. Even if I was near death.

4-now

Love Lee

P.S. Please help my friend Dawn on her phone bill and stuff. She's near to getting stuff shut off, because she's in a financial bind as of now. I just thought I'd mention it. She'd just reimburse once her share came through or whatever. I hope you could help her. Or the publishing company help her on a bonus before hand deal. I don't know. Just thought to mention this.

October 28, 1992

Dear Lee:

Hope this letter finds you in a good space--and getting ready to enjoy the day that NBC Dateline "exposes (some more of) the corruption...."

Lee: There is a huge difference between a movie for the sake of entertainment and trying to find expert witnesses to assist your lawyers. If I write a law review article about your case—there are no investor-Johns, no advertiser-Johns, no network-Johns. Our main and only "profit" is justice for you and for other women in your situation.

Whether Overkill ever appears or not; whether Giroux sues CBS Republic Pictures or not—none of this will do anything for you at all. It's all just "entertainment."

Governors do not grant clemency to someone because they saw a film by Twisted Pictures (I think that's the name of Giroux's company)...

In sisterhood and with a big hug back,
Phyllis

November 3, 1992

Dear Phyllis:

I received your very exciting letter of support being cor-
roborated and convened for this next and final upcoming trial.
Phyllis, I hope you receive all the recognition and Fame you
deserve, in the major works being put together, in showing one
last time, the evil that carried on and conspired here, throughout my cases. It is high time Society could recieve a crucial
glimpse into Capital cases (and all for) ...Self-gain, power and
financial reapings in the hundreds and thousands vie books and
movies on thee condemned to die, falsely acussed, for.

I've signed a statement agreeing to be interviewed by you/I
hope to see you "Real Soon." Please draw up a contract in Dawns
name to receive any percentages you've agreed upon. (She will
take no money but we have to use her chosen title of Sound Off.
Everyone's waiting for it. So since the World heard this. It would
only make sense to leave it as I said the book would be called.

Steve tried to play another fast one on me at Dixie Counties
hearing...I said Steve! what kind of an attorney are you. I might
be waiving off because I won't reveive a fair trial. But I am ot
(not) stupid or crazy!

There's more to tell you. But I'd rather in person okee dokee!
So I do hope you'll be here soon. On Money. So far, I'm doing
O.K. I'm just worried about Dawn. She's financially hurting, her
father died recently, funneral bills, etc. If you could help her
out...She really needs some kind of helpin hand here. Dawn's a
good honest Gal Phyllis. I believe you'll see what I mean once
you eventually meet her.

Dolores Kennedy! I'm gonna sue that no good woman if I
can. Lots to tell you. But I'll save it all for our visit. Again Thank
You !!!! Million times over. And have a huge hug back! Stress

leaves me to cut this letter short. Sorry!

4-now Love, Lee.

November 6, 1992

Dear Phyllis,

Hi, recieved your letter. Thank you for taking the time out to type this long baby out. Shew! You really must be busy! I hope you find some R&R, Before you get burned out! I very well know how stress can take one. And man it can be really rough. A tough thing to handle. Matter of fact you can see it in my handwritten at times.

Well as far as media. I've been refusing any contact. Reasons is Steve is apparently asking for money then never letting me in. Thats because he has just advicing them to contact me. Yeah! Pretty sick A! So I've halted all interviews except NBC's. As far as media money. As I believe I've told you before, I recieved 10,000 from Montel Williams, and 10,000 from BBC. I kept 1,000. 19,000 went to Dawn Steve and Arlene. I've only about 6(or)700 left from it. I don't know what I'm gonna do myself when I run out. I seriously do need to make one more interview thats willing to pay. Since everyone else apparently is reaping off of me, and I'm not really seemingly cared about (or) supported financially, by doing so myself in all this.

Since I know theres no way I could recieve a fair trial, I've considered another idea. Besides so many have been closed up anyways. Thanks to Steve and Arlenes (cunning) strategy. Yeah! there only interested in the almighty evil bucks. Anyway!

The idea was instead of looking for a pro-bono attorney. How about a private investigator. Someone who would personally come see me. Let me fill her (or) him up on everything. Look for evidence. Once it! was found! Then this could re open all cases. Immediately., All and all my main concern is getting these cops, lawyers and judges busted in all this evil premediated (premeditated). Phyllis, they really framed up an innocent hitch hikin hooker, and they really need to be punished severly for this. Using the Laws to achieve such deception's. There no execuses for what they have done.

Steve is quite jeoulous of you by the way. This is diffenately because he's afraid. You could possibly with the p.i. And all expose some royal dirt, that his ass is involved in too. He's sweating, I can tell. He in a round about way wants me to drop communications with you. Hmmm! Wonder why? Arlene does also.

You say (stand) by me. Thank You! But if it costs to much and seems to late to really get into action on (attorneys). Let's go for a good "sherlock Holmes," instead of standin by me, we can all step in, mingle this baby into a Reality that will rock the nation. Then stand by and watch the results together....Still so much to tell you. Wait I've a question whats, a Law Journal?.....

Man I need, 3 days and, 8 hours just to tell you half the crap thats gone down....Cause I know and knew (never) would ever see fair justice in all the crookedness that has carried on. And you'll see what I mean once you read it all. Well need to close letter #3 on the way.

Till then. Take Good care. Love Lee.

(Author's Note: As early as June of 1992, Lee writes to Dawn that my article "was dynamite. So dam true" and that she'd "be sending (me) a huge thank you letter very soon." But, she also writes: "Both Trisha and Arlene tell her that (I'm) not all there....she's only out for a book. Your case is not a 'Feminist issue,' and she's a feminist, and it could distroy your case...' Lee still insists on having my experts there but Lee insists that Trish refuses to call us.

At the end of 1992, Lee writes to Dawn: "Back to Phyllis. When she says the money should go to her attorneys. She's talking about her associates. So this shows me right here, she's 2 face, and lying like hell." Lee does not really understand what a Legal Defense Fund is or does.)

November 7, 1992

Dear Lee:

Steve Glazer, who called and asked for my help, never got back to me with the information about the Pasco case. I'm willing to come to Pasco to testify on your behalf. Ask your public defender to contact me. Your appeal of the Mallory case has just been filed. If you talk to any media, just keep asking for a competent attorney. Steve himself now admits that he can't do right by you.

In loving sisterhood,
Phyllis

March 5, 1993

Dear Phyllis:

Can you get me a new civil attorney? If Yes! I'd be more than happy to allow you back in my life and to help me on my book. If you're interested, please except our friendship back. I only wish I hadda listened to you on your views (about Glazer). The doors are wide open, and welcome for you if your interested. I don't care if you do a dozen books on me. Here I am! But I need you...I did Jeraldo. I've only about 200.00 left to my name.

As I write this I am very grieved at how I treated you. You were O.K. Phyllis grant you I am truly sorry....I won't ask you to walk out this time. Let's make up and start over. There's plenty of money to be made. You and Dawn can have it! All I care about is my Autobiography, my fair share of the movie money, and most important, Steve and Arlene "Super Exposed."

Let's help the Women. Hope to hear from you soon. If you hear from L.B. tell her I said hi.

Lee

April 3, 1993

Dear Phyllis:

It is quite obvious your interest in my behalfs, are not in the right places. I thought perhaps you were, O.K. But, I can diff-enately sense swindle in you. I have others helping me on law-yers, etc. So this will be the final reply back. Hope you find Jesus Christ in your life soon. For he is coming back, and the way things look, any day now, to be percise. Read the Bible. Maybe you'll see what I mean.

Yours truly,
Lee

(Author's Comment: Early in 1996, Lee is still writing to Dawn about me. She writes: "I hesitate to get involved with her. But it appears...I need to bring someone in organizations for Wom-en...And she's magnified in it. Known around the world and is involved in many organizations for Women. Steve and Arlene begged me to get rid of her...She's the one that had 10 profes-sionals ready to support me on my behalf at Mallory's trial. Connections are a cinch with her." She asks Dawn to call me to tell me that she's fired both me and Glazer. But, she keeps me in mind for many years but, by then it's all over, she's well on her way to the chair.)

AFTERWORD

Requiem for a Female Serial Killer

I N THE BEGINNING, I viewed Wuornos as a prostitute who fought back—but I understood that she was no more a political actor than Valerie Solanas was. Solanas is the woman who shot the artist Andy Warhol (he lived)—and she also wrote a brilliant and slightly crackpot manifesto, titled *The Society for Cutting Up Men*, which was translated into thirteen languages.

Wuornos and Solanas were embraced by a number of radical feminist leaders whom they promptly abused, wore out, and rejected. Both women were loners: fiercely literal, concrete, explosive, and anti-social. As teenagers, they both gave away babies to be adopted, worked as prostitutes, and were lesbians, bisexual, or asexual. After she was arrested, Solanas was diagnosed as a "paranoid schizophrenic" and warehoused in an asylum for the criminally insane. When they released her, she drifted off to San Francisco, never wrote again, and died in poverty.

Solanas did not become a serial killer.

I saw in Wuornos an opportunity to extend the right of rape/self-defense to prostitutes, most of whom are on the front lines of violent misogyny every single day. Life on the edge of the ledge does not necessarily make someone "nice." I did not expect to "like" her. Our so-called first female serial killer was not required to be a role model for women who dress for success.

As far as I knew, serial killers were all men and they mainly killed women, as well as young boys.

Jane Caputi, in a brilliant book titled *The Age of Sex Crime*, describes the serial sex murders of women, often prostitutes, as similar to a "lynching;" those serial killers who pose their victims afterwards in a parody of a "gynecological exam" (the Boston Strangler did this), or "spread-eagle with their legs apart and their knees up" (the Hillside Strangler did this), are signifying the patriarchal triumph over female humanity, and over women's sexual and reproductive power.

According to Andrea Dworkin, it is a "ritual and cathartic act," one that is meant to terrify all women and keep us afraid. Such male serial "lust" killers are therefore romanticized in books, articles, plays, operas, songs, and films.

There are thousands of books and thousands of articles about Jack the Ripper, Ted Bundy, the Boston Strangler, Son of Sam, the Hillside Strangler, and the Zodiac Killer. They have, collectively, been written about many thousands of times. Films about these serial killers have appeared and been re-aired countless times; new films have also kept appearing. The obscene fascination with murdered women, murdered prostitutes, seems to be unending.

Perhaps Wuornos is guilty of having turned the tables: If men don't want to be killed, they should stay away from prostitutes—or at least stop degrading, raping, and murdering them.

As Wuornos memorably said: "If men would keep their money in their pockets and their penises in their pants, there'd be no prostitution."

I was so focused on exposing how violent prostitution is for the prostitute, so obsessed with arguing for a just trial for Wuornos (which I do not regret), that I could not, at the same time, allow myself to acknowledge that I might also be defending a serial killer.

And I was.

This is hugely ironic, since I tend to avoid all films about serial killers and refuse to watch horror films. I only began reading about serial killers and about prostitution after I became involved in her case. It was the darkest and most chilling reading I'd ever done.

Her story is complex, not simple.

Yes, Wuornos was a serial killer—but a very unique one. She was not exactly like male serial killers or like other female serial killers—nor was she like most abused women whose lives were similarly sordid.

The FBI has characterized most serial killers as mainly (but not only) white men who had been abused by their families in childhood; had often set fires or tortured and killed small animals; were bullied and socially isolated; and, some still wet their beds after they were young teenagers.

Their motives were often sexual—they were fetishists, "partialists," or necrophiliacs; angry, thrill- or attention-seekers, and/or they wanted money. They killed more than three people; they acted alone; they were mentally ill; they engaged in petty crimes, were drifters, had trouble staying employed, took menial jobs. Many (but not all) tended to have low IQs (92.8), especially the "disorganized" or impulsive serial killers who were loners with few friends.

Doesn't this begin to sound like Our Girl Lee? Abused in childhood, bullied, socially isolated, she set a few fires, had a possibly low IQ (80-81), was mentally ill, had trouble staying employed, and was a drifter and a loner; she also engaged in petty crimes, and killed more than three people all on her own. But in her case, there's even more.

She was impregnated via rape at thirteen and forced to give a child away for adoption. This is psychiatrically catastrophic for most women and something that male serial killers cannot suffer. In addition, like some male serial killers, Wuornos did not know her biological father or biological mother; was legally adopted but unwanted; had learning disorders and either Organic Brain Syndrome or a Traumatic Brain Injury; and, briefly took drugs, was a lifelong alcoholic and a criminal. Prostitution is illegal. So is buying and shooting illegal firearms and holding up a convenience store for $33.00.

There's still more. When as a child, Wuornos was being

beaten, and beaten badly, no neighbor reported it and no police officer stopped it. When she was thrown out and had to sleep in the snow and in an abandoned car, and sell "sex" for cigarettes, beer, food, and drugs—not a single adult came to her aid. No social worker, and no school counselor, offered her any refuge, or took her for hearing and vision tests, something even her loving grandmother/mother failed to do. When Wuornos stopped going to school, no one came to find her.

Wuornos' Troy, Michigan, does not seem to exist in twentieth-century America. It seems wild, beyond civilization, perhaps more like a nineteenth-century village located in some freezing wasteland in Finland where her ancestors came from.

And so Wuornos hit the highway—a loud, belligerent, incorrigible teenager, but also a rather attractive Scandinavian piece of ass. She managed to get herself married and divorced within months—she beat her wealthy, elderly husband and he took out a restraining order against her. She was arrested many times for stupid stuff: Driving under the influence, shooting a gun into the air while driving drunk, hitting a bartender, speeding, resisting arrest, assaulting men (!), trying to pass a phony check, holding up a convenience store for chump change.

Wuornos' version of these events is very different. She couldn't get a legit job because she had a record. She kept failing the tests to become a police officer or to join the military by 3-5 points, each and every time. Even when she'd gotten "physical" with boyfriends, she never understood why they took a hike. She belonged nowhere, she fit in nowhere. She made at least one serious suicide attempt. In jail, she was written up for fighting and uncooperative behavior.

How could I not have focused on Wuornos as a serial killer right away? If I had, could I have organized a campaign for justice on her behalf? Maybe, maybe not.

She was an abused child, but here's how she differed from other abused women.

Many such female victims try to re-enact their original trauma (incest, battery, rape, abandonment) in the hope that they can create a different ending. Most such girls tend to marry batterers who are also sexually abusive; they are unable to change this script. Wuornos eventually succeeded in changing the script.

Wuornos was raped and impregnated in the woods when she was thirteen. Her murder scenes were all in the woods. Did she unconsciously revisit that primal scene-in-the-woods—in order to achieve a radically different ending? Was this the way she reclaimed some power for herself? It's entirely possible.

Then there's this. She always punched up, not down.

For example, Ted Bundy killed a series of vulnerable girls and women who were smaller, younger, and not as strong as he was.

Wuornos was only 5'4" and weighed about 135 pounds. Some of her victims were more than six feet tall, and weighed far more than she did. She physically wrestled with at least three of her victims. Wuornos liked going head-to-head and toe-to-toe with men; according to Tyria, Lee would never let a man "get one over on her."

Wuornos killed grown men, some of whom towered over her. They were an average of twenty years older than she was. Perhaps she figured she could take them down.

This is an interesting difference.

Wuornos sure was different: she tried not to take any shit lying down, she knew it hurt more that way. She'd been catching shit for so long, by now she saw it even when it wasn't there. It was her built-in early detection warning system and it worked; it helped her survive a lot of misfortune. Most women, if beaten, will cringe, cower, placate, appease. Not Aileen. It only made her more aggressive, more demanding, more difficult, more dangerous. As if she were a man.

But Aileen was angry, not like a man, but like a woman, one who'd given a child up for adoption, one who'd been raped and beaten, one who'd drunk way too much.

Some of Wuornos' victims might have been innocent but two were cops, men in positions of authority, father-figures of some kind; one was a known whoremonger and pornography addict—just the kind of men who'd been messing with her since she was born. She certainly rewrote that script.

Perhaps I minimized the fact that Wuornos was serially killing men because I believed that she had done so in self-defense; and, for a "crazy," beaten-down prostitute to have done this impressed the hell out of me. She was meant to die, horribly, not to kill anyone.

Wuornos was a female serial killer. But she was not a lust killer; Wuornos did not have orgasms as she shot men, nor did she pose their naked bodies in grotesque rituals of degradation.

Unlike most "organized" male serial killers, Wuornos was not strategic. She left a trail behind her that led the cops straight to her door. There was her brand of beer, her store-bought condoms, the items she pawned nearby under one of her many aliases, the driver's seats pushed forward for a much shorter driver. Her killing "spree" took place in a short period of time. She did not plan ahead nor did she carefully dispose of evidence.

Here's what I think may have happened.

After Wuornos saved her own life in a violent struggle with Richard Mallory—I think she just snapped and became unleashed, or "liberated," if you insist. No man was going to mess with her ever again. If a guy got rough with her, threatened not to pay her, or threatened to arrest her (especially if he wanted free sex anyway), or refused to pay her for sex (when she needed the money), or if he wanted something that she thought was "way outta line," she just "blew him away." These were now all capital crimes in her book. It was her own personal Affirmative Action program.

Here's an example of how rigid Lee was about "lines."

On December 10th, 1990, William Reinauer was driving the Votran bus. Aileen seemed the same as ever to him, which, under the circumstances, was incredible, since on any given day, twelve to fifty cops were out looking for her; she was so hot you could fry an egg on her head in under 30 seconds, and there she was, as neat as ever, wearing her regulation sunglasses, her hair pulled back, in shorts and a tank top.

Reinauer was driving north. Aileen said she would go as far north as he went.

Then, Aileen informed him: "You turn off here, at Rosewood," and she prepared to get off. "No," Reinauer explained, "I go on up another half mile to the Senior Center." The Ormond police had told the bus company not to stop on Melrose and Andrews anymore. Reinauer told Aileen, "I will let you off as soon as I make the turn." Aileen exploded. "I want to get off right here!" "But," Reinauer explained, "I can't stop here," and he didn't.

Reinauer thought that Aileen was going to take a swing at him. He unfastened his seat belt. Reinauer was Ready. The turn actually saved Aileen a half mile of walking, but Aileen was furious because, even though she had to walk only two or three hundred feet, she had to do it from an unknown and unexpected location.

Aileen was cognitively rigid, she didn't like her routine to vary. Imagine what might happen if a John tried to get Aileen to do something new or different.

Many claimed that her victims were all innocent men, Good Samaritans who had stopped to help a poor hitchhiker.

If Wuornos' victims were not Johns—then why were three of the men (Spears, Carskaddon, and Antonio) naked if they hadn't agreed to have sex with her? Did Wuornos undress them after she'd killed them? I doubt it. Unlike male serial "lust" killers, she actually protected the corpses. Mallory chose to keep his pants on but both his pants and his belt were twisted off to the side. She still covered him with a carpet so that "the birds (would not be) pecking at his body." In other cases, she pulled their bodies further back into the woods and covered them, too.

Why hadn't I focused on her victims, or on their grieving widows, and other relatives? Would I do so now? Probably, yes; but perhaps not. I was led to this case by the smell of female blood, the sound of women's arms and jaws being broken, with no rescue and even less justice in sight. I undertook this journey entirely focused on how blind the world is to what is done to prostitutes, our scapegoats for male lust and misogyny.

Wuornos had been out of control but also under attack all her life, probably more than any soldier in a real war. Read the memoirs by former prostitutes, read the studies about them, and you'll understand what I mean.

As an abolitionist, I do not view prostituted women with distaste or disgust. I see them as human sacrifices. I understand all the forces that track 98% of girls and women into the "working life:" Dangerously dysfunctional families; physical and sexual abuse; drug addicted, absent, or imprisoned parents; serious poverty; homelessness; being racially marginalized; tricked or kidnapped into prostitution by a trafficker; sold by one's parents; having too little education and few marketable skills; and, having absolutely no other way to eat or to feed your children.

However, I do not view prostitution as an act of resistance any more than I view marriage as one. The proposed solutions (legalization, de-criminalization, etc.) will not abolish sexism, racism, poverty, war, genocide or rape. What will? Until we find that magic bullet, starving and homeless girls and women will do whatever they can in order to afford their anesthetizing drugs so they can endure their "work" and put food on the table. And men will keep taking their penises out of their pants.

* * *

Wuornos is not unique in killing men for money, nor was she the first prostitute to have killed a John or a pimp. There is a long history of prostitutes killing Johns or pimps—but only one John, not a series of them.

For example, in 1843, in New Jersey, Amelia Norman, a virgin, was seduced by Henry Ballard who impregnated her and another woman and set them both up in a brothel. He refused to pay any child support and, when Norman insisted, Ballard tried to have her arrested for prostitution. Norman stabbed Ballard (who lived); she was supported by abolitionist Lydia Maria Child and feminist Margaret Fuller. Author Ann Jones, in *Women Who Kill*, wrote:

When Amelia Norman stuck a knife into Henry Ballard, she ripped the familiar script to pieces. She did not take laudanum or slink off to die painfully in a whorehouse as seduced and abandoned maidens were supposed to do.

In 1871, Susan B. Anthony defended a many-times-married prostitute named Laura Fair who'd killed her pimp, a John, or her lover—the record isn't clear. According to feminist author Kathy Barry in *Susan B. Anthony: A Biography*, Anthony visited Fair in jail and came away convinced that Fair had killed in self-defense. That same night, Anthony told 1,200 people that Fair had a right to "protect herself." The audience hissed, booed, stamped their feet, and advanced on Anthony—all in an effort to silence her. Anthony stood her ground.

Newspapers nationwide branded Anthony a "heretic." Within days, she'd lost most of her speaking engagements. Anthony said she felt "raked over," and "so cut down."

But that extraordinary woman, that Mother of Us All, only blamed herself for not having been strong enough. "Defending Laura Fair without speaking of what prostitution does to women," she said, "was like going into the South and failing to illustrate human oppression by Negro slavery."

I did not see myself as a Susan B. Anthony: we'll not see her likes soon again, but our defense of Wuornos stood on historically solid feminist ground.

Here's how Wuornos is different from other known female serial killers of men: she killed strangers on the highway of life—outdoors, not inside at home; and with a gun, not with poison. Other female serial killers only killed intimates, and they did so for real money, pure and simple.

Dubbed "black widows," female serial killers married and killed men again and again, in order to obtain insurance money. Their names are legion.

Most notorious was Belle Gunness, a first-generation Norwegian-American, known as the "female Bluebeard with a profit motive." In 1900, Belle's first husband died under suspicious circumstances; she received a life insurance payout. Belle married again—and sure enough, her second husband was also found dead under mysterious circumstances—another insurance payout. Immigrant men, lured by her ads for "partners" and "hired hands," went to work for Belle and were never seen again; so were wealthy bachelors who were interested in marriage. They came bearing cash and trunks laden with valuables.

Law enforcement believed that Gunness was responsible for at least twenty-five murders and was suspected of twice that number; she was accused of doing this mainly for money, but also for the "sheer joy of it." Gunness literally butchered these men and then buried them on her Indiana "murder farm," a fact that became clear when the police dug up their bodies. Gunness presumably died in a fire before she could be arrested, but people also contended that she had escaped.

Wuornos is quite the light-weight compared to Gunness.

Some female serial killers have lured girls into brothels with false offers of employment, where they immediately had them gang-raped, beaten, deliberately hooked on heroin or cocaine, forced to work as prostitutes, and later murdered. The punishment for rebellion was horrendous.

One egregious example took place in Mexico in the 1950s and 1960s. Two sisters, Delfina Gonzalez and Maria de Jesus Gonzalez, enticed and killed many hundreds of girls, all of whom "disappeared." In 1963, the police found the remains of eighty girls, buried on the brothel grounds. Those who were still alive and whom they liberated were "nervous wrecks." The sisters were sentenced to forty years; their collaborators were also found and sentenced.

Other kinds of female serial killers were those who killed their elderly patients for their Social Security checks or for their insurance policies, which had been signed over to their nurses. Their names are also legion, both in the United States and Europe.

Some female serial killers, who had once been paid to find homes for out-of-wedlock newborns, just killed them, one after the other, and kept the money.

Always, their motive for killing was money, as much as

they could get. What was Wuornos' relationship to money? Throughout her life, it seems that she thought she had "enough" money if she could pay for two days' worth of beer, food, loud music, and a motel room. Wuornos was not thinking far ahead; she did not act as if she had a future.

But once she was jailed and saw how others were making money "off" what she alone had done—it unsettled her, obsessed her, especially now that she was "famous," a part of history. She was far more interested in "cutting deals" than in talking about a legal defense team, or appealing her death sentences.

In an interview with Tyria a few years later, Ty insisted that she had offered to work two jobs (as a laundry worker or motel housecleaner) if Lee would stop hooking, but that Lee refused to stop. Lee insisted that she had to support Tyria, who was often out of work but who still wanted beer, cigarettes, food, and shelter. At trial, Lee said that "Ty was like my pimp. I was a white slave, I didn't realize it."

In person, Ty impressed me as a close-mouthed butch hillbilly, with a large and supportive family. Ty lumbered when she walked. She seemed tough, stolid, perhaps secretive, but also loyal and kind. She allowed me to xerox Lee's letters to her— none of which she said she had answered.

You may decide whose story you believe about money.

I don't think that Lee ever wanted to stop hooking. It was the only thing she did well and it alone afforded her the illusion of intimacy and affection. And then, one night, what men wanted, and how they treated her, became unacceptable.

In jail, Lee used money as a way to bind people to her and to control what they did. Arlene Pralle got money because, as Lee told me, "I need someone to bury me." (Pralle did not do so; her childhood friend, Dawn Botkins, had her cremated and scattered her ashes around a tree in Troy.) Steven Glazer had to be paid because Lee needed him to negotiate with the media on her behalf. Botkins got money because she was the one and only friendly tie to Lee's childhood, and she'd promised to keep writing to Lee and to visit her if possible.

* * *

Many years have passed from the time I tried to organize a team of experts for Wuornos' defense. In that time, Wuornos became something of a cult figure; by now, she has fans, followers, admirers.

Wuornos' earliest "fans" were the media—journalists, authors, and filmmakers who wanted exclusives on a new kind of evil. They wrote glossy magazine articles, interviewed her on television for documentaries, published traditional true-crime books, self-published pamphlets, and fictionalized her crimes in multiple movies, including a Hollywood version (*Monster*) in which Charlize Theron played Lee and won an Oscar for doing so.

Lee insists that she is not really a lesbian. Ty agrees with her. Still, lesbian feminist academics have claimed her as one of our own. Many wrote searing articles and chapters about her "narrative," and studied the ways in which the media "represented" her. The Sisters also marched in the streets "To Free Aileen Wuornos."

I wrote three op-ed pieces (one in the *New York Times*, two in the radical feminist magazine *On The Issues*); analyzed her case in the *St. John's Law Review* and in the *Criminal Practice Law Report;*—and, introduced a selection of her letters to her friend Dawn Botkins, co-edited by Lisa Kester and Daphne Gottlieb.

Over time, grassroots fans were drawn to Wuornos as a woman who was meant to die an awful, anonymous death—but who instead turned on her tormentors, got even, and got famous.

Hit the jackpot.

Wikipedia, in its entry for her birthplace, Troy, Michigan, lists Wuornos as one of their Notable People, right along with a Hall of Fame baseball player, a Tony Award-winning actor, an NHL defenseman, an MLB pitcher and coach, a rapper, and another high-profile female killer: Carolyn Warmus (!!). Go, check this out, it's there.

The Last Resort Bar (the one I visited, and where she spent her last night in freedom) now has a large photo or painting of Wuornos behind their bar together with a list of the names of the men she killed. The bar claims that business is booming. Fans take "true-crime destination vacations" by visiting the bar and sleeping in the motel room at the Fairview (now renamed the Scoot Inn), where Wuornos once slept. They can also choose from among 80 online mementos as a way of vicariously giving Authority the finger.

These enthusiasts buy her iconic handcuffs-to-her-neck image emblazoned on T-shirts ("I'm With Her"), coffee mugs, greeting cards, hoodies, body suits ($68.00), action figures ($35.00), sweatshirts, earrings, bookmarks—and an authentic "relic," a ready-to-be wall-mounted memorial plaque with dirt collected from the ground where her ashes had been scattered ($18.00). People were still making such purchases all through 2020 and leaving satisfied comments at Etsy.

Of course, Ted Bundy has ten times the number of such mementos for sale at Etsy which range in price from $1.00 to $3,500.00.

The playwright, Deb Margolin, wrote a hilarious musical comedy about Wuornos called *Lesbians Who Kill*; it was performed by the extraordinary theater company "Split Britches" in New York City in 1992.

Carson Kreitzer, wrote a daringly dramatic play titled: *Self Defense, or the death of some salesmen*, which premiered in Rhode Island in 2001 and then in New York City. I was a character ("a famous feminist") in this play and my nom de guerre was Cassandra Chase.

A composer, Carla Lucero, premiered an opera, *Wuornos*, in San Francisco in 2001.

For two decades, popular musicians have been dedicating albums to Wuornos and writing songs about her. For example, avant-garde singer and activist, Diamanda Galas, has often dedicated Phil Ochs' powerful protest song about the Death Penalty, "The Iron Lady," to Wuornos. The Lady is the electric chair.

In 2006, the band, It Dies Today, released a song, "The Sixth of June," about Wuornos.

In 2015, the musician Jewel, who has sold more than thirty million albums worldwide, released a song titled "Nicotine Love," about which she writes: "It's an extremely dark song about a woman who had been sexually abused as a child. She turns to prostitution and ends up getting off on killing men and controlling them."

In 2015, the rock band, Superheaven, released a song: "Poor Aileen."

In 2018, William Belli, a drag queen performer, released a darkly humorous video titled "Aileen." Here are some of the lyrics: "This song's about some poor white trash/...And she became a serial killer named/Aileen.../You're more famous than I'll ever be so/Yay you, good job, bitch."

In 2019, Cardi B., a rapper with millions of followers, paid homage to Wuornos by putting a photo of herself, raising her handcuffed wrists to her own neck, Wuornos-style, on the cover of an album.

Also in 2019, Jeffrey Messerole, an award winning folk musician released his song, "Henrietta, Queen of the Highway." It's a sweet and soulful blend of country and western folk music.

I doubt that such odes to Aileen-the-Outlaw will stop anytime soon.

* * *

Helen Zahavi, in her amazing novel *Dirty Weekend*, depicts an ex-prostitute, a quintessential victim, who lives in reduced, end-of-the-line circumstances in a dark basement apartment—an Invisible Woman, waiting to die. But suddenly, a man begins to talk dirty to her on her unlisted phone number, stalks her in a park, and threatens her life. But Bella (for that is her name) can no longer take being slut-shamed and treated like dirt by men and boldly, phantasmagorically, she kills him—and then goes on to kill six more such predators in a single weekend in Brighton, England. Seven men in all.

Zahavi first published this novel in 1991, just a year after

Wuornos was out there killing men. Zahavi also caught hell for changing the acceptable narrative, the one in which the girl always gets to die at the hands of a leering, sex-starved male monster. What Johns do to prostitutes, what they pay to do, is a crime. It wrecks girls and women. I chose to see what Wuornos did as a protest against the men who both buy women and, in addition, also act as if our streets and workplaces are their private brothels. Enough. No more.

Zahavi's work is gruesome, graphic, way over the top—and yet she is also darkly humorous. One almost giggles with nervousness. Are girls really allowed to take revenge/defend themselves? Zahavi closes with a warning:

> If you see a woman walking, and you want her. Think on. Don't touch her. Don't place your palm across her mouth and drag her to the ground. For unwittingly, you might have laid your heavy hand on Bella. And she's woken up this morning with the knowledge that she's finally had enough.

In an interview with Court TV, Lee said: "It took me 17 years to finally kill somebody...but I got stone cold and said, you know, enough is enough."

* * *

Lee is at least two (and probably more) people.

She's a born again Christian who finds Jesus on death row, reads the Bible cover-to-cover, again and again, and listens to Christian radio. In a 1993 letter to Dawn, Lee asks to be buried in "white jeans, a white T-shirt with Christ on it, some type of belt... earrings that are crosses, a cross necklace. Visible please... I'd like a cross in my hands, a Bible tucked between my arm and rib cage."

This is how she wants to be received in Heaven.

Lee also chooses to die via lethal injection—"because your laid out on this table as if your on a cross. Perfect way in my book for me to split in the name of Jesus."

But being executed by her earthly tormentors requires other clothing. For this, Lee asks to be dressed in a black Harley-Davidson T-shirt, biker-style boots, and a military belt.

She also wants to be seen as a shit-kicking mercenary—someone who is going out as a renegade, at war with the ruling classes, proud and defiant, to her very last breath.

Lee is a religious Christian, a biker outlaw, a Marine, a much sinned against child, a happy-go-lucky hooker, a wheeler-dealer, and a secretive serial killer.

On October 8, 2002, her next-to-last day on earth, Wuornos refuses the traditional last meal and only asks for a cup of coffee, black.

Dawn is with her, as is Nick Broomfield, the British filmmaker, who interviews her one last time. That interview clearly demonstrates that Lee is insane. On camera, Lee insists that she'd been "tortured" on death row, that "sonic pressure was crushing her head, (through) the TV or mirror (which) were rigged," and that she had to "wash all her food because it was poisoned." Lee says: "Now I know what Jesus was going through."

By 1999, Lee was writing to Dawn about the lawyer whom Nick had found for her as being "mob connected," part of a "revenge" plot, an "inside hit on me!" Or, she thinks that Nick's lawyer and the Capital Collateral Regional Counsel lawyers are "fishy," belong to the "CIA" or the "Mafia," and are talking to her in code.

It is illegal to execute an insane or retarded person. Executing her probably helped get Jeb Bush re-elected as Governor.

Nick hopes that he can get Lee to talk about the murders, but the request only enrages her. Her eyes bug out, her face reddens—and she won't say a word. This particular information is hers and hers alone, she will not surrender it so that others can use it to make money from books and movies.

Lee's toughing it out. In her final hours, she refuses to be pre-sedated.

And now the day has come. She's walked her last walk. Ten years, eight months, and nine days after she was first jailed, the state of Florida is ready to execute her. They drive her to the

Florida State Prison in Starke, lay her down on a blue medical gurney, expertly, almost tenderly, tightly tuck her in beneath a white bedsheet, and insert the IV line that will deliver her soul to Mr. Death.

Lee's last words are delivered in a soft and barely audible voice: "I'm sailing with the rock and I'll be back like Independence Day with Jesus (on) June 6. Like the movie, big mothership and all, I'll be back."

There are 29 witnesses in the room, consisting of six relatives of her victims; 12 journalists; John Tanner, the State Prosecutor; and, Department of Corrections officials.

As in life, Lee is also alone in death. No lover, no relative, no friend, is there to see her off.

It is the morning of October 9, 2002. The lethal injection process begins at 9:30 a.m. and by 9:47 a.m., Lee is dead.

If you had been on that jury, would you have voted to put her to death? Or to keep her in isolation for nearly eleven years, where she would inevitably become even crazier than she already was? Or would you have chosen to stash her in a state mental institution on heavy medication for life?

Lee is long gone—but she still lives on in my imagination and memory. I titled this book *Requiem for a Female Serial Killer* because this is my way of finally laying her to rest—by memorializing her life, her deeds, and her death. A dirge of sorts, to mourn what can happen to a girl in this world, a horrifying and pitiful tale with an inevitably sordid ending.

As I conclude this chapter, both on the page and in my life, I am strangely sad. Well, it's a funeral, isn't it? Both for her and for some of my own youthful dreams and illusions. I did not obtain even a smidgen of justice for her, or for any other prostitute who continues to face violence and death every day. Wuornos was far too damaged to be saved; I could not save her, we could not save her, she was beyond earthly salvation.

Yes, I know she was a raging drunk, a foul-mouthed, obnoxious, unstable, contrarian—and a serial killer as well—and yet, now that I more fully understand what rape and prostitution can do to an adolescent and to a woman, and what a pitifully damaged child-woman she really was, I have more, not less, compassion for her.

When I leave this book, I leave off, perhaps forever, continuing to grapple with the issues raised by her case.

Now, it is in your hands.

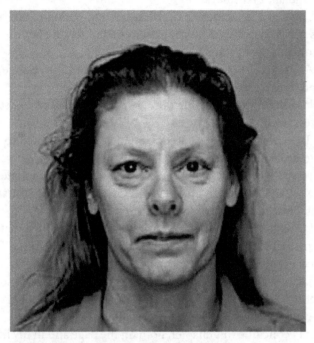

Aileen's mugshot, Florida Department of Corrections, 1991.

ACKNOWLEDGMENTS

I FIRST WISH TO THANK all those who've written about Wuornos before me. I include here the journalists, film-makers, playwrights, composers, and poets who've been drawn to her tale. I am grateful to all my interviewees, some named and many unnamed, who either knew Wuornos, worked on her case, covered her trial, or who were themselves former prosti-tutes, or who are feminists who research and write about the "working life," some of whom have gone to great lengths to offer refuge to those who wished to leave it.

I owe a huge debt of gratitude to Rebecca Bynum, the pub-lisher and editor of this work, whose enthusiasm and generosity were immediate and unparalleled, and whose professionalism and efficiency made publishing this work very enjoyable.

I am thankful to Karen Gantz of Gantz Literary Manage-ment for having so good-heartedly taken on this project.

I am grateful to my assistant, Emily Feldman, who was there for me every step of the way and who surprised me with her pre-existing interest in serial killers. I am utterly reliant upon her infinitely superior technological skills.

I must mention Matthew Greenfield, my IT guy, who skill-fully converted all my interview transcripts, notes, and diaries from my old floppy disks (remember them?) into readable ma-terial—and who is also a fan of serial killer crime stories.

I could not have so safely traveled the Florida roads without the assistance of Yemaya Kauri-Alecto.

I thank my dear friend, Merle Hoffman who, long ago, suggested that this case was meant for me, who served as an early reader, and who pronounced the work "excellent."

Finally, I am blessed with a partner, Susan L. Bender, who has seen me through the most difficult times, who was also an early reader, and who single-handedly makes my privileged life of reading and writing possible.

I thank the Almighty for having graced me with scholarly and creative skills, for having guided my every step, and for bringing me safely, thus far, into our times.

ABOUT THE AUTHOR

PHYLLIS CHESLER, Ph.D, is an Emerita Professor of Psychology and Women's Studies at City University of New York. She is a best-selling author, a legendary feminist leader, a retired psychotherapist and an expert courtroom witness. Her work has been translated into many European languages and into Japanese, Chinese, Korean, and Hebrew.

Dr. Chesler is a co-founder of the Association for Women in Psychology (1969), the National Women's Health Network (1974), and the Original Women of the Wall (1989). She is also a Fellow at The Middle East Forum. Dr. Chesler was an early 1970s abolitionist theorist and activist: She wrote and delivered speeches which opposed rape, incest, pornography, sex and reproductive prostitution, sex trafficking, and gender-based double standards of justice.

Requiem is her nineteenth book. She is the author of the landmark feminist classic *Women and Madness* (1972, 2018) as well as many other notable books including *About Men* (1978); *With Child: A Diary of Motherhood* (1979); *Mothers on Trial: The Battle for Children and Custody* (1986, 2011); *Sacred Bond: The Legacy of Baby M* (1988); *Letters to a Young Feminist* (1998, 2018) *Woman's Inhumanity to Woman* (2002); and *Women of the Wall: Claiming Sacred Ground at Judaism's Holy Site* (2002).

After publishing *The New Anti-Semitism* (2003, 2015), she published *The Death of Feminism: What's Next in the Struggle for Women's Freedom* (2005) and *An American Bride in Kabul* (2013), which won a National Jewish Book Award. She published *Islamic Gender Apartheid: Exposing A Veiled War Against Women* (2017), *A Family Conspiracy: Honor Killings* (2018) and, that same year, a memoir: *A Politically Incorrect Feminist.*

Since the Intifada of 2000, and especially since 9/11, Dr. Chesler has focused on the rise of anti-Semitism, the demonization of both Israel and the West, and the nature of terrorism; the rights of women, dissidents, and gays in the Hindu, Sikh, and Islamic world. Dr. Chesler has published four studies about honor killings, and penned a position paper on why the West should ban the burqa; these studies have all appeared in *Middle East Quarterly*. Based on her studies, she has submitted affidavits for Muslim and ex-Muslim women who are seeking asylum or citizenship based on their credible belief that their families will honor-kill them. She has archived most of her articles at her website: www.phyllis-chesler.com.

Dr. Chesler has been profiled in encyclopedias, including *Feminists Who Have Changed America, Jewish Women in America*, and in the latest *Encyclopedia Judaica.*

Dr. Chesler has published widely over the years in the mainstream media (*New York Times, LA Times, Washington Post, Times of London, London Guardian, Globe and Mail*, etc.), as well as at *FOX, FrontpageMag, Israel National News, Jewish Press, Middle East Quarterly, New York Post, PJ Media, Breitbart, Tablet Magazine, Quillette, Times of Israel*, etc.

She lives in Manhattan and is a very proud mother and grandmother.